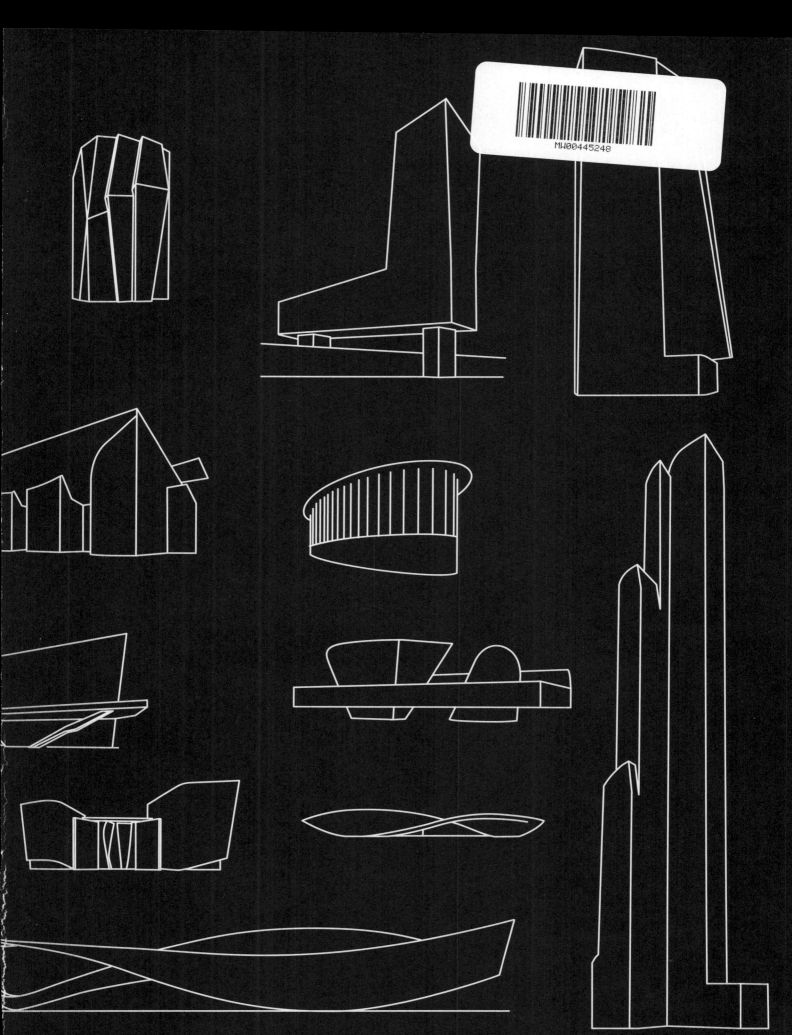

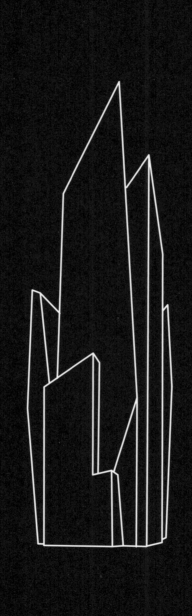

Portzamparc Buildings

Christian de Portzamparc

Portzamparc Buildings

Essay by Philip Jodidio

RIZZOLI NEW YORK

New York · Paris · London · Milan

To Elizabeth, to Serge, to Philippe

First published in the United States of America in 2017 by
RIZZOLI INTERNATIONAL PUBLICATIONS, INC.
300 Park Avenue South, New York, NY 10010
www.rizzoliusa.com

ISBN-13: 978-0-8478-4872-0
Library of Congress Control Number: 2017936724

Page 2: French Pavilion for Venice Biennale, 1990

Distributed to the U.S. Trade by Random House, New York

Printed and bound in China

2017 2018 2019 2020 2021 / 10 9 8 7 6 5 4 3 2 1

Table of Contents

Modern . . . and Now

Christian de Portzamparc

"I never want to stop being amazed by the locomotive," declared Apollinaire, one century ago, and after him Le Corbusier asserted: "We are the first in history who saw the machine." Industry, greatest numbers and the mechanical city were emerging and "mechanization was taking control," as Siegfried Giedion later wrote. Both declared in this way the birth of a new age, which intended to keep nothing of the old one to enter into. In short, they were explaining why they were modern.

The word *Modern* was the artistic banner of the twentieth century.

It was a revolution. Architecture has always had the imperative to represent civilization. For this, it had been traditionally submitted to the authority of the past, to the models of antiquity, which have been the standard. But now, suddenly, the authority of the future was proclaimed. A new task was given to architecture, which pretended to be universal: to build from zero the ultimate frame of Western civilization, with its genius for the future developed in the last century—its idea of progress erasing all of the past. This was the concept of the modern. What we have inherited is the word modern, as a categorical imperative, a semantic talisman, the emblem of our confidence in the future. But its meaning is lost, because what we have been "the first to see" in history is an entirely different world than the one of Apollinaire and Le Corbusier.

They were witnesses of the first movement toward globalization through colonialism and industrialization. We are of the second, which spreads information and trading, develops the parts of our planet that weren't previously developed, and which bloats our cities.

We have been the first to see the state of the earth under industrial efficiency: the air and climate deteriorating, life on our planet endangered. Science taught us how and invited us to be "masters and possessors of nature," in the words of Descartes; now it must teach us how to protect and save nature, and how to make livable its artefact, the city—this city that we have discovered in a continuous growth that emptied countries and passed over capacities of building properly.

We have been the first to see the car invade our cities and cut them to shreds, destroying all simple principles of the urban space, erasing streets and replacing them with specialized zones forming closed enclaves which emerged across swathes of our metropolises.

We have been the first to witness the birth of cyberspace, its wonders and its danger to allow us to forget the physical space.

We have been the first to realize that we lost control of the city as we are seeing public money diminishing, public space being forgotten.

When I was a student, we imagined time as a moving engine charging toward a future. It had to be planned through a doctrine. But this future did not last. Since the eighties there is no doctrine, no common way to think about what we are doing. It has been a major turnaround in how we see time. The first projects of this book were trying to respond to a period marked by erratic progression, reversals and blurriness. Uncertainties.

I realized that being *modern* could not remain as an outdated fetishism but it had to be about answering questions that are constantly renewed, because we live in an era of constant change.

Wishing it or not, architecture invents tomorrow, from project to project. We produce the future step by step. We learned that the best projects are often about reinventing this confidence in the future.

We are facing a real world that we want to fix where it is overcrowded, hard and disenchanted. We have to repair what had been made too quickly; we are in a time of transformation, deformation, modification, hybridization.

These questions persisted from project to project leading to periods in which I explored specific themes. I wanted to rediscover a way in which the urban space could be clearly perceived, something rejected in the modern theory. I wanted to find new ways of assembling neighborhoods that would welcome the return of the specific case, the existing building, the place, once we'd abandoned the idea of the tabula rasa.

From the very start, my work has stood at the crossroads between architecture and urban planning and this book mixes the two sides. These two disciplines have often been seen as antagonistic by those who practice them, but I enjoy combining my two fascinations: the space and the object. Having a foot on both sides of the line has probably helped me develop new ways of thinking about the city.

Urban planning and architecture have never been so vital, but they are in danger. Pressure for short-term results dulls civic awareness. We are growing increasingly blind to the shared and unintended beauty of the city and mistrustful of the vital phenomenon it is.

There is nothing less frivolous than the debate on taste in architecture and the desire to know if we all like the same future. With each project, I feel engaged in the idea of a new pathway that we open to time. Architecture is a small utopia that has become reality, a piece of the future that has entered into the present.

The first chapters of this book explore my work in the 1970s and 1980s, years of debate, years of my first architectural and urban planning concepts, such as the open block neighborhoods. The work contains urban planning projects as well as glamorous cultural buildings or everyday housing and office programs because all are relevant.

I comment on my work in the 1990s and 2000s and some evolution in the compositional working, the way I play with the space from the object systems to composite objects and then to "hollow bricks," the way I understand the old–modern opposition that had been stated between appearance and constructive truth.

Bringing Architecture to Life
The Work of Christian de Portzamparc

Philip Jodidio

When Christian de Portzamparc won the 1994 Pritzker Prize, the jury citation read in part "Christian de Portzamparc's new architecture is of our time, bound neither by classicism nor modernism. His expanded perceptions and ideas seek answers beyond mere style. It is a new architecture characterized by seeing buildings, their functions and the life within them, in new ways that require wide-ranging, but thoughtful exploration for unprecedented solutions."[1] This assessment, written more than 20 years ago still serves as an apt reminder of the accomplishments of Christian de Portzamparc. The international reach of his work, stretching beyond Europe to the United States, Brazil, Morocco, Lebanon and China in recent years is a testimony to the appeal of his designs and the significance of his role in the development of contemporary architecture.

Opposite page: Law Courts, Grasse, France, 1993–1999

Christian de Portzamparc was born in Casablanca, Morocco, in 1944, he thus received the prestigious American award just as he was turning 50, young by the standards of major international architects. He studied at the École des Beaux Arts, Paris (1962–69) and created his own firm in 1975. It became apparent quite early in his career that he would not limit himself to work in France. In 1982, he completed his first project in Japan (Nexus World, Fukuoka), but it was with the Pritzker that significant international projects came to him. The elegant LVMH Tower on 57th Street in Manhattan (1996–99) actually had been discussed in February 1994, shortly before he was granted the Pritzker Prize, and it was followed shortly thereafter by the prestigious French Embassy in Berlin on the Pariser Platz next to the Brandenburg Gate (1997–2003). The Philarmonie in Luxembourg (Grande-Duchesse Joséphine-Charlotte Concert Hall, 1997–2005) and another cultural complex, the Cidade das Artes in Rio de Janeiro (Brazil, 2002–13) are other international commissions that he won. Portzamparc's wife, Elizabeth, a noted designer, architect and urban planner in her own right, is a native of Brazil, a country that has had an influence on him in various ways, including an appreciation of the tradition of Niemeyer. The extensive use of concrete in the Cidade das Artes is indeed an homage to the Brazilian master. As opposed to the geometric rigor of a Tadao Ando, Portzamparc's use of concrete in Rio is lyrical in its essence, an element that runs through his architecture from his earliest work to the present.

Back in New York, Christian de Portzamparc has continued to mark the city's skyline, completing the 306-meter tall One57 building in 2014. Briefly the tallest residential building in Manhattan before it was surpassed by Rafael Vinoly's 432 Park Avenue, One57 made the Frenchman the only living architect to have designed two buildings on 57th Street. As this book was going to press, Portzamparc had just completed the 144-meter high Prism Tower at 400 Park Avenue South (at 28th Street).

A Sophisticated Stylist

The late American architecture critic Ada Louise Huxtable, a member of the 1994 Pritzker Prize jury wrote "Portzamparc is both a sophisticated stylist and sensitive urbanist—qualities usually considered antithetical. In his housing, sociology coexists comfortably with aesthetics and an insightful understanding of the nature of public and private places. Although it is not uncommon for able architects to court disaster when moving from small to large scale, he is equally capable of handling the bold monumentality of the Cité de la Musique and the knowing and subtle certainties of a small addition to Paris's Bourdelle Museum."[2] Huxtable's points are well taken. Few of today's major architects seem capable of adapting to the different scales seen in Portzamparc's Café

Beaubourg and his Cité de la Musique, both in Paris, but of entirely different natures and sizes. Unlike a number of his French colleagues, Portzamparc never allowed himself to create buildings, apartment structures in particular, without paying careful attention to the city environment, inventing what he called the "open island" (îlot ouvert), to bring light, air and a sense of openness to otherwise closed modern complexes. Although the 1994 Pritzker Prize jury citation refers to the "urban scale" of the Cité de la Musique, no specific mention is made of the architect's early and continual mastery of urban design, taking his own esthetic and social sense to the level of entire city neighborhoods, as he has done on several occasions in his career. Appropriately, Portzamparc was the winner of the 2004 Grand Prize for Urban Design (Grand prix de l'urbanisme) given by the French government.

From Caprarola to Ronchamp

As he describes his youth, Christian de Portzamparc did indeed take an early interest in painting, sculpture and cities. He was particularly marked by drawings of Le Corbusier in a book by Jean Petit. "In a naïve way," he says, "I imagined a painting or a sculpture that one could walk through or live in, and that would be as large as the landscape." He entered the Ecole des Beaux Arts in 1962 at the age of 18 and worked in the atelier of Eugène Beaudouin (1898–1983). Beaudouin was a noted architect, who worked on the urban design of the Maine-Montparnasse area of Paris amongst other large projects. After two years Christian de Portzamparc left the atelier of Beaudouin to join that of Georges Candilis (1913–1995) who had worked with Le Corbusier on the Unité d'Habitation until 1952 (Marseille, France). Candilis and his partner Alexis Josic (1921–2011) were both known for the modernity of their approach. Portzamparc's exposure to both the modern and academic aspects of the Ecole des Beaux Arts might be summarized in drawings he did at the time of the Villa Farnese (Caprarola, 1573), and of Le Corbusier's chapel at Ronchamp (Notre Dame du Haut, 1954). As modern architectural theory as such was not taught at the Beaux Arts, he plunged into the books of Le Corbusier and visited such sites as that of the Berlin Philharmonic by Hans Scharoun (1963).

Art and Revolt

In 1965, Christian de Portzamparc with a number of other young architects, who would later become well-known figures of the contemporary French scene such as Roland Castro and Antoine Grumbach, openly questioned the teaching methods of the Beaux-Arts. Christian de Portzamparc felt that filmmakers such as Godard and Antonioni showed the

Pastel. École des Beaux-Arts, Paris. *Le tombeau d'un poète*, 1964

European city in its real hybrid nature, mixing modern and ancient elements, in a much more tangible and "real" way than modern architectural theory had accepted.

Subsequent to this early revolt the architect took time to read, to paint, and to go to New York in 1966. "It was the underground scene there that fascinated me, art, music and poetry seemed so vibrant while architecture was boring. I was fascinated by the sheer urban power of New York. Then 1968 and the student uprisings in Paris came along, and for me that made architecture and urbanism seem outdated or worse, authoritarian."

In 1970, he participated in a psycho-sociology group led by Jacqueline Palmade and Françoise Lugassy that looked into the life experience of the residents of new neighborhoods in France. Open to the influence of the Structuralism, which beginning in the 1960s posited that elements of culture had to be understood in terms of their relationship to a larger structure. From discussions with the inhabitants of France's new residential areas, Portzamparc found that architecture and urbanism after all had a role to play, giving form to ideas that had their basis in theory.

A Roundabout and a Water Tower

A first practical occasion for Portzamparc's transition from art and theory to practice and construction came when he worked on public spaces for the areas around the new town of Marne-la-Vallée with Antoine Grumbach in the context of a plan conceived by Michel Macary. The architects travelled from Genoa to Amsterdam to study the public spaces there, and in 1971 Portzamparc proposed a water tower (Chateau d'Eau) to be placed at a juncture of roads and intended as a kind of symbolic point of reference in the new development zone. The structure completed in 1974 in a roundabout can immediately be identified as having an esthetic interest—rather than a Modernist totem, the architect chose rather a stepped form that has been called "Babylonian." With this gesture, he immediately placed himself in a different category than many architects of his generation, both in terms of esthetics and in his interest in the city and its symbols. Without being self-consciously referential in the mode of the rising school of post-modernism, Christian de Portzamparc from the first sought a personal vision of the city based in history and an openness that would be contradictory with the oppressive residential "bars" so favored in the new cities of France at the time.

Before this rise in the national reputation of Christian de Portzamparc however, he entered another competition that was important for his career, in the La Roquette area of the 11th arrondissement in Paris, on the site of a former prison. Here he proposed to place the 150 housing units and retail spaces around the periphery of a 1.5-hectare central green area. "I wanted to imagine a planted monument in Paris, a garden open to all uses, bordered by retail, cafés, restaurants, public services and housing," says the architect.[3] Above all, Portzamparc sought here, as in later projects to change the very logic of urban development, privileging open but inhabited public spaces against the prevailing logic of overweening density and rigid geometric plans.

The Open Block

Portzamparc's participation in the La Roquette competition for housing (not built) did bring him an invitation to participate in another competition organized by the Régie Immobilière de la Ville de Paris (RIVP) in the 13th arrondissement of Paris. The competition was related to far-reaching plans made in the 1960s to rebuild areas of the French capital. Rather than attempting to group the 209 social housing units in a single block, Portzamparc chose to design six buildings of varying height and configuration. Significantly, the architect looked at old plans of this area of Paris and found the name that he gave to his own submission: the Hautes Formes. This name (which can also refer to a top hat) is related to the existence on the site of open chalk pits. As Portzamparc's plans and images of the completed project demonstrate, he uses passages and green space to create a convivial urban space, inaugurating his concept of the open block (îlot ouvert), contrasting with the obviously closed blocks of Modernism which he rejected.

He says, "With the Hautes Formes, my preoccupation was with just how contemporary architecture can deal with an existing city, how to transform the city without eradicating what was there."[4] He sought here, and elsewhere afterwards, to address the issue of an intermediate scale, somewhere between an entire neighborhood and a building. Moern French architectural theory had imagined that new buildings should be purely geometric and thus somehow egalitarian, but Portzamparc took the position that such intervention in a city ignored history, geography and what existed prior to construction. His feeling was that the "crystalline objects" thus proposed obviously had to be built on "virgin territory" and that was certainly not the case of Paris. Portzamparc's logic in his urban design as elsewhere has often been one of fragmentation, of breaking up a program in order to create a more sensitive, living space, where air, light, and the movement of people animate architecture. This concept, developed with the Hautes Formes can also be seen in the Cité de la Musique, divided into its constituent parts to create a living entity rather than a "crystalline object." Prisms that might well be considered crystalline in their essence do of course make an appearance in more recent work by Portzamparc, but these are largely a reaction to more modern city spaces.

The architect then participated in a number of other competitions, including that for the Ballet School of the Opera national de Paris (Nanterre, 1983–87), for which he won the prestigious Equerre d'Argent award in 1988, the Tête Défense (a project won by Johann van Spreckelsen), the Opéra Bastille (won by Carlos Ott) and ten years after the Chateau d'Eau, he won the competition for the Cité de la Musique in Paris.

Islands in the Stream

Referring to the Hautes Formes, Christian de Portzamparc writes, "I did not start by imagining the buildings that had to be built, I thought instead of a passage, or rather the possibility of movement through a passage, a street, a square, I don't know which. This movement would cross through the block the way one makes a passage between the branches of a tree. It was from this point on that the built volumes could be accumulated in a rational way. From this standpoint, the overall density and the mass of the architecture did not worry me in the least, I reasoned in terms of empty volumes before thinking of built ones."[5] Though the theories of the French architect may sometimes seem complex, his explanation of the open block he imagined for the Hautes Formes and used on numerous occasions thereafter seems very clear.

From the Empty to the Full

The word "revolutionary" is certainly overemployed, but real revolutions occur when relatively simple ideas meet with appropriate circumstances. In post-war France, housing was often conceived rapidly and precisely in terms of the built volume—how to squeeze in as many square meters as possible on a given site. The architect's attention was often entirely focused on the object that could contain the program, rather than on the end users, their needs and what might be called the life of the architecture. By reversing the cognitive process of conception, starting with what is empty rather than what is full, Portzamparc conceived of a revolution in housing and even in city planning. His way of approaching design had esthetic and practical elements, but the end result is to put the user, the resident back into the center of the equation, and not to deal with the life of the architecture as a secondary, almost insignificant part of the work of the architect. Portzamparc sought neither undue complexity nor specific reference to city patterns of the past. Rather he looked at sites and their urban implication and imagined that contemporary architecture could very well fit into the old city, not by mimicking its forms like the post-modernists hoped, but by isolating and using its essence, the passageways and movements that still give life to old cities.

Liberty and Rigor

Having worked with a housing complex, Christian de Portzamparc found that some of the same ideas could be used in larger urban development schemes, such as the more recent Rue de la Loi in Brussels (2008) or the mooted Sea Extension of Monaco (2007), just as they could be applied to a single building complex like the Cité de la Musique or the French Embassy in Berlin. In 1994, he carried out the design development of the Masséna district in the Paris. Here, he says that he associated two contradictory principles, that of the liberty of the "full" or built forms and of the rigor of the "empty" or public spaces. He explains that the idea was to see the entire neighborhood as an "interaction of architecture. My objective," he concludes "was to open the city to diversity, to randomness and to an uncertain future." The bold concept here consisted in saying that it was neither the built volumes nor the streets and walkways that determined the form of the city, but the interaction of the two. Part of his process has generally be a rejection of adjoining buildings that tend to block all possibility of passage, forming urban walls. In the case of the Masséna project, Portzamparc left an unusual degree of liberty to the other architects participating in the project, operating at the limit between architecture and urban design.

The idea of avoiding adjoining buildings has to do not only with offering easier passage at ground level, but also with bringing more light and air into residences within a city block. The fact that buildings no longer form continuous walls, as is often the case in Paris, for example along the avenues laid out by Haussmann in the nineteenth century, means that an even older conception of urban development, one of individual buildings not necessarily laid out according to a geometric plan, takes pride of place in the new city. This is a constructive and modern use of history.

Liberating the Architect

Portzamparc's plan for Masséna defines the built zone in terms of large "envelopes" that contain more than the allowed built volume, thus freeing architects to express themselves and relying on the overall city zoning density regulations to bring the whole into line in the final analysis. Nor did he attempt to impose specific materials or types of facades, resulting in a diversity of architectural expression and even a variety in the orientations of the buildings within each block. "The idea," he states "is to give real liberty to the architects. The 'esthetic' system of the open block controls the overall result without imposing artificial unity. Rather than an urban design based on restrictions, this method relies on openness. This is often the way to incite architects to be creative, and the resulting buildings are indeed quite different. It is obviously more interesting for an architect to design an entire building rather than a simple façade in a carefully aligned street of adjoining buildings."

Living Art

An interesting side-light of the Masséna plan is that Portzamparc specifically states that all architects are not good and that in such an area of the city, it is necessary to admit the possibility that every new structure will *not* be a masterpiece. "We have to make do with ordinary architecture," he says. The open block is one of the essential ideas of the work of Christian de Portzamparc. As the urban planning and architectural projects presented in this section make clear his is an inclusive architecture, one that retains the essential connection to the users, to making space that is convivial and not exclusively the province of the architect as artist or "genius." Modernism consecrated the idea of the architect as a maker of forms often with little or no relation to their specific site or to history, while modern urbanism privileged geometric patterns constituted of solids (built forms), often made up of adjoining building. Portzamparc's architecture and his urban design on the contrary break these molds, creating passages and openings, basing his work as much on emptiness as on solids, on the interaction between buildings and their environment, be it in a historic or an esthetic sense. Portzamparc is surely an artist, as his drawings and paintings demonstrate—he makes harmonious, attractive buildings, but he has never allowed his sense of art to dominate what constitutes the essential element of his open blocks, which is to say the life of the architecture and its users.

A Relation to the City and to History

In the larger projects that would follow such as the Cité de la Musique, Christian de Portzamparc continued to develop his concept of the relation of a building, or a group of buildings to its urban site, and his consistently sought to create passageways and openings that would better integrate his own work into its specific location, both in terms of esthetics and in the very real and practical sense of day to day life in the city. Always lyrical in his forms, and never ceding to the sirens of post-modernism in its tendency to create pastiches, Portzamparc has nonetheless sought out the deeper links to history in an urban environment, a history that is expressed in names, in shapes, in an evocation of life that has gone on in places such as Paris for centuries.

The reputation of Christian de Portzamparc did not only develop in France because of his increasingly large-scale work, but also because of a number of smaller projects. His 530-square meter Café Beaubourg (1985–87) designed for Gilbert Costes occupies the lower levels of three historic Paris buildings, on the upper square of the Centre Pompidou. With not only the space itself but also the interior finishing and furnishings and a number of more painterly interventions, Portzamparc demonstrated his obvious capacity to undertake works of design as opposed to pure architecture. Le Tracé Intérieur edited the Café Beaubourg Lounge Chair in 1987. Christian de Portzamparc's intervention here is quite obviously contemporary, but it is neither post-modern nor for example minimalist, it is made up of space and light and materials that do not conflict with the exterior environment, made up of the old city together with the high-tech fantasy of Piano and Rogers, but also bring a new energy to the area.

Surely because of his theory and because of realizations like the Hautes Formes, Portzamparc began in 1988 to receive commissions to design or build in the urban environment. He entered competitions in Nantes (Atlanpole), Strasbourg, Metz and Aix-en-Provence. He also worked in Toulouse and Montpellier. As he states, he was fascinated by each case, because of the differences in the projects, and because of the need to find new solutions. For Nantes, he took his open block concept one step further, imagining an urban scheme that would be open to different types of architecture, volumes uses and even unexpected change. The 1988 urban design competition involved a four-kilometer long area of Nantes destined for housing, research and industrial use. Alternating built and green areas, the architect also took into account the possibility of perceiving the larger scale of the project, an element not often taken into account in contemporary urban design. The open blocks were to be situated in a grid plan with no pre-defined masses—rather the intention was the urban designer would place given clients and functions according to their needs. Again, this project was not carried out for financial reasons linked to the overall economy.

In Strasbourg for the Place de l'Etoile project (1991) Portzamparc studied the 500-meter wide corridor separating the old city of Strasbourg from the nineteenth century town of Neudorf. This corridor was used for a canal and a highway. Rather than proposing to simply fill in the empty areas with new buildings, the architect sought to enlarge the canal and create a park. In the center of this space, he proposed a kind of administrative island with the existing headquarters of the urban community and a new congress center, which was part of the program. Throughout the scheme, street alignments and empty spaces create a kind of "hybrid" link between the two existing urban areas.

Opposite page: Le Café Beaubourg, Paris, France, 1985–1987

Logic and Originality

These and other urban design projects by Christian de Portzamparc were presented under the title "Urban Situations" at the MA Gallery in Tokyo in 1991. In 1990, he won the Architecture Prize (Grand Prix d'Architecture) of the city of Paris, attesting to his rising status in France. Beginning in 1989, Portzamparc participated along with Rem Koolhaas, Steven Holl and others in a master plan laid out by Arata Isozaki for the southern Japanese city of Fukuoka. This project surely participated in international recognition that culminated in the 1994 Pritzker Prize. The words of Ada Louis Huxtable at the time continue to have a resonance and to apply also to the career that Portzamparc has carried forward since the mid-1990s. Betraying her own quite American point of view, she nonetheless wrote: "To dismiss this work as homage to a trendy vernacular, however, one must overlook the logic and originality of Portzamparc's plans, the expert and effective way in which his solutions flow and function, his sure grasp of scale and proportion, his superior sense of urban amenity, his lyrical use of light and color. Given cultural distance and European perspective, his sources transcend shallow sentimentalism. This is no artfully retro exercise; the timeless elements of architecture are being dramatically reinterpreted. These colorful, light-filled forms serve a functional and social organization of exceptional skill. Portzamparc transforms his obvious delight in Arp-like curves and giant cones and candy colors into a pop monumentality that takes serious high camp into the realm of serious high art. Make no mistake; this is serious architecture. It is also serious hedonism and profound French chic. But unlike so much French architecture, where the chic is skin-deep, this is seriously innovative work with an impressive range of invention."[6]

Paris–Tokyo Express

With the mid-1990s Portzamparc took on a number of projects that have come to identify his work in the public mind. Beginning in 1994 he created a very visible extension to the Palais des Congrès in Paris, situated along the axis that leads from the Champs-Elysées to La Défense. The east wing of the Cité de la Musique was completed in 1995, as was the Crédit Lyonnais Tower in Lille. Part of the Euralille master plan by Rem Koolhaas, this unusually shaped tower, straddles the high-speed train station on narrow structural foundation columns and a 328-foot clear span over the tracks. In describing this project the architect refers to the "sculptural" or "expressionist" nature of his designs, which were unexpected at the time. In part due to its unusual form, the Crédit Lyonnais Tower, now known simply as the Tour de Lille, has become one of the favorite landmarks of city residents.

During the same period, Christian de Portzamparc won the competition for the Bandai Tower (Tokyo, 1994) against Jean Nouvel with a sculptural design that proposed an unexpected artistic lighting scheme. The lyrical nature of Portzamparc's (unbuilt) Bandai Tower was visibly quite the opposite of Nouvel's more geometric proposal. A 1996 exhibition at the Centre Pompidou in Paris (Scènes d'Atelier) was his first major show and included 900 sketches, drawings, models and plans, as well as paintings that showed the continuing role of personal artistic expression in the work of Portzamparc. The goal of this exhibition was to explain his creative process.

An Event in the City

An essential step in terms of visibility came with the LVMH Tower in New York (1995–99). Set near the corner of 57th Street and Madison Avenue, the LVMH Tower represented a shift in the design of tall buildings in New York. Rather than the more common undifferentiated facade generally seen in Manhattan, this 23-story office building boasted a complex glass facade designed to avoid direct reflections of the black IBM Tower located just across 57th Street. By carefully studying New York's then even more complex zoning laws, the architect managed, through the use of a sophisticated series of setbacks to increase the overall height of his building, surpassing the neighboring Chanel Tower. This gave him the possibility to create the so-called "Magic Room" atop the tower—a spectacular three-story room with view on three sides onto 57th Street, or toward Central Park. Portzamparc's contribution is in good part limited to this room and the facade, since the office decor, and even that of the ground floor boutiques is the work of other architects. A sophisticated lighting system inserted into a "fault" line running up the facade gives the building a real nighttime identity in the cityscape. As the architect described his project at the time, "We didn't want it to be a twin of the adjacent Chanel Tower. I never worry about image, I was focusing here on the problem of how to give a presence to this building which risked disappearing in the reflection of the huge IBM block opposite. That's all. Here the oblique lines, the rejection of a single plane, the ultra-white sandblasted glass, the bands in the windows and the lines, which affirm the vertical presence. But there was no image in my mind, no conscious translation of what LVMH should be."[7]

Unlike some noted contemporary architects who rely on private clients to a great extent, Portzamparc works frequently with government authorities. In France, the division between architects who do private work and those who do public work is marked, whereas in most periods, Portzamparc had a portfolio that was roughly half and half of each. In New York for his first project there, the architect owed his selection to Bernard Arnault, head of LVMH, owner of the Dior and Louis Vuitton brands amongst others. Arnault explained his choice in a 1999 interview: "Once we had opted for a tower project, I obviously considered the importance of the American market for the group, the highly artistic aspect of our firm's professions and our attachment to quality at all levels. It was therefore indispensable to erect a building that was in itself a message strong enough to express at first glance the LVMH group's image—in other words, creativity, beauty, and charm. That's why I contacted Christian de Portzamparc and asked him to reflect on and design the building for this site, right in the heart of Manhattan."[8]

The work of the French architect was enthusiastically reviewed by American critics, such as the architect and writer Joseph Giovannini, who stated, "An event in the city comparable to the Chrysler Building with its illuminated tiara, the LVMH Tower, designed by Parisian architect Christian de Portzamparc in association with the Hillier Group, at last reverses New York's long architectural slide into commercial banality. Not since the Seagram Building, the Guggenheim and the TWA terminal at JFK were finished in the 1950s and 1960s has an architect given New York such a significant and jewel-like intervention."[9] With the Pritzker Prize and the completion of the LVMH Tower, Portzamparc emerged as a significant international architect.

A second LVMH project on Madison Avenue was called off for economic reasons, but Portzamparc kept good relations with Bernard Arnault, recently completing the Cheval Blanc Winery (Saint-Emilion, 2011). Chateau Cheval Blanc wine is only one of four in France to have the highest distinction (*Premier Grand Cru Classé*), and the winery belongs to Arnault and his associate, the Belgian businessman Albert Frère. The twisting concrete walls designed by Portzamparc form a promontory-belvedere overlooking the vineyards. The architect also designed 52 vats in which the wine is kept in the building, as well as a more classical cask storage cellar with an openwork brick wall to facilitate natural ventilation. The lyrical purity of Portzamparc's use of precast concrete in this instance is readily apparent, perhaps underlining a somewhat less complex vision in his mature work.

Cascading Skyline

Both the Pritzker Prize and the LVMH Tower surely had an impact on the selection of the architect to design a 75-story, 306-meter (1,004-foot) high residential and hotel tower on West 57th Street just across the street from Carnegie Hall (One57, 2010–14). This was a direct commission from the promoter Gary Barnett. He and the architect studied structures that would have gone as high as 400 meters,

but One57 was built as it stands within Manhattan's current zoning code and air-rights regulations.

The so-called as-of-right procedure means that a building is allowed within the zoning code and thus does not have to go through the complex and limiting procedures set down in the city's Uniform Land Use Review Procedure (ULURP), a fact that has led to a proliferation of super-tall buildings south of Central Park in Manhattan with the influx of mainly foreign money for expensive condominium apartments. As the London daily The Guardian explained, "none of the tall new towers in New York required city permission (although they did require clearance from the Federal Aviation Administration, given Manhattan's proximity to three airports). The city doesn't limit height, just floor area ratio, and developers, can buy 'air rights' from adjacent buildings, letting them go super-tall 'as of right'."[10]

Things have changed clearly changed in New York since the LVMH Tower was built, and 57th Street has become a new center for high-rise condominiums with extremely expensive apartments, often bought by foreigners. The penthouse duplex in this building is reported to have sold for over one hundred million dollars[11]. The same developer (Extell) is planning to go even higher one block west of One57 with the Nordstrom Tower (Adrian Smith, Gordon Gill) due to top out at 523 meters (1,775 feet). One57 includes the Park Hyatt Hotel whose interiors were designed by Yabu Pushelberg. Residential interior design was by Thomas Juul-Hansen. The architect states, "The building's volumes are linked by an ascending and descending cascading movement that flows over curved transitional surfaces containing inhabited terraces. A vertical pattern of contrasting stripes comprised of two different glass types (with uniform visibility from the interior) distinguish the north façades and recall the vertical energy of New York's cascading skyline, in contrast with the east and west façades that resemble the aesthetic of the Le Monde and Nantes projects." The headquarters of the Paris daily newspaper Le Monde were designed and built by the architect between 2001 and 2005. The lateral volumes of the facades of that building were 'composed of glass and aluminum marquetry" that does bring to mind the blue and gray patterns of the glass surfaces of One57. The Nantes Tripode project (2006–12) is a large open-block design including housing, offices, a hotel, retail and parking areas.

The scale and nature of One57 differentiate it from the more "jewel-like" design of the earlier LVMH Building, it is one very tall piece of real estate, but calling on Christian de Portzamparc has clearly added to the value of the structure and to its integration in the rapidly changing Manhattan skyline. Especially when contrasted with the strict linearity of Rafael Viñoly's taller 432 Park Avenue, Portzamparc's skyscraper does conserve the lyrical essence of his designs, both in its color patterns and in its soaring curves.

From Berlin to Rio

Though he has completed prestigious projects in other countries, one of Christian de Portzamparc's most noted realizations was the French Embassy in Berlin (1997–2003) located on the prestigious Pariserplatz almost next to the Brandenburg Gate. The new French Embassy was built on a site already occupied by the French delegation between 1860 and the War. Severely damaged during the War the building was too close to the Wall to be of any use until after 1989. It was in 1993 that the Berlin Senate announced plans to rebuild the Pariser Platz while conserving its original neo-classic volumes. Requirements imposed by the authorities included the use of stone cladding and glazed surfaces not to exceed one-third of the façade area. Aside from Christian de Portzamparc who won a 1997 competition for the French Embassy design, architects Josef-Paul Kleihues, van Gerkan & Marg, Günter Behnisch, Ortner & Ortner and Frank Gehry (DG Bank, Pariser Platz 3) have built on the square with greater or lesser degrees of success. Working with the landscape architect Régis Guignard and his wife Elizabeth for the interiors, Portzamparc designed an 18,000 square meter structure with 4,000 m2 of office space and 1,400 square meters of reception areas for a budget of 33.9 million euros. Aside from the strict zoning problems he faced, the architect also had to deal with a complex architectural program and a site that was enclosed (except on the side of the square) by twenty-meter high blank walls. Portzamparc created an interior garden and assured that the reception areas opened onto this quiet inner space. In an interesting use of his open block concept, the architect managed to lodge the complex program and to still bring natural light into the office spaces. His close collaboration with Elizabeth de Portzamparc for the interiors allowed him to propose a coherent whole, with interior spaces and furnishings also carefully designed by the couple. An earlier example of Elizabeth de Portzamparc's work in her husband's buildings was the Café de la Musique in the Cité de la Musique, completed for Gilbert Costes in 1995. Today, Christian and Elizabeth de Portzamparc share an office building in the 9th arrondissement of Paris.

The same year he started work on the Berlin Embassy, Christian de Portzamparc began another significant public project in Luxembourg, The Philarmonie in Luxembourg (Grande-Duchesse Joséphine-Charlotte Concert Hall, 1997–2005) is located on the Kirchberg plateau near administrative offices of the European Community and next to I.M. Pei's MUDAM (Musée d'Art Moderne Grand Duc Jean, 2006). His original idea was to plant a ring of trees around the building that would have encouraged visitors to forget their surroundings before a concert, but he opted instead for a peristyle made with 827 steel columns that also differentiate the building from its more bureaucratic surroundings. These columns filter light, with some of them bearing the structural load of the roof and others carrying down rainwater or service conduits. Noted for its excellent acoustics, the Philharmonie hosts 400 performances a year and is considered one of the main concert halls in Europe.

Christian de Portzamparc completed his Cidade das Artes in Rio de Janeiro in 2013. This 46,000-square-meter complex is located at the crossing of Americas and Ayrton Senna avenues in the midst of an area of the city originally laid out by Lucio Costa. The Cidade das Artes forms a single large structure with a vast terrace set ten meters above ground level. Intended for an 1800-seat Philharmonic Hall, a Chamber Music venue (500 seats) as well as use for popular music, three movie theaters, dance studios, ten rehearsal rooms, exhibition spaces, restaurants, a media library, the design is characterized by the two horizontal plates that form the roof and the main terrace. Between these two horizontal limits, curved concrete walls contain the halls and establish an interplay of solids and voids. At the personal request of former Rio mayor Cesar Maia, the Philharmonic Hall can be converted into a 1,300 seat Opera.

The architect describes this work as a "public symbol" and a landmark for a new area of Rio. Its concrete work is surely an indirect tribute to the work of the great Brazilian master Oscar Niemeyer. Although it's concept has been partly compared to that of the Cité de la Musique in Paris, the Cidade das Artes also shows the ways that Portzamparc has taken up the influences of earlier masters, much as Le Corbusier had an impact on his earlier career. This was indeed the opinion of the Pritzker Prize jury, who's citation reads in part, "His is an architecture that draws on French cultural tradition while paying homage to the master architect and countryman, Le Corbusier. It is a lyrical architecture that takes great risks and evokes excitement from its audience."[12] If the curves of the later work of Corbu found their origin in Rio and the work of Oscar Niemeyer. Ada Louise Huxtable preferred to cite the "Arp like curves" of Portzamparc's work prior to 1994, she might also have thought of Oscar Niemeyer in a case such as that of the Rio building.

Although the Rio project like the Cité de la Musique before it were complex from the point of view of relations with the municipalities and governments concerned, Christian de Portzamparc carried through right to the end, obtaining the essential elements of what he wanted. This too is a considerable quality at a time when many well-known architects wind up in endless lawsuits over large public projects, in France and elsewhere, or do not succeed in getting their original concept realized. One clear indication of the success of Portzamparc in his major cultural projects, is that he has other large ones underway outside of France.

Opposite page: Cidade das Artes, Rio de Janeiro, Brazil, 2002–2013

Culture in China and Morocco

The Suzhou Cultural Center is one of a series of projects commissioned by the city as part of the Wujiang Lakefront Masterplan. It is considered the flagship project of this new district. The 100,000 square meter site is located at the convergence of one of China's most beautiful lakes and the urban perspective of the new city. The Cultural Center is to include a 1,600-seat Opera House, a modular 600-seat hall, a 24,000 square meter Museum, an 18,000 square meter Exhibition Center, a Conference Center cafés, restaurants and cinemas, as well as a 14,000 square meter shopping center for a total floor area of 202,000 square meters. Employing vast curves that bring to mind his design on a smaller scale for Cheval Blanc, the architect essentially takes into account the pedestrian access that divides the site, linking the Opera House on one side and the Museum and Conference Center on the other with his ribbon. These arching curves are designed in metal as opposed to the precast concrete used for the Cheval Blanc Winery. Portzamparc creates a generous foyer for the Opera and entrance for the Museum at the center of the complex, forming a belvedere or window looking out at the lake.

Though substantially smaller than the Suzhou project, the CasArts project in Casablanca is to be Africa's largest theatre complex, including a multi-purpose hall with 1,800 seats, a flexible theater with 600 seats, public rehearsal rooms, special events rooms and, shops, a restaurant, café, cyberspace, library, showroom and art gallery. The project is located on the one remaining free side of the Place Mohammed V, a classic rectangular 1920's composition dating from the period when Hubert Lyautey was the Resident-General of French Morocco (1912–25), and designed by the urban planner Henri Prost. Prost (1874–1959) was the author of a comprehensive city plan for Casablanca, but also for Fes, Marrakesh, Meknes and Rabat. Portzamparc won the international competition for the project in July 2009 against the likes of Zaha Hadid, Frank Gehry and Rem Koolhaas. As the architect describes the project, it "gives the impression of being composed of several detached houses, like a medina in the city. Instead of an autonomous architectural object . . . this fluid ensemble defies symmetry without opposing it, inviting visitors to enter the shadow of (an) interior universe through several slim, gaps and entrances that lead to a vast . . . public gallery . . ." The architect turned the façade of the complex into an outdoor stage in itself. Slightly angled vis-à-vis the square as was implied by the streets entering the space on the side of CasArts, the complex as seen in plan recalls the architect's designs for open blocks, and emphasizes a fragmentation that allows for internal courtyards and unexpected angles and juxtapositions of the volumes. It appears too to reconcile the somewhat martial regularity of the square with the ore complex accumulations of buildings in neighboring blocks; here as elsewhere, the architect reconciles the site, its history and the function of the new structure. Modernity in his hands clearly is not meant to be a break with the past, but rather a sign of continuity in the urban environment. As Christian de Portzamparc was born in Casablanca, this project is a return to his own point of origin, with the now-distant French colonial presence giving way to a modernity obviously accepted by today's Morocco.

Relating to the Context

The work of major architects can often be likened to that of artists. They take the substance of a program and a site and model it according to their own personality and convictions. The task of architects today is surely linked to a transition from the certainties of Modernism and its underlying concept of the tabula rasa, to a more uncertain world, where the idea of "progress" has been abandoned. Architects who still indulge in the creation of singular objects would seem to be intellectually anchored in the time of Modernism when it was deemed necessary for the new to entirely replace the old. Christian de Portzamparc is indeed a product of the spirit and culture of France as the Pritzker Prize jury pointed out in 1994. Very early on though, the architect in training that he was led a revolt against the outdated teaching methods of the Beaux-Arts. If his country is France, it is less that of classicism than it is the modern nation that gave rise to such concepts as Structuralism. Relating elements of architecture to its larger context, never ceding to an attempt to create a pastiche of the past, Christian de Portzamparc adds a lyric sense of esthetics, grounded in his own drawings and paintings. Concepts such as his open block are by no means an esthetic whim, they are based in careful thinking about what life in the modern city is, and how modern structures can fit into the old cities of Europe without creating a feeling of rupture and disenfranchisement.

The main contents of this book are based on the work of Christian de Portzamparc since 1995, when he attained a degree of international notoriety and was given major projects. The division of the chapters is that suggested by the architect, according to his sources of inspiration, the building types concerned and the chronological order of the work. Thus tall or vertical buildings have become an integral part of his oeuvre, with such buildings as One57 but also the recently completed 144-meter (472-foot) Prism Tower at 400 Park Avenue South in Manhattan.

Though more angular than most of his other buildings, the Prism Tower is yet another demonstration of Christian de Portzamparc's ability to integrate a structure into its urban

Opposite page: rue de l'Abbaye, Paris, France, 1975

environment, even when regulations have entirely changed as is the case in Manhattan at present. This project is in part the result of policies implemented by Amanda Burden, New York City Planning director from 2002 to 2013 under Mayor Michael Bloomberg that aimed to foster architectural creation by requiring developers to negotiate air rights at the district level, allowing them to build more easily under city regulations. Referring to Mayor Bloomberg, Amanda Burden stated, "In terms of design, he always said, 'good design, great design is a priority for the city. It is essential for physical and economic and social wellbeing.' He said we had to raise the bar for what's expected, for both public and private development."[13] Portzamparc has also made skillful use of New York City zoning laws that he had already mastered for the LVMH Tower, in the oblique or prismatic forms of the building that optimize views and substantially enliven the exterior appearance of the building. Christian de Portzamparc states that Rick Cook, the architect of the 3,658-meter (1,200-foot) tall Bank of America Tower located at 6th Avenue and 42nd Street (2009) discussed the idea of such oblique angles with him prior to the design of the taller building.[14]

Museums and buildings for music are another signature element of Christian de Portzamparc's built work. From the Cité de la Musique and the Cidade das Artes in Rio to the upcoming Suzhou Cultural Center in China or the CasArts complex in Casablanca, he is leaving a mark in an area where few other architects have such a prestigious list of projects. These buildings, together with smaller scale culturally oriented buildings ranging from the Cheval Blanc Winery to the new Dior building in Seoul (2011–15) represent the point of juncture between Portzamparc's obvious artistic sensibility, long expressed in his paintings and watercolors, and the sensitivity required for the commissions concerned.

To Serve a Purpose

Christian de Portzamparc has never developed signature elements in his designs like Richard Meier's white grid, or Frank Gehry's sculptural expression, he has sought to respond to each programmatic situation with the best possible solution. Portzamparc has managed to be identifiable in his work even without introducing specific signature design elements. His forms are surely more lyrical (gently curved) than the work of many other contemporary architects, he has a fondness for pastels and sometimes bright colors in his work, and above all, in plan and section he has a sense of fluidity that sets him apart without ever becoming repetitive or formula-driven. He has never rejected history like some of his Modernist predecessors, rather he has taken to heart the Structuralist belief that the

Prism Tower, New York, U.S.A., 2002–2016

"phenomena of human life are not intelligible except through their interrelations. These relations constitute a structure, and behind local variations in the surface phenomena there are constant laws of abstract culture."[15]

Portzamparc's innovative use of the open block expressed in early projects like the Hautes Formes, and more recently in the French Embassy in Berlin or the Tripode complex in Nantes reflects a philosophical desire to engage contemporary architecture in everyday life, to look at what makes people comfortable, what makes them interact, and to set aside Modernist tenets that went quite clearly in the opposite direction. Basically, Christian de Portzamparc took some of the geometric building blocks of Modernism and made holes in them, and then he accumulated them in the slightly irregular ways in which cities most often develop. There is an order in his open blocks, but it is more akin to the living city than it is to a mathematical grid. In this respect, the practical implications of construction in an urban environment, and one is tempted to say the success of his architecture does reconnect at a certain level to the idea of interrelations in culture in the broadest sense of the term. Nor is the suggestion that Structuralism, which emerged before Portzamparc was an architecture student, may have something to do with his thought a way of limiting his importance to the past. The ideas expressed in the open block have to do with behavior and its connection to contemporary architecture, and to the relation between architecture and urban design. Rather than trying to build a sculpture or a monument to his own artistic creativity, Christian de Portzamparc has been *engagé* in the French sense of the word, engaged in his architecture, engaged in the esthetic and philosophical implications of designing and building, engaged with the future users of his buildings. In this sense, he has done a great deal to bring contemporary architecture back to what it was always supposed to do— to serve the city and its inhabitants, to uplift and to shelter, to serve a purpose.

Notes
1. http://www.pritzkerprize.com/1994/jury accessed November 25, 2015
2. http://www.pritzkerprize.com/1994/essay Acessed November 25, 2015.
3. http://www.portzamparc.com/en/projects/paris-la-roquette/ accessed December 1, 2015.
4. Christian de Portzamparc, Grand prix de l'urbanisme 2004, Ministère de l'Equipement, 2004, Paris.
5. Quotes from Christian de Portzamparc here are from an internal office document entitled *Ilots – Quartiers – Rues* (Islands – Neighborhoods – Streets) written by the architect in June 2004 and provided to the author.
6. http://www.pritzkerprize.com/1994/essay accessed November 25, 2015.
7. Christian de Portzamparc, in The LVMH Tower, *Connaissance des Arts*, Paris, 1999.
8. Bernard Arnault, in The LVMH Tower, *Connaissance des Arts*, Paris, 1999.
9. Joseph Giovannini in The LVMH Tower, *Connaissance des Arts*, Paris, 1999.
10. "Supersizing Manhattan: New Yorker Rage Against the Dying of the Light," *The Guardian*, January 16, 2015. http://www.theguardian.com/cities/2015/jan/16/supersizing-manhattan-new-yorkers-rage-against-the-dying-of-the-light?CMP=share_btn_link accessed December 2, 2015.
11. Martin Filler, *New York Review of Books*, April 2, 2015 http://www.nybooks.com/articles/2015/04/02/new-york-conspicuous-construction/
12. http://www.pritzkerprize.com/1994/jury accessed November 25, 2015
13. Amanda Burden quoted at http://www.archfoundation.org/2011/10/something-about-amanda/#sthash.FVPueVht.dpuf accessed on December 2, 2015.
14. Christian de Portzamparc in discussion with the author, Paris, November 8, 2016.
15. Simon Blackburn, *Oxford Dictionary of Philosophy*, second edition revised, Oxford University Press, Oxford, 2008.

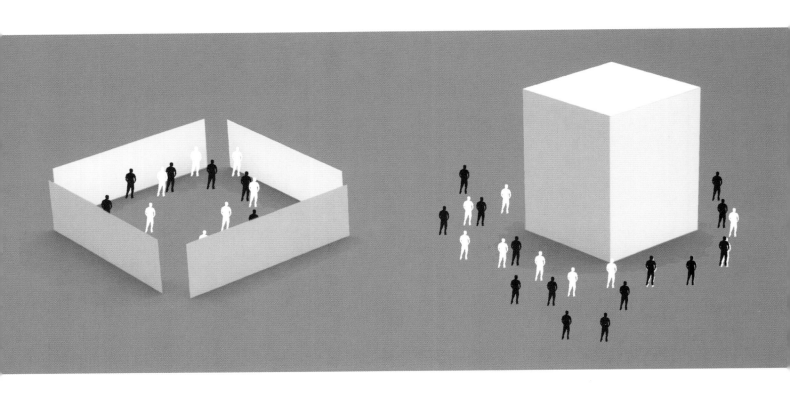

Chapter 1
Perception of Space

Program and Site

As a teenager in the 1960s, I would go and watch the modern town advancing into the fields surrounding Rennes in Brittany. The regiments of tall white buildings near the city's inner suburbs loomed menacingly over the earthen farmhouses and copses. From mid-century onwards, cities broke their banks, and a period of upheaval spread around the world. More than one hundred people a day were arriving in the big cities; one thousand a day in the future metropolises. I saw the city of objects and boxes conquering the city of streets and hollow spaces, and at the time I thought it was a good thing. I did not know at the time that I would embrace architecture.

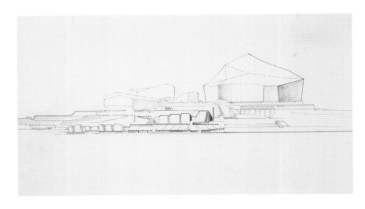

Studies for a philharmonic ensemble. École des Beaux-Arts, Paris, 1964

In France, homeless campaigner, The Abbé Pierre, was leading the attack on country's shantytowns and slums. Rural exodus and mass immigration were upon us, and we responded with industrial organization and a quasi-military conquest of the land. Europe was breaking with the nightmare of war and was rebuilding a new world. It was an earthquake, a big bang that can be understood as a delayed effect of the industrial revolution that went on to undermine cities and landscapes everywhere.

From the nineteenth century, the steam engine, factories and automobiles entered the landscape. Very soon, metal girders, concrete, plumbing and elevators penetrated our buildings. These "alien" technologies led to a decorative frenzy to cover, hide, forget and embellish technology, pulled along by a mainstream of fear about the future. Gustave Eiffel was forced to suspend an arch at the base of his tower to make it esthetically acceptable. Architecture had always had a duty to represent the stability of civilization. Since the Renaissance, the past had held sway over architecture, which was regularly urged to return to the modes of Antiquity, the supreme tradition.

Then everything changed. When Le Corbusier placed a photograph of a Citroën opposite one of the Parthenon in "Toward an Architecture" he jump-started the modern era. Technology became a fixture of civilization and culture. It became a passion, an esthetic, an emotion. In architecture emerged the ideal of fusion between beauty and utility that never existed before. For centuries, architecture relied on authority and imitation of the past. Following that, future had dominion over architecture. The new "stability" had arrived.

This is what fascinated me. I first discovered the architect's profession when I saw a drawing of Chandigarh in a book by Le Corbusier. I used to draw a lot and I suddenly realized that a drawing could be used to imagine a place where you could walk and live. I used to go and see Le Corbusier's work. The doctrine of the Modern Movement, forged in the pre-war years, had become a democratic and international virtue. The idea that the beautiful and the useful could form a same reality became the foundation on which we based our judgements, and it remains so, even if we play at contradicting it. It was the start of a new era. It was as just as obvious as the Quattrocento.

On entering the École des Beaux-Arts, I initially studied under Eugène Beaudoin before moving to the studio of Georges Candilis, a follower of Le Corbusier. The school remained as it had been for centuries, attached to the famous Beaux-Arts system, totally detached from the present, and we struggled against this "system," its outcomes and timeless programs.

In the commotion that muddled its way to May 1968, the prevailing academic tradition pushed my generation to call everything into question.

Project for a nursery school. École des Beaux-Arts, Paris, 1965

Under the search of addressing a new time, it was a period of certainty. Time was a machine marching unstoppably toward progress. Never had the idea of historical determinism been so strong and maybe it never will be again. Science mastered matter; it mastered nature. The modern movement gathered momentum in the technological era, affecting every field of human activity and transforming every area of our lives and cities.

Back then, in the early sixties, there were plans to demolish and rebuild two thirds of central Paris. The streets were "subject to frontage setback." They needed to be widened to accommodate higher buildings. Modernization would arrive and a new age would begin. It was inevitable. We were very excited about it. This official plan was a watered-down return to Le Corbusier's "Plan Voisin," in which the center of Paris would be razed to the ground and replaced by cruciform tower blocks. As early as the *Salon des Arts Décoratifs* in 1922 he presented an astounding representation of a city for three million people under the striking title "The City without Place." No place, no site; the city could be anywhere; but there is a program. "We were entering a period of imminent certainties," wrote the author. Demography and industrial methods of the technological era imposed for Le Corbusier the absolute authority of needs over the site. The predominance of program over place, *logos* over *topos*, went on to become the main thrust and strength of Modern thought: a powerful force for construction but also for the destruction of the planet. Architecture had always sought to strike a balance between what Rimbaud called "the place and the formula," the site and the program. From now on, the formula would be king.

Whereas Haussmann, in transforming Paris, cut through the flesh of the city, opening up avenues and voids, Le Corbusier wanted to put solid objects down on a razed and empty ground. He had witnessed Fordism and its streamlined mass production, and Leninism for which tabula rasa was a pre-condition to bringing the new into being. This period seems long gone now and the intervening decades have seen a turnaround in our awareness of the future. Despite my enthusiastic trust in the genius of science since my very first architectural projects I have always questioned the technical certainties that structure our world.

I gradually began to doubt this destruction program. Total tabula rasa of Paris seemed improbable. At the very least, it failed to take into account the reality of the city, which I saw as a temporal phenomenon as much as a spatial one; a vast repository, of the collective memory. Movies of Antonioni and Godard were showing us the real, contemporary and contradictory city as it travelled from the brand new suburbs of Milan or Paris to their ancient centers.

City is time materialized, time intimate and time shared; permanent proof of the passing of generations; a vast metaphysical calendar that is never completed. We live in the present in places from the recent or distant past that we transform to create the future, which is immediately integrated as a present and then as the past.

1966

In 1966, I spent several months in New York. The city fascinated me. It was the extreme archetype of the Greek city, with its grid of streets, the modernity of the nineteenth century, with its feeling of nature and central park, and the modernity of the twentieth century, with its dense verticality, which could not be further from European modernism. I was absorbed by the newness of its artistic life—painting, performances, poetry and music. I put architecture to one side. I left behind my studies and the avant-garde architectural ideas of the period: Archigram, systems theories, self-construction and megastructures. When I returned to Paris I expected the protests against the Vietnam War and the libertarian hedonism of New York to spread across Europe. I was also increasingly aware of ecological issues. What I found were earnest theories of linguistics and Marxism, and the political activism that led to May 1968.

1969

Man's first steps on the moon and the success of the Apollo mission stunned the world. We had taken a leap into the future. Leaving the earth, conquering the wide-open spaces, living in vehicles and nomadic objects: it was the stuff of science fiction. And it was coming true. Already the ambition of modern architecture was the expansion of machine objects on stilts lifted above the ground.

Science fiction had popularized the image of mankind's destiny, and this image was being revealed by the Apollo mission. The lunar module—the absolute object, detached from terrestrial attachments—was a symbol that could easily have been designed by Peter Cook. But I remember, at that exact moment, astounded by the wonderful images I was watching on the screen, I said to myself that despite this mastery of the far-off, the off-ground, back on Earth we were increasingly unable to build livable neighborhoods to expand our cities. The success of Apollo was the absolute victory of program over space and place but it was clear that the rational technical method, which was supposed to sweep everything before it, had come up against the stumbling block of the city.

1970

Thinking that architecture was an outdated and obsolete discipline, I distanced myself from it. Until I was invited by Jacqueline Palmade and Françoise Lugassy to join their multidisciplinary team in researching experiences of people living in France's new housing projects. The team included sociologists, economists, psychologists, psychoanalysts and semiologists. The work was based on analyzing "daydreams," the transcribed recordings of the people who lived in these projects.

Through the words and silences of the peoples interviewed, I perceived in them a sense of ill-at-ease and even a feeling of pain amidst their new surroundings and buildings . . . too far away, too loud, too small or too big. Depending on their discipline, each specialist had his or her own approach to these dreams: Oedipus, social class situations, and so on. The searchers were aware to find the presence of concepts in the talking. It appeared to me that most of the problems were purely spatial: distance and light, isolation and lack of privacy, noise and images. And that opened my eyes. There was a rejection of these new spaces. And the complaints were surprising because the new housing replaced slums and insalubrious buildings. I was hearing what language often expresses through silence: the experience of space. Semiology was very fashionable at the time, it reduced everything to language. I realized that space and language are two distinct mediums and that our space experience cannot really be translated or understood by language. It has to do with the body. It crosses immediate sensation, perceptions, feelings, memory, with rationality and numbers, it is about motion, colors, noises, dimensions. It is before language.

It fell squarely within the field of architecture. I had moved away from it, but I had to go back to it. We are linguistic beings but more archaically we are inescapably spatial beings. At every moment, our awareness of existence comes from our constant inner monologue, our conversations and what we read, but our self-awareness is about the position and place where our bodies are situated in space.

Around that time, I was walking through a new housing project and I asked myself a question that suddenly appeared to be vitally important even though it had never been raised during my studies: what dimension and what form should we give to the empty space between two buildings? If we don't choose, norms will choose for us, a fact that has subsequently been confirmed, and increasingly so. The architect's profession, which we thought had been made obsolete, had to continue to exist! My subject was this space, this concept. And yet since the war this urban space had been severely shaken across the world.

After the "City without Place" and the Plan Voisin, Le Corbusier constantly returned to the solid obstacle

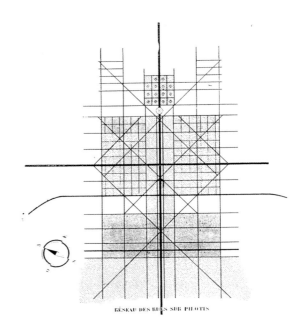

RÉSEAU DES RUES SUR PILOTIS

6. MORT DE LA RUE

8. UNE NOUVELLE VILLE REMPLACE UNE ANCIENNE VILLE

Le Corbusier in 1935, calling for the death of the street. © FLC/SIAE 2015

that, as he saw very well, resisted his vision of total overhaul: the street. He decreed the "death of the street," a dark, unhygienic "corridor." This was stated in all his lectures and in the article 8 of the celebrated Athens Charter of 1933. The high-tech speed lines belong to the train and the car techniques, but the theory erasing the street as a tool of the past was also driven to the zoning theory, replacing the block by huge enclaved zones of buildings between the roads. Nobody opposed such a simple statement that adapted cities to the speed and the growing number of cars.

In the middle of last century, technology was working wonders in every field with the industrial method. Its analytical approach was sectorial and produced effective answers, each in its own field of performance, through the dedicated company that was supposed to move forward alone in its schedule and dictate its demands. But in some fields the very sectorial nature of the answers produces aberrations in another field.

Specialized and closed zones and the enclaves carved out by highway channels later demonstrated the extent to which life, the city, architecture and "good political government" are not the simple sum of technical performances. The city seems at first to be a technical artefact. It is produced by combining numerous different techniques. But this blinds us to its deeper reality: it is not a technical object like a boat or a train. It is a complex anthropological reality. It is not a pure rational matter, it is history in space. It only exists in time. It is time made place. It creates a place-time. Blinded by the efficiency of transportation we didn't anticipate the inanity of the spaces and enclosed dead-ends that will emerge in the new suburban territories. That mistake had serious consequences for cities worldwide.

1971

Initial Projects: Space

With the radicalism of the "death of the street," Le Corbusier had stated that "one city should replace another." There were now two opposing mental constructions. There would be two ages: the traditional city of blocks and streets inherited from Millet and Pompeii in the center, which would soon be surrounded by the expanded and streetless city we're now familiar with in every suburb around the world, filled with constructed and autonomous objects and intercut by highway "channels."

Since antiquity it was the "void" of the streets that encircled the inhabitants, which dominates the perception and dictates the organization of the cities, creating a system of concave community spaces for traffic. In modern cities, the void, the space is unlimited everywhere, it can no longer be perceptible as a system, what is perceived is

The city of the street

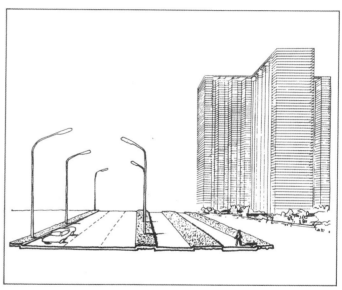

The city of objects

Presentation drawings of the "Liaison Organique" for Marne-la-Vallée with Antoine Grumbach, 1970

the proliferation of solid built objects. The centuries-old perception of urban space had been turned on its head.

In one of the new town built in the Paris region, Marne-la-Vallée, urban planner Michel Macary wanted to tone down the radicalism of modern urban planning. He asked Antoine Grumbach and myself to work on a multi-transport route linking housing sectors in a landscape that was shaping up to have no links or streets.

We were discovering the second wave of post-war urbanization: the new towns of Paul Delouvrier, were intended to house millions of people. However, the rural exodus was about to run out of steam and the huge effort that had been made to rehouse people from the slums and the vast shantytowns around Paris was almost complete. The public authorities were going to pass the torch to private investors and builders. Everything was going to change.

In the presentation for Marne-la-Vallée, I wrote: "It is a common space. The automobile has invaded the city. It makes the city. To a large extent, it also tends to make urban planning. All development projects tend to be arbitrary and subjective. Its laws are pressing and beyond question.

"In new towns, even when the buildings are still on the drawing board, the band of asphalt is ready to be rolled out. It imposes a pre-determined course and standardizes shapes. It cuts decisively through the site. These are technical predefined elements.

"From the moment, the bulldozers cut into the soil, the landscape is marked in an irreversible manner. The future urban space has already been laid out by footprints, bend radii and grass buffers. It opens up possibilities and closes others. It's the degree zero of the new town." (*Le cours du Val Maubué, Aménagement et équipement de la liaison organique, Téta Aménagement Urbain, January 1973*.)

Space and Object
The Water Tower

One of the suggestions I made in this study was to replace one of the large planned road hubs with a traffic circle. I noticed on the plans that they were going to build a water tower five hundred meters away. I suggested moving this large technical object and placing it at the center of the roundabout like a plant-covered landmark to signify a place in this otherwise undistinguished space emerging from the plans. With this tower, I diverted something technical and gave it a second function.

Far from the debates on megastructures of the sixties, when I was designing the water tower, my goal was to provide a place, a landmark where will be numbers of slabs of housing. And it was also about looking through

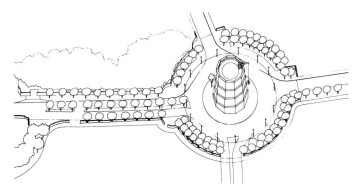

A water tower/urban signal

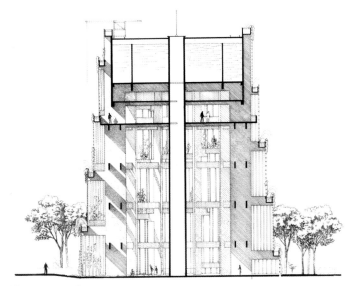

Water tower section

Green Tower at the roundabout of Quatre Pavés, Noisiel, France. Program: A water tower, an urban signal. Height: 37 meters. 1971–1974

architecture to what man wants to be in relation to nature, technology and the city. It was no longer about dominating nature, but protecting it, taking place into consideration, learning how to evolve gradually and transforming what was already there rather that erasing and relaying foundations. Modernity addressing a different time.

1974
La Roquette, Paris, France
With the water tower, I had begun my work by moving decisively away from the legacy of the Moderns, although it was warmly received by them when it was built in 1974. The following year, my competition entry for a development at La Roquette in Paris was also praised although my plans were a manifesto for a type of space forbidden in new urban theory: an empty space with a shape. In 1974, it went against the "doxa." The Moderns, apart from Fernand Pouillon, were uneasy about enclosed and recognizable voids.

Le Corbusier went to absurd lengths to avoid anything that looked like a traditional space: the corridor street, the square or a courtyard. He hated when buildings created a concave space, whether it was the shell of a place or a square. Although he had loved Camillo Sitte's precepts as a young man, his vision of "outdoor rooms," which squares actually are, he went on to reject them. He wanted to see objects, as his urban theory was to mark a shift of no return between the street, perception of hollow voids, and solid objects, products of the machine by nature, "placeless" and generated by the needs of the future users.

Space, Object, Void and Solid
If we were to adopt the structuralist analysis, according to which the city can be analyzed as a linguistic reality, we could say, as an extension of this metaphor, that the language of the city was replaced, not only in terms of its vocabulary—the buildings have been changed—but also in its grammar, the principles by which the buildings were assembled.

Set against this new, unreadable landscape that was emerging, with the water tower and La Roquette, I was demonstrating two basic ways in which we are situated in space. Our consciousness of being takes place through two media. The language, which can be our constant internal monologue, our listening, talking or reading. And the space in which we are always situating ourselves, either near an object or inside an enclosure. Inside or outside. The totem or landmark around which we place ourselves and the enclosure or clearing that englobes and surrounds us.

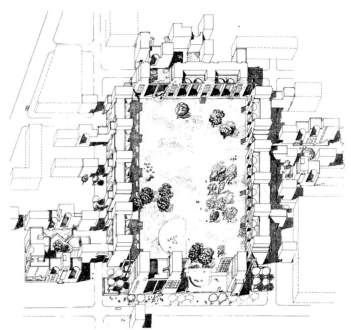

The "Programme Architecture Nouvelle," 1975

La Roquette competition, rue de la Roquette, Paris, France, 1974

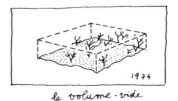

In the void: the empty volume

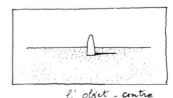

Around the solid: the center-object

Many people don't see space because it isn't visible. What is visible are the objects, the faces of people, the cars, the printed letters on paper or the line of horizon, but not the distance between these objects, and that is about architecture.

But when I gave talks, the audience never understood what I meant by the word "space" or "void." "What do you mean when you talk about this? This idea of void is harrowing." Later, as I was reading *Tao Te Ching*, I discovered Lao Tsu's phrase: "My house is not the wall; it is not the ground; it is not the roof; it is the void between these 'things', because that is where I am dwelling." What he's talking about is the sensorial experience that everyone has and not an abstract concept. From then on, before I used the words "void" or "space," I would quote this sentence. And people immediately understood.

The Invention of Modern Infinity

And yet the modern way of imagining space seems to be the opposite of how Lao Tsu imagined it, since it carries the notion of infinity. Emerging in the age of Kepler and Galileo and their discoveries, it infers the idea of an unlimited, continuous, homogenous and "isotropic" environment. When Pascal wrote: "The eternal silence of these infinite spaces terrifies me," he established a new vision of the world that was no longer seen as a cover, as believed by Lao Tsu and the Greeks, for whom space was a "closed world" with a sky-lid under which they imagined a series of places reserved for things that could only have a consistency in a place or by defining a place.

This infinite space as conceptualized at the time is not something we can experience with our senses; it is not a primary experience. It is a truth learned from science that becomes part of our consciousness and reality; it is imaginable and almost perceptible through the telescope, navigation, cartography and representations of the solar system.

Has Lao Tsu's phrase been superseded as a way of presenting space to ourselves? Is it misleading? No, it's still relevant today. The experience of the enclosed space has been, since Neolithic times, the physical experience of inhabiting it. And we're still the same man.

Of course, we're mechanized man, the man of the industrial era, of planes and space shuttles. We're also rapidly becoming the man of cyberspace, defined by our high-speed virtual exchanges, the storage of Internet data, and geolocation. But we're still the man who walks, sees and hears at the same distance as our *homo sapiens* ancestors. We are living in several strata of evolution and several types of spatial experience. And it's vital to understand it within architecture and within the city.

And precisely, many architects and planners are afraid not to be modern if they understand this, maybe feeling that it is too ancestral, too philosophical or too metaphysical! They are used to think about space only as it derives from new technology transforming distances and links, connections, localization . . . Technology is transforming humanity, but let's not forget we have not yet fly out of our earth, our body and our lifespan.

If architects are not guarantors of the initial body's space as one of our two mediums of consciousness and of relationship with our common world, space that is constantly transformed, helped by prostheses but roughly handled, who will be?

End of "The Universal"

In France in the 1970s, the government was developing a "models policy" for architecture, following industrial technical methods to provide a standard, universal, mass-produced solution. A national competition program, the PAN (New Architecture Program), used to select designs for standard buildings to reproduce across France and to furnish models for families, older people, schools, and so on. They were "placeless" projects. I presented my designs for La Roquette, which was not a model of a universal object but on the contrary a place to integrate into a neighborhood, or to create it. I was told it should have been eliminated. To my surprise, I was accepted. We had moved into another era of urbanization. The figures were changing.

Public funding was being replaced by private developments and smaller projects. We wouldn't build over huge beetroot fields anymore. We would have to fit our designs into sites that would already be partly constructed, or sites on leftover land. The specific and contingent were to become more important than the generic. I had the impression that history was faltering because the march toward the universal, once so inevitable, had been stopped in its tracks. Each project was being looked at on a "case by case" basis. There was a return to contingency, an ironic reversal of Universalist principles. You had to analyze places and use your cunning to find the best way of using them.

Another theoretical vision of the future emerged and its path was no longer straight. The new line of a modern project would be about transforming rather than founding, it would have to be attentive to its surroundings. We had to take back ownership of territories that were often poorly constructed and bend the program to the place, not the other way around.

1975

Transforming the Existing City

Thanks to the PAN and the project for La Roquette, I found myself in another competition, a practical one this time, against two other PAN laureates, for which we were asked to apply our ideas to a difficult plot in the Paris 13th district. There were plans to build two towers on this plot accessible from a narrow side. A single eight-story building could also be suitable for two hundred housing units with an entrance onto the street. This is what my competitors were proposing.

Taking the void, possible flows, the light and views as my starting point, I initially designed a common public space surrounded and generated by a built environment. Rather than a single building I proposed a thoroughfare, a square and a set of five tower-buildings, two low buildings and one special tripod tower building with two elevators. It was dense but not claustrophobic. Each place and housing unit had a combination of near and far views. The rhythm of the façades, the trees in earth, the street and its opening onto the city provided two hundred and ten housing units with a quiet, light inner architectural space. This was where I applied my work on the void and the defined space between buildings.

With La Roquette, I had formulated a manifesto for space. With this concrete project, I wanted to create a link between contemporary architecture and the existing city. This project had been perceived like a manifesto and I kept the name of the site, which was called Passage des Hautes Formes, a former pottery works. The Hautes Formes made a mark on the time and were my first attempt at an open block. I went on to develop the thought in the 1980s.

Esthetics and the Technology of the Greatest Number

Looking over the drawing for the Hautes Formes again, I distinctly remember saying at the time that I claimed refusing repetition or to pile up equal-sized or "standard" windows, balconies and habitats. I wanted to finish with the modern axiom advocated by George Candilis, according to which it was essential, on a housing project, wherever it was built, anywhere would be the site, to provide everyone with the same conditions, advantages and cells. And at the time, it was always necessary to drastically limit number of types of built elements in order to keep to the deadline and budget. But the idea of repetition had another aim: equality. If the buildings were a series of standard elements that answered to a production logic, the inhabitants themselves should enjoy the same conditions, based on the logic of democratic distribution.

Although equal rights are enshrined in law, by applying this repetitive logic, intended for industrial and democratic

La rue des Hautes Formes, Paris, France, 1975–1979

Aerial view of Les Hautes Formes, 13th District, Paris, France

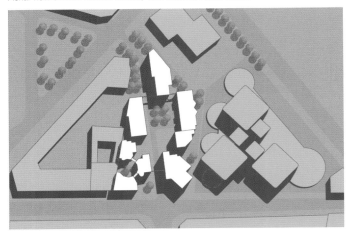

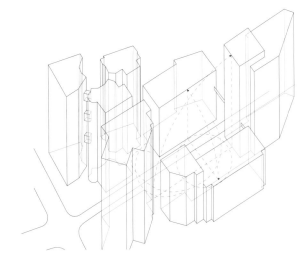

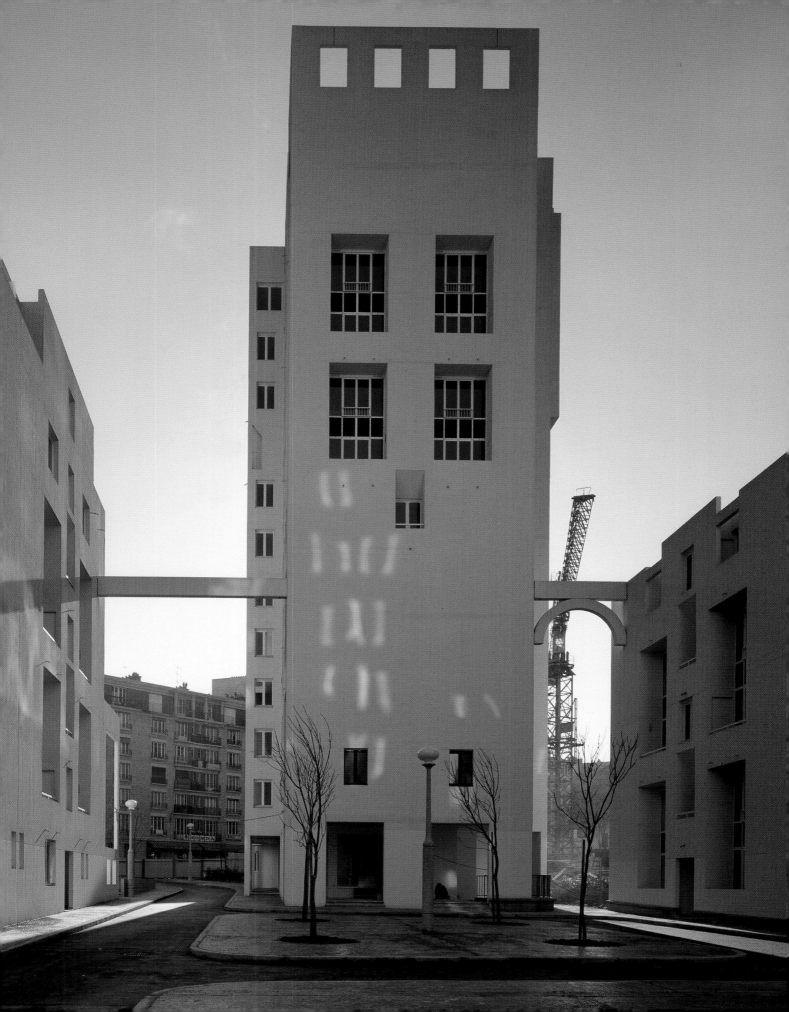

purposes, we overlooked the potential of the spaces and spoilt their use. Conditions of strict equality don't exist in spatial terms in a dense city with buildings over five stories high. On complex sites already surrounded by buildings, it is impossible to prioritize a single orientation or a perfect height for living without ruining qualities of the majority of the apartments. I saw the need for a different approach to building for large numbers of people that takes into account multiple cases, positions in space, situations and individuals.

The twentieth century addressed the "greatest number" with series and mass production principles. Industry, administration, the army and political parties approached the large quantities of the modern world by subdividing them into serial groups modeled according to a standard and ordered into a hierarchy with a leader at the top.

Around the end of the sixties, this order, which appeared to have been a fatality of runaway demographic growth, was no longer the only model. The greatest number was subdivided into countless units. Did the genius of the digital revolution combined with virtual networks and the Internet created this, or did it arrive at just the same moment when the notion of individual subject raised up? They responded to a world of multiple individuals by breaking free from the strict limits and delays of arithmetic administration. This made possible to scale things down to small quantities, tribes and provide multiples options. Our metropolises and architecture are those of a period in which series, repetition of a model and unique formula are no longer an absolute imperative and are overpassed by the richness of the multitude. An invisible order makes possible the breathtaking disorder of the profusion of numbers.

The Broken Timeline — The word Postmodern

The change in consciousness I mention above occurred in the seventies. We experienced a crisis in our representation of time; a slow and long reversal of our western consciousness of time established over two millennia through a genius for the future and an idea of progress. Even if in the sixties already, possible conflict between industrial and environmental logics were first recognized and introduced doubts about this vision.

The first crisis of 1974 interrupted the march of history, which no longer seemed to be going in a straight line. What would become of the becoming itself? Was the world in which time was an arrow pointing toward the future still ours if the route no longer seemed to be going in a straight line? The future had not endured. We couldn't see the horizon anymore. For unemployed youth, there was "no future." Planning, seen in France as an earnest necessity, lost its abilities.

La rue des Hautes Formes, Paris, France, 1975–1979

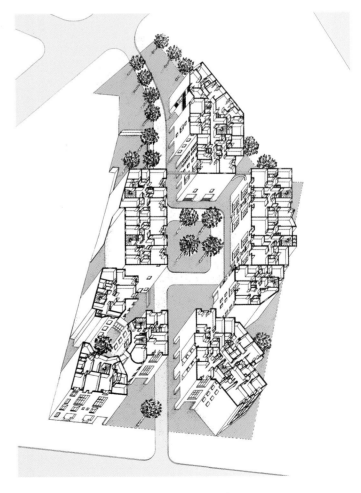

Les Hautes Formes, La rue des Hautes Formes, 13th District, Paris, France.
Program: 7 buildings, 210 social housing units, six different unit types; surface area:
11,460 square meters; in association with Georgia Benamo. Client: The City of
Paris Housing Office. Date: Competition Pan VII, 1975; completed in 1979

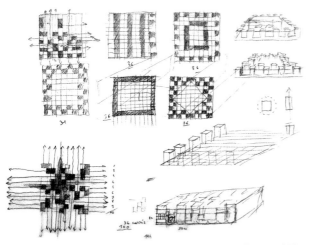

First open-block study for a competition in Cergy-Pontoise, France, 1979

Tête Défense competition drawing, Paris, France, 1983

First stage of these convulsions came in the 1970s and 1980s as a return to the past. The word postmodern appeared, borrowed from the world of dance and open to interpretation. Applied to architecture, it was a critique of modernism as an esthetic "style," favoring an alternative of columns and pediments over piles and roof terraces. Applied to urban planning, it learned to conserve the lessons of history but soon called for an eternal model of the "classic" city, the fantasy of an ever-lasting urban space, the unchangeable essence that justified a return to pastiche. It lacked the analysis of modern urbanism that still represented the only doxa.

However, cities in Europe began to stop building slab-like developments and highways inside town and engaged a major shift toward heritage conservation, to shrine "places of memory" with the inconvenient of turning city centers into museums and ignoring their immense suburbs.

1979

Between Architecture and Urban Planning—Toward the Open Block

At the end of the 1970s, I started working on neighborhoods with open blocks, but I was reluctant to turn the theme into theory, aware of the need to experiment with reality and the danger of an absolute model, the Achilles' heel of the Athens Charter. I knew that the complexity of the city and the composition of its neighborhoods required each case to be looked at on its own merits and in relation to its stakeholders and their demands, which were always specific, rather than the promulgation of a new schematic universal model.

So, I went forward with practice, in the 1980s, by entering competitions suited to blocks in a wide range of urban situations in Paris and elsewhere. They were years of experimentation. Despite incomprehension of the judges, I opened up irregular blocks in leftover parts of the classic city and for planned renovations. The projects were refused because of the new fashion for returning to the former city and its closed blocks. For me, the classic building adjoined to its neighbor on a street was no longer legitimate. But neither did I feel that the autonomous modern building was relevant in itself as a way of structuring space.

1982

Grands Projets

In the 1980s I entered designs for several of the Grands Projets competitions launched by Jack Lang (Minister of Culture) during the presidency of François Mitterrand: the Opéra Bastille, the "Tête de la Défense," the École de danse de l'Opéra and the Cité de la musique. They were monuments because their locations interacted with the void, the urban space and its axes.

The strict Modern Movement obviously rejected the idea of the monument as a dramatization of the space, and the word remains taboo. However, no one was surprised by this curious return of the monumental in the 1980s. My entry for the competition for the Opéra Bastille in 1983 was in the six selected for the second round on five hundred entries.

Opéra Bastille, Paris, France, 1983

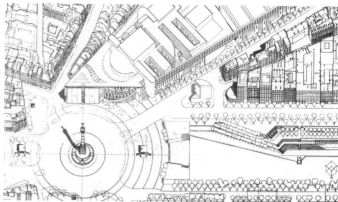

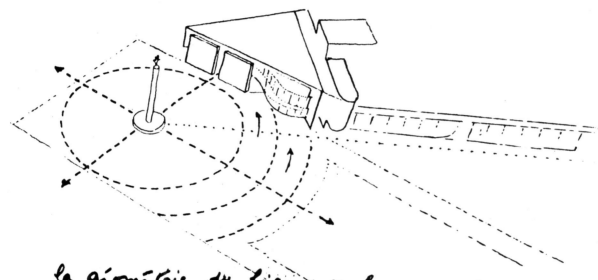

la géométrie du lieu : cercle et carré,
— centre,
— lignes cardinales,
— enroulement, rotation,
— grande oblique de la rue de Lyon

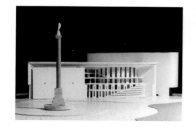

Competition drawings and model for the Opéra Bastille, Paris, France, 1983

Opéra Bastille, Paris, France, 1983–1987

My designs for the Opéra Bastille took into account the site and its offset placement. I considered that "the plan of the Place de la Bastille is based on its central totem but has no form in its limits." So, I introduced a geometric element, a geometric layout to link the column and the drawing of the future opera to give form to this unfindable square. There were two opposing registers: on the one side, the solid wall of the Maison de l'Opéra, split along its axis, which stabilizes the position of the column and whose axes define a new circular square. On the other side, the crescendo of the elliptical concert hall and lobby, which give a turning motion to the whole and integrate the site's challenging dissymmetry. These two great masses form a "canyon"—a large public passageway. Depending on the event, several vast sliding panels could seal off all or part of the façade and transform the opera house into a more or less closed space, or a public space open onto the Place de la Bastille for music festivals, concerts, balls, etcetera.

École de danse de l'Opéra de Paris, Nanterre, France, 1983–1987

The same year I won the competition to design the École de danse de l'Opéra de Paris in Nanterre. The Ministry had decided that this École needed to have better facilities and should abandon the Palais Garnier and move close to the Parc de Nanterre near Paris. Whereas previously dance students went to school in the afternoon after a morning at the Opéra before returning home at night, they were now going to become boarders.

I won by proposing to retain this separation between these three major moments of the day in order to avoid the feeling of being locked into a single place. I split the school into three distinct buildings: the dance building, the teaching and administration building and the wing of bedrooms overlooking the park. I wanted to avoid claustrophobic feelings.

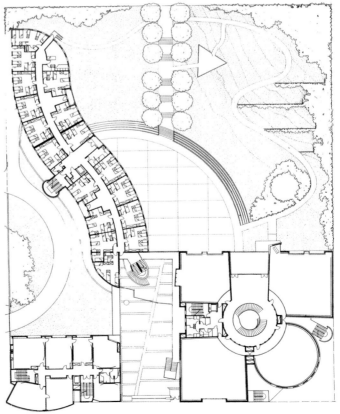

top: The central staircase for the École de danse de l'Opéra de Paris. bottom: Plan

top: A dance hall with painted acoustic canvas by artist Pierre Buraglio. bottom: The school and dance building. opposite page: The dance building and the students' rooms

École de Danse de l'Opéra de Paris, 20, allée de la Danse, Quartier du Parc, Nanterre, France. Program: Cultural facility, dance school for 150 pupils, student accommodation (50 rooms with 3 beds), refectory, offices, meeting rooms; surface area: 11,000 square meters. Client: Ministère de la Culture, Établissement public pour l'aménagement de la Défense (EPAD). Artists: Pierre Buraglio, Roland Cabot, Béatrice Casadesus. Date: Competition entry, 1983; completion, 1987. Award: "Équerre d'Argent," delivered by the French Minister of Culture in 1987.

Between each part is a garden. A high glass portico links the tree buildings and forms the entrance to the whole. When completed in 1987, this realization won the Prix de l'Équerre d'Argent.

In 1984, we were twelve candidates to enter the two-stage competition for the Cité de la musique, which I won in 1985. This project combines an urbanistic reflection on space, on the city and the monument, and also an architectural thinking on the life of a huge school and the dense concentration of musical activities partly opened to the public.

The Entrance to the Parc de la Villette, Two Wings of the Cité de la musique, Paris, France

Located along avenue Jean-Jaurès, at the southern entrance to the Parc de La Villette, the Cité de la musique consists of two very different wings, which contrast and complement each other, on either side of the Grande Halle.

From the 1984 competition, I placed, to the west, the Conservatoire National Supérieur de Musique et de Danse, reserved for teaching and public classes. To the east stands a complex of spaces open to the public, including concert halls, the Instrument Museum and rehearsal rooms, and the home of the Ensemble Inter-Contemporain. Together it formed a unique group of spaces for music and dance.

The western part had a large curved white façade reflected in an expanse of water and regularly punctuated by transparent thin openings. This complex concludes the dimensions of the long avenue Jean-Jaurès. I gave fewer urban attachments to the east wing, I opened a large triangular piazza, creating an opening from the city onto the park.

By doing this, I eluded the axis of the Grande Halle and avoided creating an overly-obvious symmetrical square for this entrance to the parc de la Villette, which would have hidden it. So, this triangular space installs a communication all around it from the city and its avenue, the two wings of the Cité de la musique, west and east, the Grande Halle, the Park and the Follies.

The rhythm of the façade of the east wing, along this piazza, would lead people toward the future Philharmonic hall.

The interior organization of both wings are led by one principle: all of the opaque volumes with highly diverse dimensions and shapes formed by the acoustic shells of the musical spaces stand shoulder to shoulder. Instead of isolating one big building "making every space deaf," I isolated the different volumes dedicated to music pieces by pieces, groups by groups, opening an interstitial tissue of transparent volumes and light breaks, which links them.

These are places of movement and encounters, fully glazed or open to the sky. So, despite the program's density, everywhere there is light and views onto the exterior and the ear can decompress, sounds coming from afar.

It is a lively, fluid, multiple city; an architecture that you can move around in and that cannot be understood at a glance. And it's precisely in this experience of movement, its duration, its sequences, its breaks and its discoveries that architecture and musical experience meet.

Completed in 1990, the Conservatoire National taught us, as the Hautes Formes, to find quality collective life in a dense ensemble, as it will be seen later in the French Embassy in Berlin and the Rhône-Alpes County Council Hall in Lyon.

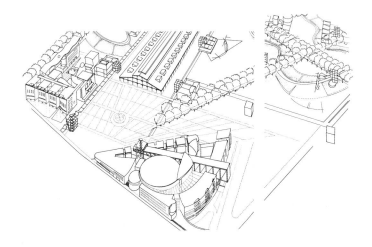

Cité de la musique, Paris, France, 1984–1995

The two wings of the Cité de la musique, 209, avenue Jean-Jaurès, Parc de la Villette, Paris, 19th District, France. Date: Prize-winning entry to competition, 1984; completed in 1990 (west wing) and 1995 (east wing)

Cité de la musique, West Wing, Paris, France, 1984–1990

To the West, the Conservatoire National Supérieur de Musique et de Danse de Paris (CNSMDP), completed in 1990, provides 40,000 square meters of facilities for 1,200 students. More than 5,000 people work or teach here together and the building provides everyone with a space of their own. Each discipline, each "tribe" has its own house. It creates a vast network of passageways and places where students can meet up.

Vertically, this west wing divides into two large families of space: 186 study rooms served by vertical and horizontal "streets" and situated on the upper floors, small and medium sized rooms (studios, study rooms, listening areas, media library and offices) and the large spaces. Whether opened to the public or not (concert hall, interdisciplinary studio, organ room, orchestra room, jazz room) all occupy a sunken level set at the heart of the site, surrounding a cloister and a garden.

It is a modern monastery open onto the city.

This solution decongested the site and satisfied draconian acoustic requirement, which precluded certain super impositions.

Horizontally, the building is structured into four north south spans separated by corridors of light, forming a boulevard front on the south side. The four buildings are brought together by a large inclined wall, which forms an acoustic shield for the upper floors.

The western span wing is a long continuous band housing the media library, the gymnasium, and student housing. It is topped by a large undulating roof. The eastern span, facing the fountain, houses the dance building. Between the dance and study rooms, a transparent cleft marks the entrance to the public spaces.

Unlike these calm exteriors, the inner court discovers contrasting architectural events and the spatial effects of music: from the patio/garden emerges the conical form of the organ room and that of the backstage premises. A colorful, structural sequence galvanized by the undulating west wing. In the middle, the large halls open onto a patio garden. And thus, you forget that you are seven meters below the street level.

Inside the Conservatory, the walls picturality due to variation of materials and colors offers a varied landscape for students.

Cité de la musique, West Wing, 209, avenue Jean-Jaurès, Parc de la Villette, Paris 19th District, France. Program: Cultural and public facility accommodating the conservatoire de Paris, 66 teaching rooms, 3 examination and competition rooms, 7 orchestra sets, 1 electro-acoustic auditorium, 3 amphitheaters (50 seats), 100 rehearsal rooms, 3 public auditoriums (organ, singing, multidisciplinary), media center, audiovisual center, 53 student housing units, gymnasium, restaurant-cafeteria, offices, medical center, parking; surface area: 40,000 square meters.

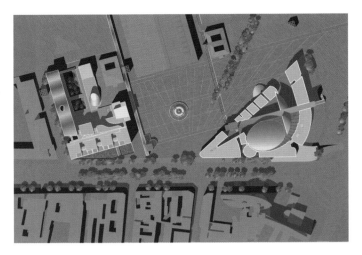

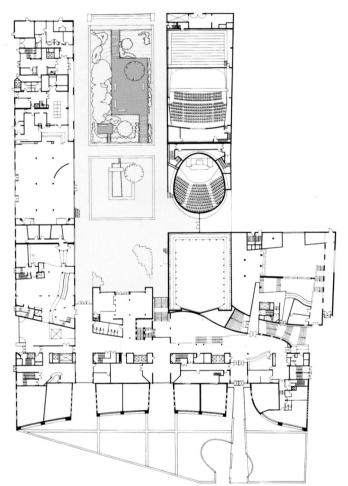

Ground floor plan showing the different "enclosed buildings"
opposite page: At the west, the entrance to the conservatory

Client: French Ministry of Culture and Communications. Developer: Établissement Public du parc de la Villette (EPPV). Furniture: Elizabeth de Portzamparc. Acoustic: ACV, Xu Acoustique–Xu Ya Ying. Scenography: Jacques Dubreuil. Lighting: Jean Clair. Artists: Christian Boltansky, Pierre Buraglio, Aurélie Nemours, Georges Noël, Yann de Portzamparc, Antonio Semeraro. Date: Prize-winning entry to competition, 1984; completion, 1990

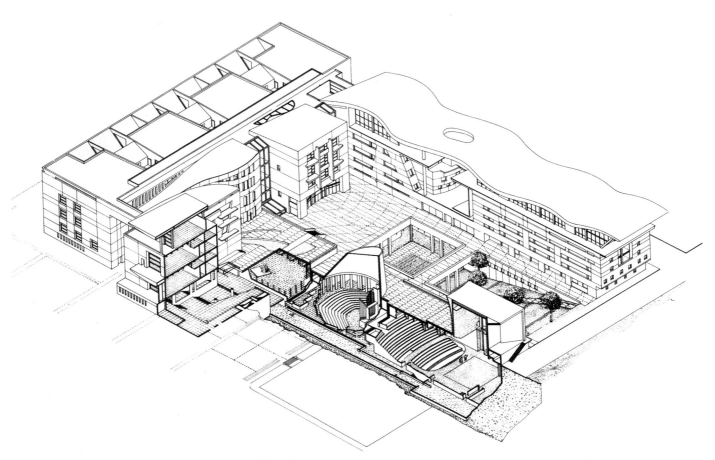

Axonometric drawing showing the multipurpose room, organ hall, and opera house

From left to right, organ hall, chamber music hall, administration building, mediatheque (multimedia library), singing rooms, student rooms

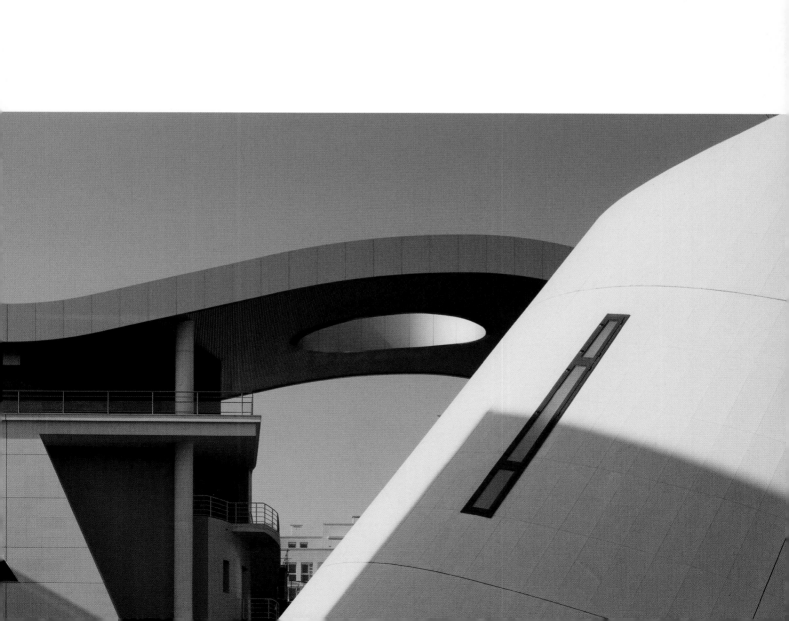

top: Piano room. bottom: Interior corridor or "street"

54

top: Below the entrance, the students' foyer. bottom: the public foyer

Cité de la musique, East Wing, Paris, France, 1984–1995

The east wing of the Cité de la musique, was completed in 1995. It brings together all of the spaces opened to the public over a surface area of 50,000 square meters. It is a highly-varied series of programs forming a real neighborhood composed of various volumes within which you can walk: concert halls, the museum of music, the organology center, the auditorium, the student residence, the teaching institute, the media library, offices and the headquarters of the Ensemble Intercontemporain, rehearsal rooms, music stores and the Café de la Musique.

Each program has its own shell with a specific form and all of these distinct volumes fit into a puzzle assembled into a vast triangular block crossed by the large spiral gallery forming the "foyer" that surrounds the famous elliptical concert hall.

This hall has become a benchmark for its acoustic quality, its exceptional form, the range of possibilities it provides in terms of the relationship between stage and audience.

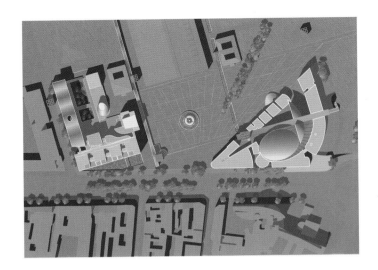

This project opened a long triangular piazza, between its east blocks and the Parc de la villette, designed by Bernard Tschumi.

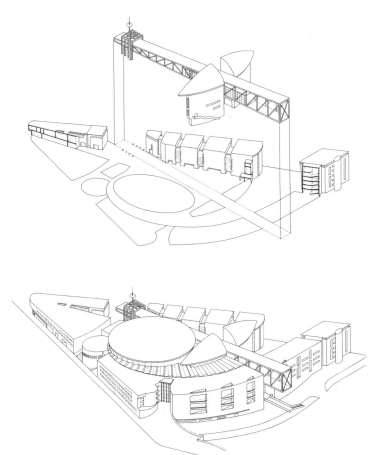

Cité de la Musique, East Wing, 209, avenue Jean-Jaurès, Parc de la Villette, Paris 19th District, France. Program: Cultural public facilities accommodating the headquarters of the Ensemble Inter Contemporain, a 800 to 1,200-seat concert hall, a 240-seat amphitheater housing a baroque organ, 3 rehearsal studios, a music room for the apprentices of Gamelan, museum of music, multimedia library, information center offices, offices of the public institution of the Cité de la musique (EPCM) and the SACEM, the Institute of Musical and Choreographic Pedagogy (IPMC), the Café de la Musique, artists' changing rooms, parking; surface area: 40,000 square meters. Client: French Ministry of Culture and Communications. Developer: Établissement Public du parc de la Villette (EPPV). Interior design and furniture of the Café de la Musique: Elizabeth de Portzamparc. Acoustic: Commins bbm, ACV, Xu Acoustique. Scenography: Jacques Dubreuil, Jacques . Lighting: Gérald Karlikoff. Artists: Louis Dandrel, Yann de Portzamparc, Antonio Semerano. Date: Prize-winning entry to competition, 1984; completion, 1995. Award: "Équerre d'Argent," delivered by the French Minister of Culture in 1995

opposite page: Entrance of the concert hall top: The concert hall. bottom: Museum amphitheater with baroque organ

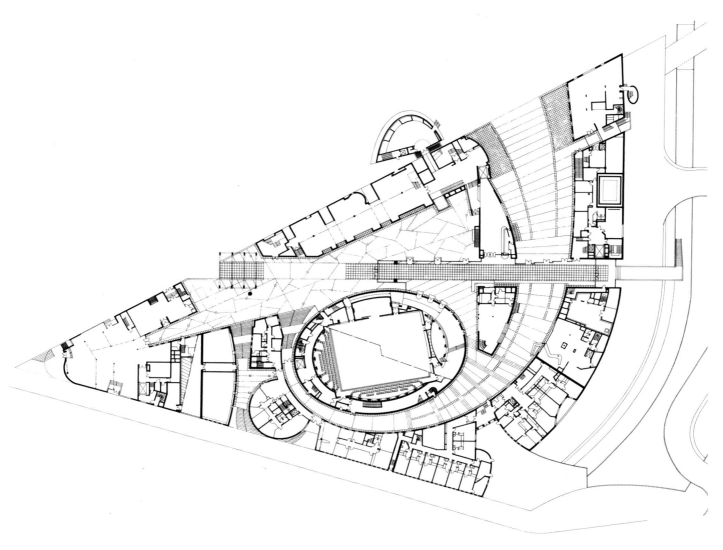

Ground floor plan

opposite page, top: The interior curved "street," which encircles the concert hall; here, the main foyer
opposite page, bottom: The main lobby of the Cité de musique, under the long bridge housing the multimedia library.
Outside, in the background, the façade of the music museum can be seen.

Interior and exterior spaces of the multimedia library

Musée Bourdelle, Paris, France, 1988–1990

The existing Bourdelle Museum in Paris, designed by Henri Gautruche in 1948, is settled around the sculptor's studio. In 1988, the city of Paris decided of an extension to present the numerous studies of the sculptor. This extension installs on the neighboring ground, inserted between four gable walls within a block, on a ground three meters lower than the existing structures. The course of the visitor descends to the new sculpture showrooms.

The extension showrooms being necessarily enlightened by a top lighting, I used the reflection on clear walls to obliquely enlighten the works.

In this space for statues, each sculpture finds its own home: backdrop, light, perspective. Each base is adapted in size, shape and material stone, cement, or untreated metal. It is an interplay of levels and planes: between white stone walls, grey cement walls absorb light, provide a backdrop for the dark bronzes and avoid placing them against the light on the white. In this itinerary, which, in the end, breathes life into the academic concept of museum space, major works can be seen from a distance, in uncluttered spaces, while large numbers of Antoine Bourdelle's preliminary drafts and studies are concentrated together in a way that evokes the artist's studio.

With the Cité de la musique and the Café Beaubourg, the Bourdelle Museum was a confirmed pictorial experience that played with materials, lights and colors.

Musée Bourdelle, 15 rue Antoine-Bourdelle, Paris 15th District, France. Program: Extension of the Museum of the French sculptor and painter Antoine Bourdelle; sculptures showrooms, temporary exhibition space, paintings and drawings exhibitions areas, audiovisual room, documentation room, offices, reserves; surface area: 1,655 square meters. Client: Direction des Affaires Culturelles de la Ville de Paris. Museography: Christian de Portzamparc. Date: Competition entry, 1988; completed in 1990

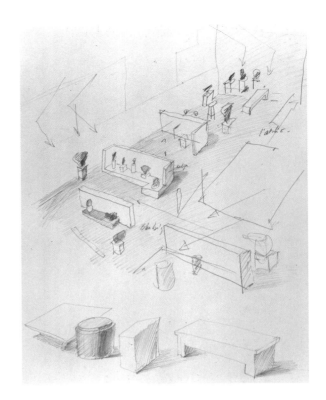

1984

Designing with the Void—Systems of Objects

In the catalogue of the exhibition devoted to me by the Institut Français d'Architecture, the interview I gave with François and Olivier Chaslin reveals an obsessive focus on the notion of perceived space. I criticized the chaotic proliferation of objects that characterized the new landscape.

However, the projects I had worked on in the seventies and eighties were most often formed as distinct object systems. There were not isolated objects. This fragmentation was often a response to the functional organization of the program in the site, but it was also what happened between these objects that interested me. This is the space Lao Tsu talks about. The build substance was organized from the shaping of the inside void between objects. My architecture at the time was white and approached from the point of view of solids and voids, the numbers and proportions and the attempt to give space a presence effect.

In the Hautes Formes project, seven built objects create a system of spaces that follow on from each other, accommodate the square and the street and offer the exterior a plasticity that adapts to the surrounding buildings. The program for the École de danse de l'Opéra led me to create three distinct objects for three aspects of a student's life: dancing, learning and living. The following year, I separated and apportioned the different concert halls of the Conservatoire National de la Cité de la musique into nine objects linked by light corridors. I wanted to soundproof the halls in sub-groups of four in separate sound-proofed enclosures to avoid silent corridors. This provided 1,500 students and their teachers with good living and working conditions by giving each teaching section and every class light and acoustics.

On the other side of the esplanade, from the first stage of the competition, I planned to provide areas for the public in the eastern part of the Cité de la musique. It was composed of thirteen objects between which a sequence of varied spaces was extended (spiral lobby, courtyards, etcetera); they were unified and held within a large virtual triangular shell. This is an urban block. In this wing of the Cité de la musique, the objects system turned out to be a lucky strategy: the program changed a lot and the system allowed us to develop the evolution of each object independently at the study stage without disrupting the whole because the interstitial empty spaces absorbed variations in dimension; a little like when you see boats change position between themselves in a port.

This fragmentation reappears in the project for the Berlin Embassy, where it literally expands the space in a narrow and closed block interior.

A Silent Return

Between the seventies and eighties, there was a silent revolution in Europe. Modernist rules were surreptitiously sidelined. Urban planners in cities reversed their practices without any real statement of doctrine. In Paris, local authorities explained to us that the rules of "the new frontage," which required buildings in a lot of streets to be setback in order to be built higher, were still in force. But they added that if we didn't follow them, our plans would not be refused! The idea of systematically clearing sites was abandoned. There has been serious work on the history of the city recognizing the qualities of Haussmannian Paris and the rejection of the modern urbanistic theory generated a desire to restore a mythical idea of an eternal city and the return of the closed block became a new dogma. I was going against the grain.

On some architecture courses, they were teaching that modernism had been a dark interlude. There was no analysis of the new chaos emerging in suburbs and the theory, which produced it. They ignored the fact that, across Europe, thirty years of the big bang had created new urban expanses much larger than the old centers and home to half the population. It was no longer the eternal city! Out of a sort of laziness, professionals reconciled themselves, together with elected officials, to the tentative idea—seeming reasonable but impossible in reality—of a return to a classic model. They renounced the heroic projects of above the street planning, slabs and towers and returned to the continuity of aligned buildings on streets, plots, and so on.

This silence on the part of the decision-makers, this understated return, had the inconvenience of ignoring the absolute necessity of thinking about the city in its transformed state, about the present, and the new needs for the city's forms.

The Moderns were determined to continue recognizing the contribution of the magnificent pre-war benchmarks and to believe in progress through technical innovation. They had remained loyal to a doctrine whose simplest and most persistent rule was to allow nothing that might suggest a return to the past. The "urbans," in contrast, wanted to return to the existing city and perhaps the architecture of a bygone age. It had the quality of placing civility and welcome high in their priorities. But a regressive movement toward the past was leading nowhere.

Both reduced their ideas to a binary warrior system. The question they asked themselves was: "Who are my enemies?"

History shows that, to move forward, it was necessary to remove this divide and return to a sort of text of the city, the "language" of which the Moderns had wanted to change—not only the vocabulary (the buildings) but also and above all the grammar (the way in which one thing led on to another)—making it illegible. I went this way to work on this molecule—the block—in order to transform it.

System of Objects

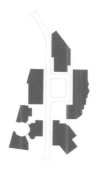

Les Hautes Formes, Paris, France, 1975

École de Danse de l'Opéra de Paris, Nanterre, France, 1983

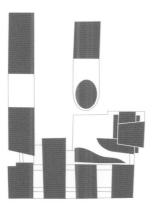

Cité de la musique (West Wing), Paris, France, 1984

Cité de la musique (East Wing), Paris, France, 1984

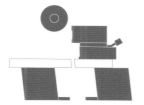

Nexus II, Fukuoka, Japan, 1989

French Embassy, Berlin, Germany, 1997

Disparity

At this time, there was a confrontation between increasingly contradictory architectural styles and building types. It was a nightmare for urban planners. I got firsthand experience of this when I was invited by Arata Isozaki among six other architects to design buildings on sites along two boulevards. Each of the six was invited to build something "unique" in this neighborhood of serial slabs without being shown the designs of their colleagues. It was what the Surrealists called "an exquisite corpse," and it showed that Isozaki's vision of the future was spot on.

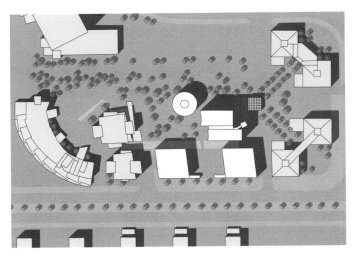

Nexus II, Fukuoka, Japan, 1989–1991

At first I installed my project in one building along one of the boulevards, but the proviso that all of the living rooms faced south led me to break it and orientate three buildings toward the sun around a courtyard. "This is now Portzamparc!" said the client, who was looking for a "signature" or stylistic "label," something I have never in mind and that I am opposed to take as a goal.

They are two white symmetrical buildings facing the sun and aligned with the boulevard. They surround a courtyard, at the end of which emerge a "rock" building and a golden tower. The buildings interact with the existing housing blocks that stand on the opposite side of the boulevard. The program is composed of 37 apartments in four different housing units for a total surface area of 4,000 square meters.

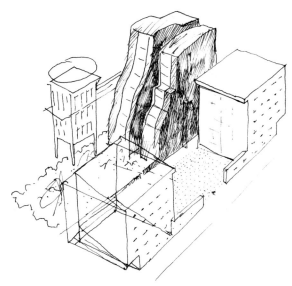

Nexus II, International Housing Exhibition, Nexus II, Fukuoka, Japan. Program: Apartments; surface area: 4,000 square meters. This project, located along two boulevards, forms part of a master plan for which Arata Isozaki brought together several architects of different nationalities. The brief included 37 apartments, which the architect divided between 4 different housing units. Client: Fukuoka Jisho Co., Ltd. Date: Commission, 1989; completion, 1991

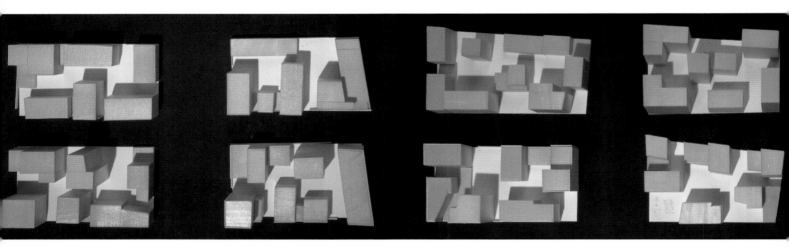

Chapter 2
Urban Situations:
Birth of the Open Block, 1990s

From 1988 to 1990, I entered a series of competitions for which we were asked to transform large swathes of wasteland into neighborhoods in various French cities such as Aix-en-Provence, Metz, Strasbourg, Marseille and Toulouse. Most of them were city-center sites, but the Jardins de la Lironde in Montpellier, and the Atlanpôle project in Nantes were large suburban spaces.

At the closing symposium of the Fukuoka project, one word was appearing and used frequently: "chaos." It was like a new way of defining suburbs, which the architects acknowledged as experiencing something of a crisis, which was at the same time special and architectural.

In the space of the new territories, there was no longer the unique and universal simple way to assemble buildings that the street constituted, as a "grammar." We inherited from the last century a chaotic space.

Furthermore, due to an increasing number of options of materials produced by the building industry, an exploding diversity of "style" between the built objects was rising up, as if architects had to differentiate from each other as they felt the end of the modern architectural doctrine. Nowadays, as soon as a public or private authority impulses an ambition of architectural quality to a development, the neighborhood becomes a zoo with different built animals.

Both in the classical centuries and in the modern twentieth, the notion of harmony had always been synonymous with homogeneity and similarity based on the repetition of types or models. Buildings had to look alike.

We like coherence and unity but we saw how the recurring economical and rational building principles produced a "generic" (Rem Koolhaas) worldwide repetitive style in mono functional zone, either offices or dwellings, which is often more boring than the chaos of the zoo.

This required us to change our vision on the pluralism we were forced to work with in our cities. I saw this as one of the challenges facing the city of the future: accommodating randomness and diversity, taking into account an uncertain future and inventing an esthetic of successful pluralism.

In interviews in the 1980s, I talked about the end of homogeneity in the city and its "multifaceted" future.

These competitions in different towns of France raised a number of vital challenges. Unaware or unprepared for urban planning, municipalities let the destiny of their city be decided over the course of a single morning by a panel of judges. They would meet us for ten minutes and sometimes refused even to let us explain our projects. It gave rise to all sorts of possible misunderstandings and humiliations.

In Aix-en-Provence, there was a real panel of judges, but they chose, against all the evidence, a tortuous project that refused to simply continue the Cours Mirabeau, and decided instead to follow, on this large site, a street from the medieval center that turned out to be illegible. Coming second and given the chance to do a building, I found it impossible to subsequently fit into this plan, which has now made the neighborhood difficult to understand.

Three competitions entries for central urban areas, including: an extension of the Cours Mirabeau, for Aix-en-Provence, France (1989; top left); Les Catalans, Marseille, France (1991; bottom left); and for Coislin Square in Metz, France (1990; opposite)

Place Coislin, Metz, France, 1990

Many projects were poorly grasped and opportunities were missed, like the Catalans in Marseille and Place Coislin in Metz. This Place Coislin is a site where the confrontation between different urban fabrics produces a caricature of a hybrid city with two visible periods: the Middle Ages and the 1970s. The medieval center of Metz, has become a lively commercial hub. At the side of it, the rather heavy, gloomy towers of the 1970s and housing blocks of the Place Coislin have been transformed into a coach station. On this square, the program that the developer proposed was an ensemble of highly diverse offices, housing units, hotels, sports facilities, movie theaters, a parking lot and, above all, a ground-floor store network continuing that of the medieval center. I proposed a series of building blocks with commercial units on the ground, over two levels, topped by small towers for housing and offices. This system of blocks produced a street network continuing the city center, rising and leading to a central hyper-dense square. This small, high, central, electric neighborhood with its tight "staccato" rhythm integrates and absorbs the towers and existing housing blocks of the seventies to form a mini downtown in the old city. Between the old quarter, the new quarter and existing towers, the new structures cut vertical ridges out of the sky. They keep the width and privacy of the traditional streets; the height of the buildings bordering them is increased and continuous; a well-spaced rhythm, a scansion of voids and solids, an entry point for light and views, replace the traditional and horizontal alignment of the buildings.

The object systems of the projects I was working on in the 1980s prefigured the open block.

With urban projects, I turned a new page and entered a new period. My focus was now the city's "plural" aspect and I left behind the white architecture of my previous projects. I had hesitated to use three different materials for the three volumes of the École de danse. I would learned to do that successfully later on, in Berlin. I understood later that the experience of the Cité de la musique enabled me to move from a personal architectural work on projects of blocks to the elaboration of a shareable urban doctrine, open to the multiplicity of the city. This vision included experimentation on materials and colors that I had worked on in the Café Beaubourg project.

In France, the debate on urbanism was polarized between reductive positions that reflected the fact that, when it comes to communication, only simplified, radical ideas staged like TV games or sport matches actually get through. There were two caricatural positions and one debate. On the one side, there was the culturalist but regressive even technophobic line; its supporters in

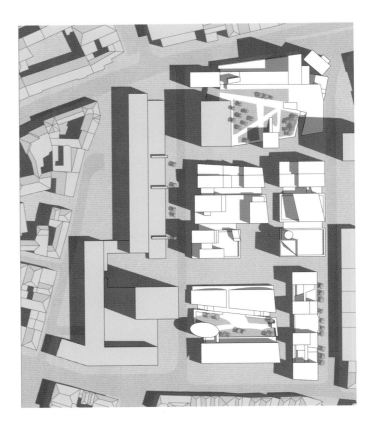

Competition entry, including model and renderings, for Coislin Square, Metz, France (1990). The aim was to establish an urban network that continued the medieval city and transformed existing towers of the 1970s, creating a school, hotels, shops, and housing.

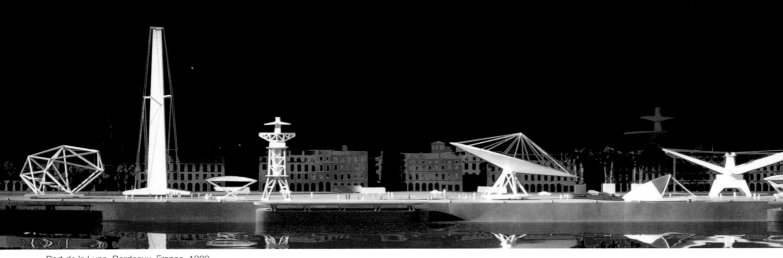

Port de la Lune, Bordeaux, France, 1989

favor of a return to the classical city, its dimensions and even its architecture. On the other side, there were those who were worried by this regression. It was a line taken by orthodox modern architects and advocates of a new modernity who saw urban planning as an academic discipline that had reached it sell-by date. They advocated a new autonomous architecture capable of "boxing" in the chaos of the large suburb.

Proposals were judged according to two camps— postmodern or high-tech, backward-looking or modern— and took a simplistic form limited to an appreciation of style that short-circuited thought. I talked about the importance of space, of the concept of the street, and rejected as much the return to the closed block and the arguments for chaos. Because I failed to conform to the slogans, my voice was not heard.

Joyful and heterogeneous, an example of the modern picturesque, the Eurodisney project provides a colorful example of my interest in the plural city.

On the Île-de-France plain, at the entrance to the Eurodisney site, I was asked to design a 1,000-bedroom hotel. I proposed two buildings with five hundred rooms shaped like mountains. In front of this ridge, I placed small colorful architectural objects containing suites, restaurants and common areas. As a tribute to Rio de Janeiro, the buildings create an interplay between city and nature, construction and geology. The thematic image is been seen from a point in space, but this is just a starting point: the perception generated by the movement of the viewer in the space through the lines the colors and the distances creates a spatial anamorphosis. Designed to overpass an illusion, this approach produces a "site" and a system of

Project for the docks of the old port of Bordeaux on the Garonne River. All along the 4 kilometers of docks, pavilions move slowly on the rails that once supported harbor cranes.

spaces. To the north, the city is reflected in the lake, and to the south, the pure cutout of the mountains creates a visible and distant entrance to the site.

Along the same spatial lines, the study for the Port de la Lune in Bordeaux is based on the idea of the movement of unique objects in the city. The harbor of Bordeaux along the Garonne had been moved out of the city, downstream. I wanted to imagine a future use to the long beautiful façade and the magnificent quays along four kilometers. I proposed to use the remaining rails of the cranes, made to carry enormous weight, to support mobile pavilions for shops, cafes, children's nursery, meetings shelters, sports, boxes of earth with trees, green houses. A clock tower would move all along the 24 hours from each extremity of this "linear alive center" of the city.

bottom: Competition entry for the Americas Hotel, Euro Disney (Now Disneyland Paris), Paris, France, 1988

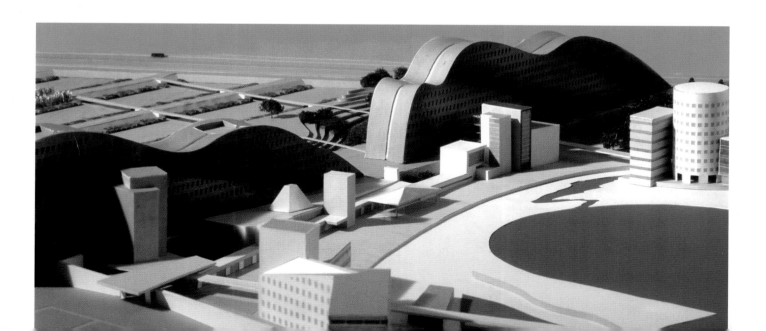

Atlanpôle, Parc de la Chantrerie, Nantes, France. Program: Plan for the development of a technopolis on the banks of the river Erdre ; surface area: 22 hectares. Client: City of Nantes, SEM Atlanpôle. Date: Competition prize-winning project, 1988; design phase: 1988–1994, interrupted by Nantes Town Hall

Atlanpôle, Nantes, France, 1988

Atlanpôle, in 1988, was the first among these urban projects for which I put forward the idea of a neighborhood of open blocks with a random program. It was a project for a city of knowledge and technology launched in Nantes by Olivier Guichard called a "technocluster." There were lots of different requests for laboratories and colleges. Jean-Yves Delaune's idea was to create a synergy between the knowledge economy, technical designs and business incubators, in order to promote industrial development. I was hearing the words "random" and "variety of programs" a lot and the principle that I set myself was to accommodate this programmatic diversity, to link together unique elements, and to be open to an unknown future. The volumetric freedom of the open block allowed for this.

It was a very large site, four kilometers in length, in the countryside with two small hamlets on the banks of the Erdre. I started by working on the relationship between the city and nature and the large-scale perception of the site by forming built "islands" with "open edges" in a large expanse of ecologically interesting countryside and marshland, while preserving the existing villages.

The site formed an archipelago and I called these islands with constructed fronts facing nature "Mont Saint Michel." The project created four large islands. A large 60-meter-wide gap, in the axis of the highest tower in Nantes city center, provided a large-scale view of the whole and allowed people to physically appropriate it.

This large-scale perception, which I think is important, is almost always lacking in suburban areas. I also placed cross-cutting lines through the site to maintain the countryside and make it habitable. They marked the territory every

417 meters. These physical structures allowed the urban site to be perceived in its wider dimension.

But what was really new about Atlanpôle was the way the blocks functioned. It was the first time that I had applied open blocks, something I had had in mind since Cergy. I clearly formalized the open block rule on a "Hippodamian" grid. These blocks construct the streets, give the buildings autonomy and allow for a large degree of uncertainty. We tested a large number of varied programs from various institutions and companies which had asked to the public development leader to be installed, such as advanced schools, laboratories, living accommodation. We did volume-based simulations for the layout of each of the programs based on the open block design. My idea was for the future occupants to supply us with their program, architectural drawings and surface requirements. The urban planner and development specialists then found them a place in the grid; there was a grid but no longer a fixed block plan. The block's compulsory openings optimized perspectives onto the street for each program, giving each of them clearance and light.

Because of the property crisis in the beginning of the 90 and political developments, Atlanpôle never got off the ground. Atlanpole stayed without large realization. What remains from our work on this site, were natural open spaces and conversation areas that I defined from the beginning. I was disappointed but I knew I had jump a great step: the seeds of a new approach to urban planning had been sown.

From this point onwards I refused imposed block plans and experimented with the unlimited versions of my decisive concept of a grid of open blocks as a rule for a group of buildings in a neighborhood, a definition of a new urban planning that I had thought about after Les Hautes Formes.

Model

General Mass Plan

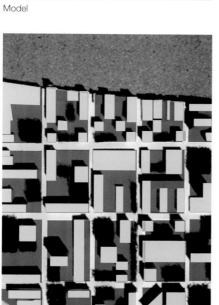

Studies for the Open Streets and the Open Blocks

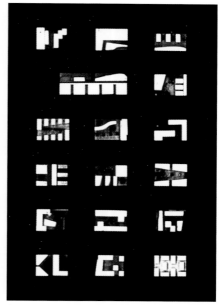

Studies for the Open Blocks

The Jardins de la Lironde, Montpellier, France, 1991–2012

The Jardins de la Lironde in Montpellier, in 1990, was something else entirely: a city in the countryside.

When Alphonse Allais joked "We made a mistake with cities. We should have put them in the countryside," he squared an impossible circle. And yet the city/nature hybridization is one of the most important issues facing us today.

The Jardins de la Lironde is close to the center of Montpellier but surrounded by countryside with its own very special charm, including olive groves and farms.

I was asked to create a neighborhood with two-story buildings and streets. On my first visit to the site in 1990, one thing really stood out: the construction of 2,000 housing units was going to destroy its charm and what made it so special. I rejected this program. Rather than divide it into a series of plots covering the whole site, I proposed to keep large sections of countryside by concentrating the construction into some separated free standing built "blocks" of four to five levels high on top of parking lots.

The design freed up the ground, preserved some of the vines, olive groves and farms and transformed the rest into gardens to be used jointly by the owners or as a public garden.

Each unit in the built blocks has a double exposure with closer views onto the inner courtyard, private and cool, and into the distance toward the expansive views over the natural landscape and to the sea for the upper units. Most of the blocks were built by two or three developers and architects from the region.

My attempt there was to provide for edge of town housing with new own qualities that would compete with those of the highly prized city center. Even though it was the opposite of the program, this principle was immediately adopted by the mayor, the Société d'aménagement (SERM), the property developers who were surprised and interested, and the residents, who liked the idea of preserving the landscape.

Suspended in 1992, the project was relaunched in 2000, with exactly the same concept and plan as the 1990 project. Our idea had been ten years in advance of its time, according to the promotors, and it came just at the right moment because it created, on the edge of town, housing with qualities that did not exist in the highly-prized city center.

Unlike Masséna, where three years later I introduced the freedom of architectural "style," where contrast was allowed and brought together by the straight line of the street, here we needed to avoid scattering architectural objects over the landscape. I laid down the shared principles each architect was to apply: a type of relief concrete basement, a color code and specific materials, and superposed roofing for natural roof ventilation. It was important for the buildings to correspond and form a whole.

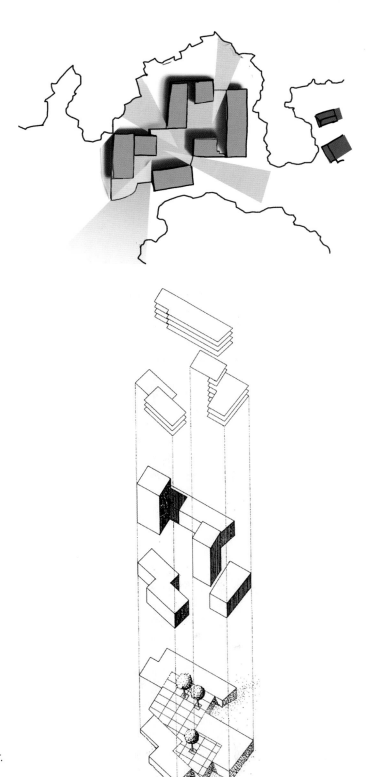

Les Jardins de la Lironde, Port Marianne, Montpellier, France. Program: Definition of urban and architectural orientations of the ZAC La Lironde, 2,000 housing units, 114,848 sq.m of offices and facilities, a school located in "built islands" within a Landscaperd park ; surface area: 623,376 square meters, GFA (of which GFA housing is 459,333 square meters) on 40 hectares. Developer: Société d'équipement de la Région de Montpellier (SERM); Date: Commission, 1991; project completion, 2012

One of the built islets, by Christian de Portzamparc

Built islets in the Jardins de la Lironde

A view of the natural preserve made possible by higher building blocks

Views of one of the built islets, by Christian de Portzamparc

Urban Transformation of a 1960s Neighborhood

In 1991, Michel Lombardini, the property developer of Les Hautes Formes, asked me to work on a subject that has since become vital: the transformation of 1960s housing projects without moving their residents out.

In this traditionally working-class 13th arrondissement of Paris, the same district as Les Hautes Formes, the renovation operations of the 1960s and 1970s had created a hybrid city: left over old blocks and slabs coexist with horizontal blocks of flats and towers characteristic of the time, that the urban planner had placed on a virtual grid with two perpendicular directions to prevent the new buildings from aligning with the streets. It was a way of giving the impression of modern urban planning, which produced stupid left over public spaces between street and façades.

In fact, the modernist tabula rasa had not been completed and the result was a mix of two entirely antagonistic concepts of the city. An Age I, a city with streets and an Age II, a city of objects.

The project of transformation was primarily about the neighborhood and not simply its buildings. Afterwards came matters of architecture, transforming access ways, façades and isolation.

The Urban Planning Project:

There were four large existing buildings of housing. The space between them and the streets was neglected and redundant. I reduced these public spaces and clearly separated them from new private common spaces (entrances and gardens). I requested the demolition of just one small "block", which casted a shadow, and the construction of two new buildings that restored the street alignment. Between these new buildings, I placed the entrance giving onto a garden shared by the residents.

The Architectural Project:

The ground-floor housing units were removed and replaced by new lobbies with through views of the eastern and western gardens.

The transformation included new acoustic and thermal insulation, inhabitants staying in their apartments, the woodwork was changed, the balconies widened from eighty centimeters to one meter eighty-four and fitted with shutters, turning them into living spaces. This transformed the façades, from which we removed the structurally useless vertical lines.

On the rear garden, the smallest "block" became a new building with the creation of small balconies and the addition of insulating cladding. The residents suddenly discovered to open their French windows onto the terraces overlooking the garden.

Nationale District, Paris, France, 1990–1995

National District, Paris, France: in the 1970s, before transformation (at top), and after transformation (at bottom)

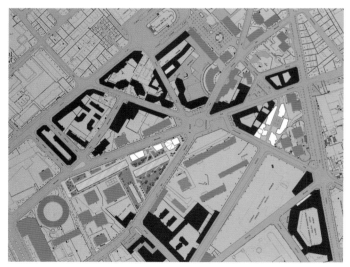

■ Age I The buildings of the city are aligned with the street

■ Age II The buildings of the modern age resist conventional alignment with street

□ Age III A re-evaluation of the relationship between buildings and street

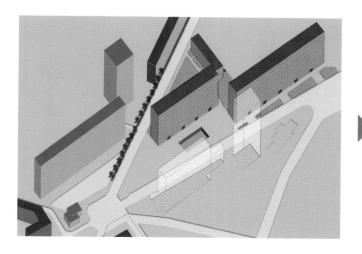
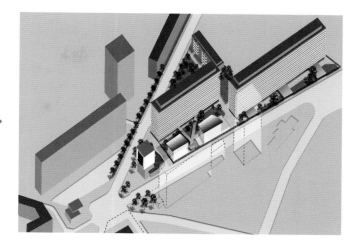

Before

After

For the large Place Nationale, I wanted to place a public symbol on this square that was surrounded by housing on all sides. The art school run by the City of Paris was composed of two superposed cubes that would replace the small "block" and its former garden. There were artists' studios at the top of the art school. It gave meaning and new life to the square that had previously been a simple crossroads.

Fuck Context: the Anti-Space Program

As I was working on the rue Nationale project, globalization was beginning to take hold. Within the space of fifteen years, the suburbs had become highly chaotic in Europe, gripped by social problems caused by deep-rooted inequalities. The caution exercised by town councilors in charge of urban planning extended and also the reject of anything that appeared to be new. Rem Koolhaas issued a warning: "fuck context." With those two little words, he denounced, like many of us, the tendency to conserve and turn cities into museums, to reject invention and to reproduce heritage.

Seventy years after "The city without place," this "fuck context" puts its finger on the divisive point between modernity and regression, from the point of view of the heroic tradition of the Moderns. It was enunciating again that the doxa of the modern project was the program as law, not the context or the place. According to this vision, the place is what exists; it is the past. And the future is in the program.

This slogan, as beautiful as if it were a poem written especially for the moment, was provocative and therefore, in communication terms, very powerful. It contained the idea anamorphosis and expressed clearly that we shouldn't regress, that radicalism alone leads to brave new decisions, especially in a swamp of cautious indecision. But yet, in terms of the city, we know that turning division into a principle was the error made by the Moderns. Saint Paul and Lenin proclaimed that to found the new, you needed

to destroy and reject everything that already existed. Prophets need to create a division between before and after.

However, the city goes beyond us; as it went beyond the Moderns. The key to the quality of the city does not primarily lie in the extent to which it represents a break with the past and context. In the world fragmented by the industrial revolution and migration, resilience and continuity are virtues. More than ever, urban planning projects like neighborhoods pointed toward this way of thinking. I always considered the place as the basis of a past to transform but also the program as a reality to transform.

In his own projects, Rem Koolhaas did not reject context; he used it; he brought it back to life in wonderful ways; and I had the pleasure of being part of it in Lille and Almere where his planning program pushed the architect to go beyond

Nationale District, 119–123 to 131–135 to 149, rue Nationale, Paris 13th District, France. Program: Rehabilitation: apartments; 75,000 square meters; implementation: apartments and shops: 3,500 square meters; art school: 5,500 square meters; multi-purpose urban project with housing, shops, public facilities; rehabilitation of 3 residential buildings with 608 apartments ; demolition of a building; implementation of 2 buildings with apartments and shops; implementation of a building with an art school, concert hall and art studios. Client: City of Paris Housing Office (RIVP). Landscape design: Lydie Chauvac. Date: Commission, 1990; completion, 1995

The new school (at left), the "Pavillon" facing the street, and the renovated long building, in background

himself. The plans for the rue Nationale, for example, were none other than an attention to context and the complete transformation of its urbanistic meaning through the invention of a hybrid. This work obviously became increasingly important after the post-war building decades. Transformation would be the modernity of the future.

The Ages of the City

At a series of urban planning workshops organized by the Caisse des dépôts, the investment arm of the French government, in Lyon in 1990, I described the three ages of the city, in order to respond and oppose to those who wanted to return to the city of "the past." Stating that we could not return to the classical city, I got my message across by describing, in simple terms, what characterized our time. After Age 0, with its medinas and distribution corridors, came the street, followed by two thousand years of the city with streets that followed on from each other. But there had also been another episode, the "death of the street," and, since the middle of the last century, another age of the city arose, the streetless city, which followed the precepts of the Athens Charter. This ultra-fast age second age, with its large housing projects, tower blocks and vast suburbs constructed urban surfaces bigger and more densely populated than the city centers. The forms of these two ages were fundamentally conflicting as the moderns presumed that Age II would replace Age I, the classic city. Then in this conference, I stated that this idea was obsolete, that Age II could definitely no longer be our model, but that we could not regress to Age I, as many planners believed, because the economy, the technique and the expectations of the people had changed.

We could understand that if the idea of the tabula rasa had been rejected when the Age II had not yet replaced totally the Age I, the city would obviously no longer consists in one single unity growing. It would at least be dual or hybrid forever. We were the heirs of this dual urban planning history, which determine our urban geography everywhere.

We had entered Age III. This was not understood by modern urban planners and still less so by the supporters of a return to the city of "the past," because this move to Age III wasn't born from the invention of a new model but with the dereliction of any main unique model. There is no longer dominant doctrine. We lived through this lack of analysis it in the following years.

The reconstruction of the Berlin Mitte neighborhood, for example, shows that it was right to return to the historic grid pattern of streets, but adapting our time to this plan should have led us to rethink the volumes of the block, rather than claiming to return to Age I by building higher

Nationale District, Paris, France, 1990–1995

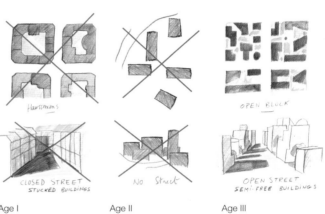

Age I   Age II   Age III

top: The school on the square. Bottom: Nowadays, the traditional enclosed block is no longer the ideal model.

The new building demonstrating respect for the street

and wider blocks with inner courtyards that were often too dark for the northern European climate. New types of blocks would have allowed for density while opening up the views and letting in the light.

In fact, the modern city didn't have time to remove the ancient city entirely, but we cannot apply these two models but reinvent them. This is the city with which we live and find ourselves working, the hybrid system in which the two contradictory models coexist. Discreetly, between the 1980s and 1990s, the cities of Europe abandoned modern urban planning without developing a line of thought appropriate to our own age.

Masséna and Open Blocks

After Atlanpôle in 1988, my ideas about an open block neighborhood had matured. I was able to finally put them into practice in 1994 when I entered the competition for a part of "Paris Rive Gauche", a section of an enormous swathe of wasteland previously occupied by factories and railroad infrastructure.

I saw that a street network linking the thoroughfares of the 13th arrondissement to the Seine would clearly allow me to construct the open blocks I had been considering for years.

We started by studying blocks for one hundred accommodation units with two or three operations per block. I wanted to set urban rules that gave architects a freedom and no longer fix ground plan and volumes. There were two successive competition stages and the judges were very divided. At the final session, the judges came down on the side of innovation and my project's new method.

The block is open in two ways: it is open because it welcomes a diversity of programs (housing, university, school businesses and offices) and because it is open to views and the light.

The Characteristics of the Open Block

1: Autonomous Buildings

The opening of the block is characterized by autonomous buildings. They don't adjoin each other but let visual openings between them, making up 30 percent to 40 percent of the block's perimeter. This scheme avoids the shadow of courtyards and corridor streets. The buildings face all directions to provide multiple views, near and far.

The block is therefore open in volumetric and spatial terms; it involves light and flows; it is a method of working with the space between buildings, courtyards, gaps and the street, to "inhabit" the dense horizontal city.

This new block is "hollowed out" and divided into solids and voids, according to a controlled alternating pattern.

Masséna new district, Paris, France, 1994–2010

Masséna new district, Paris, France, 1994–2010

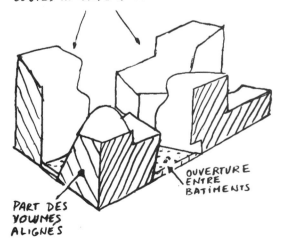

AUTONOMIE DES BATIMENTS
VOLUMES LIBRES DANS L'ILOT
COUPÉS AU CORDEAU SUR LA RUE

OUVERTURE
ENTRE
BATIMENTS

PART DES
VOLUMES
ALIGNÉS

opposite page: Competition model of Masséna new district, Paris, France

It's an approach that's halfway between urban planning and architecture within which several architects can work. I was looking for what gave the city its shape, what makes it perceptible to us. It's not just about the buildings or the roadways. It's the link between the two.

2: The Open Street

Here the street is the volume of empty space framed by the continuous plane of the alignment of façades that unifies the discontinuity between façades and ground. A certain proportion of the surface of each building is aligned along the plane of the street. The open block produces an open street that can be straight but bright thanks to the gaps and voids between the disjointed volumes and varying heights. It took a year of discussions with the city' street department because the 11-meter-wide streets were contrary to regulations and we finally agreed on 11.60 meters. On the ground floor, the blocks are closed using see-through railings or walls with trees visible behind them. The spatial limit between private and public is clear.

3: Sustainable Because Transformable

According to the rules of the open block, the surface or volume define the constructability and property limits. It is a three-dimensional plot that allows for the future development of property sales, the possibility to resell and rebuild within an expanded shell to change the purpose of a plot. For Masséna, we provided shells of building space that exceed the building rights. We called them "oversized coats" and they provided architects with the freedom to compose their volumes.

4: Uncertainty and disparity

There is another form of opening allowed by the open block: the infinite variety of programs and types of architecture. The independence of these buildings frees up their volume. The project addresses disparity and the limits placed on the freedom of architects to design as they wish, an increasingly common problem in urban planning.

Classic cities have been designed around the idea that harmony comes from homogeneity, resemblance and variations on a type, with a style that varies slightly with each century. The twentieth century made a clean break with this idea, but the modern model, with its serial repetition, confirmed nevertheless the notion of repetition and homogeneity between buildings. This urban homogeneity approach more or less exploded in the recent period. The disparity that has since emerged often defies any notion of order and harmony of resemblance and is a nightmare for urban planners. It represented a major challenge, which had to be met. The variety of programs and the unpredictable diversity of architectural "styles" that appeared and exist

Masséna new district, Paris, France, 1994–2010

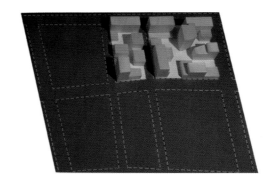

Study models showing interaction of buildings and open blocks for Masséna new district competition, 1994

today led to see urban esthetics, in another way, adopting another vision and to pay attention to the flavor of a heterogeneous, contrasting environment.

From Atlanpôle onwards, I developed the open block to "open up" the city to uncertainty and to assemble this multiple disparity in the dense city.

To achieve this, I wanted to confront various architectural styles, knowing that the flavor of multiplicity can only be revealed in a composition that is both interlinked and in confrontation. In this instance, the street is used to achieve this with the "cheese wire" formed by the strict alignment of portions of the façades. In fact, here, two contradictory principles are married: the freedom of individual "solid" forms and the strictness of the "empty" forms of the street's public space. This is what guarantees the unity that links up a series of separate architectural designs by offering a maximum of possibilities and diversity in a very obvious continuity. The singular and the plural.

I would never impose a "demanding" rule that the city should be diversified. I see coherence between buildings as a quality but with the Masséna project I wanted to bring into play this plurality. I wanted to experiment, express the absence of censorship, without recommending diversity, and give esthetic and practical grounds for a certain freedom contained within the rules as an esthetic test necessary for our times.

A different neighborhood of open blocks could be ordered according to a required unity of "style" by imposing the architecture and materials. The open block does not imply diversity of architecture but it does lend itself to pluralism and the addition of different programs and volumes.

In the Masséna sector you find programs that are extremely different in their volumetric needs, from housing, offices, a school, laboratories and classrooms to a university; buildings which are part of the urban heritage, the history of the city and this neighborhood are preserved and absorbed into its framework.

During the various consultation stages and competitions for the Masséna block, we had to choose between projects proposing very different volumes on the same plot. Rather than urban planning based on restrictions and prohibitions, these "oversized dimensions" offer a certain degree of freedom and open up possibilities. It often encourages us to be more creative. It is a lot more interesting and rewarding to design whole volumes with a choice of shapes and materials than to design a façade between two adjoining buildings.

The challenge presented by the city of tomorrow is to welcome the unknown, the future, without itself being deformed or destroyed. You need to allow time to play

Imagery demonstrating various open blocks within the whole, with free volumes that allow for light to reach the street

Masséna New District, On the South Bank of the River Seine, Paris 13th
District, France. Program: Urban project; conception of urban rules: volumes,
division of the blocks, drawing of the network and public gardens ; surface area:
339,100 square meters; GFA total on 12.5 hectares. Client: City of Paris. Devloper:
Société d'Économie Mixte d'Aménagement de la Ville de Paris (SEMAPA). Date:
Competition award-winning project, 1995; completion, 2010

1

2

3

4

5

6

7

8

Paticipated Architects

Thirty-one architects were involved in the project:
Anthony Bechu, Beckmann N'thépé, Bellecour &
Barberot, Badia-Berger, Bofill-Heckly, Bolze & Rodriguez,
Frédéric Borel, Brenac et Gonzalez, Chaix & Morel,
Pierre Charbonnier, Arte Charpentier, François Chochon,
Christian Devillers, Jean Guervilly, Epstein et Glaiman,
Foster and Partners, Catherine Furet, Henri Gaudin,
Edith Girard, Antoine Grumbach, Michel Macary, Nicolas
Michelin, Jean-Philippe Pargade, Gaëlle Peneau, Philtre,
Rudy Ricciotti, Marc Rolinet, Francis Soler, Antoine
Stinco and Robert Turner.

1. Marie-Hélène Badia, Didier Berger, architects
2. Jean-Philippe Pargade, architect
3. Antoine Stinco, architect
4. Aldric Beckmann, Françoise N'thépé, architects
5. Wilfrid Bellecour, François Barberot, architects
6. Frédéric Borel, architect
7. Nicolas Michelin, architect
8. Marie-Hélène Badia, Didier Berger, architects

its role, respond to the progressive and changing nature of development, organize diversity, sometimes-contradictory singularities, and manage to create a whole within this disparity. The open block welcomes a mix of designs and avoids the monofunctional principle that is often characteristic of new neighborhoods.

It is true that architects are not always good or, put another way, no one likes all types of architecture. There are no absolute criteria and it would be delusional to imagine that a neighborhood is going to contain an alignment of masterpieces. You need to work with ordinary architecture. But you also need to add a few lively and intelligent buildings.

The neighborhood took fifteen years to complete, a reflection of the economic climate, and in all thirty architects and property developers produced buildings for the project. It was said before this achievement of Masséna that I was the only one who could follow my own rules. But all the architects told me that, rather than limiting them, these rules had been easy to follow and allowed them enormous freedom and flexibility to realize their programs.

In the early 2000s, the mayor of Paris organized a visit to the site. One of the visitors, a town planner, started with a criticism: this plan did not enable him to resell and rebuild on a plot like in a classic city. I explained how, on the contrary, there is more flexible space if you need to rebuild. The buildings face in four directions without being caught between two neighboring walls. The visit obviously proved the quality living environments of the apartments.

The most interesting comment was made by Amanda Burden, chair of the Department of City Planning of New York, during a round table meeting organized by the City of Paris, who described the project as a "stratification of periods in miniature"!

The open block is a method that subsequently proved useful in allowing unique adaptations for various urban projects with very different uses. We used it as a tool for projects in São Paulo and Beijing to avoid large closed areas. In New York, the height-staggered vertical block was used to link road systems, the block and towers. In Brussels, the open block technique was also used to transform a major road, the rue de la Loi. The open block became a benchmark for new neighborhoods everywhere.

Hestia—Hermès

In every city, at each moment of our lives, we are either still or moving—steady, seated, idling; or running from one place to another. We need places and links according to a system. The Greeks always paired the temples of Hestia, the goddess of the hearth, and Hermès, god of movement and trade (Jean-Pierre Vernant underlined this observation

which Bruno Queysanne then took up in his writing on Los Angeles). Since the invention of the street, in Millet 2,500 years ago, and in China probably before that, the same system of streets and blocks plugs all places into a network of links. Hestia and Hermès are united at any place. They are placed side by side within a continuous space, from proximity to proximity. With the death of the street, the rise of rapid motorized transport and the creation of specific functional areas, a second urban age emerged.

The link was separated from the place. The tentacles of highways and railroads pushed the new neighborhoods far out and the city broke up along the vast channels of highways into camps, zones, ghettos and parks cut off from one another in a fragmentary way that the new networks of cyberspace have moderated but not resolved.

The street was rejected in theory and practice by modern urban planning of the last century but it goes beyond us. The street is our past and our future. It is order and freedom.

This neighborhood, Massena and its open blocks, reveals a street of the future. The street is an interface between society and individuals. It creates a link between the multiple private and the public in a single form, a single line forming the unity of a public space accommodating infinite diversity. It is a theater for meetings and the system that allows for space to be practiced, for us to recognize addresses and places gradually, to find our bearings, to know where the others are. The community, even though vast and anonymous, is represented here. It is like a "search engine" where lines of movement, routes and avenues are also lines for exchange and the dissemination of information and business.

The city of streets silently teaches each child the public thing, the world outside, as an accessible and attainable richness. When we remove the street, we abandon its system of multiple distribution along their route. I have always created thoroughfares, passages and streets.

It alone comprises the esthetic of the fragmentation and modernity described by Baudelaire and taken up by Nietzsche, then Walter Benjamin and Aragon. It offers us the fugitive and multiple, stability and unity. In the 1950s, Guy Debord caused a scandal when he targeted Le Corbusier because his urban planning wanted to "finally kill the street." He knew the street had and would always be the support of the randomness, the very immediate life and he made it the vital territory of the "by-products" and adventures of life that he felt should be invented not imposed, a concept he saw reflected in André Breton's "The Lost Steps": "It used to be that I never left home without bidding farewell to all the binding memory, to everything that I felt to perpetuate in myself. The street, which I believed could furnish my life with its surprising detours; the street, with its cares and its glances, was my true element: there I could test like nowhere else the winds of the possible."

1

2

3

4

5

6

7

Streets, Crossings, Passages

1. Tripode, Nantes, France, 2006
2. Rue de la Loi, Brussels, Belgium, 2008
3. Masséna new district, Paris, France, 1995
4. Masséna new district, Paris, France, 1995
5. Riverside City Center, New York, U.S.A., 2005
6. De Citadel, Almere, Netherlands, 2000
7. Logistic Port, Bejing, China, 2003

Our city today

After declaring the "death of the street," Le Corbusier had to replace it. Imitating the industrial method, he promoted the idea of zoning. Shocked by the countless uses performed by the street (transportation, light, air, addresses, stores, a mix of homes and businesses and amenities) he separated them and located on their own site to optimize their operation according to the famous list: live, work, recreate and travel (which needs rapid transit systems running along separate channels that would section the land often creating enclaves).

Although intended to be applied as a public planning principle for the locating and scaling of common utility services and residences this zoning proved rapidly its efficiency for private large investment in urban territories, industrial "camps" and other activity zones, vast trading and leisure zones, followed by residential parks and private towns. Lined with highway channels that distributed nothing to the places they passed, these camps and parks are enclosed "bags" with one entrance. And so began the era of special-ized territories, private zones, more or less confiscated from and in symmetry with the most deprived areas. Our world is a world of channels and enclaves. Camps for the wealthy and their opposite, the housing projects, then the areas inhabited by the most deprived. It is precisely in this type of city that the Cidade das Artes, which I built in Rio, should find its raison d'être.

Surprisingly, this program, which did away with the street, a form two millennia old, was implemented in all developed cities. This cannot be explained by the needs of the car alone. The street had to be portrayed as a nuisance, archaic and bothersome. Bucharest and the Berlin of Stalinallee were exceptions to the rule because this approach to urban planning was considered as a western capitalist feature. But streets were destroyed from Singapore to Beijing, and forgotten in Europe as in what is now called the Greater Paris.

The analytical method that cuts up production (in this case, the city) into sectors of distinct technical fields is necessary for producing engines but cannot be applied

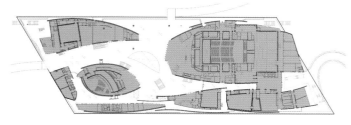

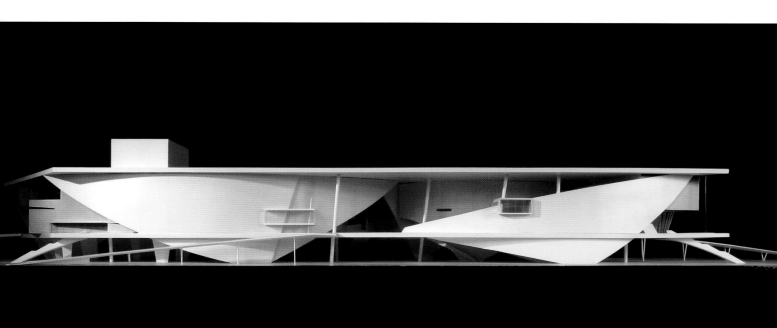

In 2004, for the Lille exhibition, we were confronted with two projects of the same size: one singular in Rio, one multiple in Beijing.
above: Cidade das Artes, Rio de Janeiro, Brazil, 2002–2013

to the living, communities, politics, cities.

The death of the street was planned, programmed and decreed as a benefit by twentieth-century urban planners during the boom years of the "mechanical city." And this decree was understood by urban planning departments worldwide as the lifting of a millennia-old obligation. Remove the street and you abandon this public responsibility to put links everywhere, to defend the concept of public space, a "res publica" as applying to everyone.

It meant breaking forever with what we might call the anthropological institution of the city and the metropolis. With streets, places like Barra da Tijuca in Rio and Orly-Rungis in Paris could have been protected, lived normally, and coexisted perfectly with technical requirements.

This is our world, our city. Our condition. We cannot deny or reject it. We need to abandon the Manichean tradition of being for or against. We need to think in hybrids. We need to transform it, sometimes through cunning, in line with practical demand. There will be several worlds in one, several continuous cities.

Singular and Multiple

With the "Singular and Plural" exhibition in 2004 in Lille, I realized through three decades of our projects, how our thinking about space is always political and requires us to think in terms of numbers—classify, add, share, divide—and therefore in terms of dimensions ("the scale" to use the vocabulary of architects).

I have rarely designed pure units; I have sometimes accentuated or sanctioned unity, as in Seoul or Rio, but in general, I brought into play the plural at the risk of losing unity. I fragmented and brought into play the city. And I introduced the void, the space, rather than the solitary object and the solid. And although I started Bercy, Fukuoka and Luxembourg as pure unities, I only liked these projects from the moment I had to bring in plural additions.

I like small and large unities and I also like the profusion of multiplicities. I have always created thoroughfares, passages and streets. I don't see another link between the singular and the multiple than the street.

From then on, we assess the great and the small, and we evolve from the singular to the multiple, from the street to the object.

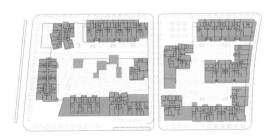

Logistic Port, Beijing, China, 2003

Along the Park of Bercy, Paris, France, 1991–1994

As an example, in the new district of Bercy, in the urban plan and the volume designed by Jean-Pierre Buffi, the presence of a chestnut tree appeared to be protected and to hold up our construction permit. I proposed then to open a breach in the northern side in order to keep the tree, dividing the building in two.

The end result a nice transparency in the block; the double-height glazed elements let in light from the sky and a layout that judiciously positioned the living rooms, gave everyone views into the distance and perfect light, despite the density and the fairly close proximity of the buildings opposite.

This positive experience of density highlighted the qualities of breaches and openings as Les Hautes Formes had already demonstrated.

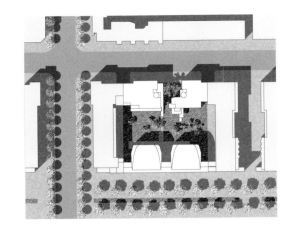

Housing along the Park of Bercy, rue de Lambroisie, rue Gabriel-Lamé ZAC Bercy, Paris, 12th District, France. Program: 4 buildings, 67 housing units, retail, parking lot, restaurant, office areas; surface area: 12,860 square meters. Client: C.A.R.C.D., PromoReal. Developer: SEMAEST. Date: Commission, 1991; completion, 1994

opposite page: The opening of the block allows for
light to reach the building entrance

TV Channel Canal + Group Headquarters, Boulogne-Billancourt, France, 1996–1999

The site forms a gateway to the town of Boulogne on the banks of the Seine, and the promotor Nexity explained during the competition that the building along the Seine would be put in the spotlight whereas the buildings at the rear of this triangular plot, which would be enclosed on the courtyard side, would be worth a lot less.

I started with the idea that we needed to challenge this prejudice and give all of the offices that I had to build the best views and light possible, by finding a way of opening up secondary views over the Ile Saint-Germain.

Here, I applied a three-dimensional open block strategy, designing four blocks among which the two along the river are lifted. The whole works with multiple openings, views, perspectives horizontal and vertical views from inside to outside, transparency and materials.

The two buildings along the Seine are not continuous, they open a wide window between them. Being raised ten meters above the ground on a trellis formed by thin metal columns, they free a large transparent space, providing view on the Seine for the second line of building and open the garden onto the Seine riverside and the Ile Saint-Germain through the slim columns of the trellis.

In the transparent lobby, which opens to the bright south, Elizabeth de Portzamparc was commissioned to design the reception area.

The building had to be suitable for purchase by two or three companies. The whole fragmented building is therefore linked like a single piece, a continuous ribbon, with filming studios inside a basement hill (it has been the headquarters of the TV channel Canal+ production companies).

The whole block demonstrated the efficiency of the open block system. On this site, next to the Seine, the area on the edge of the district was considered to be crowded, dense, but we obtained a similar "FAR" which felt like the opposite, like an open and bright ensemble.

TV Channel Canal + Group Headquarters, 48, Quai du Point du Jour, Boulogne-Billancourt, France. Program: Office building for the audiovisual production activities of France's leading private television network, the Canal + Group; surface area: 31,400 square meters. Interior architect: Elizabeth de Portzamparc. Client: Nexity-Sari. Date: Competition entry, 1996; completion, 1999

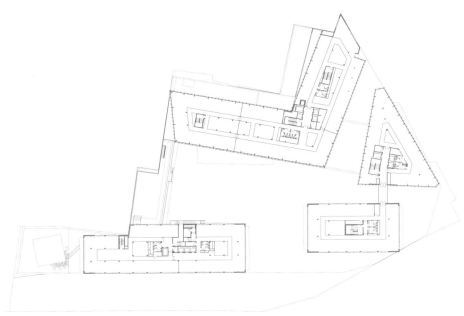

Fourth Floor Plan

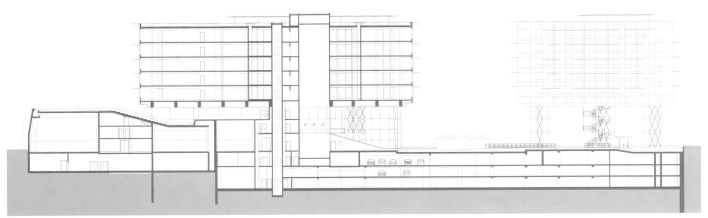

Elevation

Building entrance facing the city of Boulogne-Billancourt

View to the river and park

French Embassy in Germany, 1997–2003

In Berlin, when I visited the site, I first decided to quit the competition, having to work in such a tight enclosed block of the site in the Parizer Platz.

Curiously, it is the open block experience and strategy, which saved the study and allowed one of our greatest achievement.

In 1945, there was nothing left on Pariser Platz except the Brandenberg Gate: the French Embassy, the US Embassy, the Adlon Hotel, and all of the buildings on the square had been destroyed. When the competition to rebuild the square was launched by the ministry in 1996, I entered it as a team, with Elizabeth de Portzamparc for the architecture of the reception areas and Régis Guignard for the landscaping.

When I visited the cleared site, I realized that both the 100 meters long and the tall closed wall of the abutting buildings planned for the adjoining offices of the Bundestag coupled with the number of offices required to put in this future confined block were the very contrary to my whole approach to urban planning.

In early November 1996, I told myself that if I hadn't managed to overcome this impression of claustrophobia after a month of working on the project, I wouldn't enter the competition. I didn't want the distance left over between buildings be too little to create courtyards, even if accepted by the urban rules.

However here, the strategy of fragmentation combine with a subtle game of the illusion of openings expanded this narrow, closed block and gave comfort to house a multi-functional embassy building.

I began by analyzing the functions and flows, the offices required and the links between them, and produced a series of hypothetical models. I used the interaction between six solids and two large voids to give the interior space of this closed block the impression of being a series of spaces, one leading infinitely onto another. I gave it light by different height of buildings respecting the legal section.

The six buildings and two garden courtyards are linked together and crossed by a long, planted walkway at a height of sixteen meters. It disperses the spaces, brings in light, gives the impression everywhere of expanding the volume and provides close and distant views in all areas of the building. It is a building whose interest is in discovering the richness of the inside and outside interior of the block. On the ground, a six-meter wide interior street with extremely vertical proportions links the two entrances from the city: Pariser Platz and Wilhelmstrasse and enables visitors to immediately grasp the block as a whole, to see depth and the sky too. The square's paving is continued into this covered passage and running in the courtyard. On the corner of this angled interior street, Elizabeth de Portzamparc has designed a café.

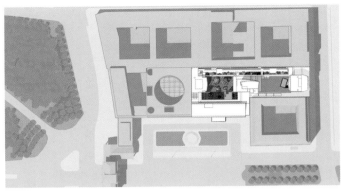

Mass Plan

Model of the French Embassy in Berlin, Germany, 1997–2003, with the Brandenberg Gate in foreground, and, beyond, Parizer Platz

View of the embassy from the Parizer Platz

On the second floor, taking up Elizabeth's idea, the reception areas all open onto an interior in-ground garden, at a height of five meters, for better lighting. These rooms and meeting spaces form the *piano nobile*, *bel étage* in German, on the garden side. Lower down, on the Wilhelm-strasse side, the courtyard provides open light and access to the consular services and the public consultation areas.

The long walkway suspended at a middle height to the adjoining wall of the Bundestag successively crosses the garden and courtyard. It is lined with birch trees on one side and, on the other, with a vertical garden by Régis Guignard, which grows up onto a structure installed on the long wall.

opposite page: The reception garden at main floor

During a visit in 2003, one of the visitors congratulated me for creating "voids," and asked me why I had used four types of materials and colors. For me, without these contrasts, all of the spaces would have become enclosed courtyards; the colors distinguish and separate the different buildings: beige split-block concrete for the exterior base and the pillars of the offices along the wall, white plaster for the three buildings of the middle span, glass for the curtain walls of the interior sides of the south-facing offices, and black, matt metal for the southern interior façade of the chancellery.

On the square, the building regulations applying to the Brandenberg Gate vicinity require buildings to have a base, here in split-block concrete. The combination of this base, like the piano nobile is a tribute to Karl Friedrich Schinkel, the architect who has designed this beautiful part of the city of Berlin.

Above this base, the windows were not allowed to be larger than the surface area of the largest of the Brandenberg Gate's arches.

The lessons drawn from the open block concept here allowed for the transformation of a closed block and demonstrated how architecture can make a tight and enclosed space appear to be large.

Eisenstein said of the movies that they can handle time like an accordion, a year might pass in a minute, and then the following minute might last much longer. Architecture

and the landscape play with this possibility of transforming the perception of space and distance. That was my approach to Les Hautes Formes, the French Embassy in Berlin, the Conservatoire at the Cité de la musique in Paris, which are very dense projects, on very narrow plots of land. I could describe in detail how we expanded the volume in each design, but there's no formula, no absolute certainty. I was only really sure at the end. Everything counts: the colors, the way the materials contrast with each other, the entrances, how the light and sound are reflected, the proportions between the different elements, the openings to the square or toward what you assume is a distant view. In the Embassy the amazing game of the illusion works, given through the impression that there are other spaces that continue beyond its apparent limits even if these limits protect us. Every good project is made with joy, as in this case. It was not hard work. My pleasure as an illusionist discovering the efficiency of transforming was incredible, unexpected and effective.

French Embassy, Parizer Platz, Berlin, Germany. Program: This public facility accommodates the Ambassador's Residence, the Consulate and Chancellery offices, the cultural department, function halls, a cafeteria, an amphitheater, housing and multifunctional spaces, all divided into seven buildings; surface area: 20,000 square meters. Client: French Foreign Minister. Interior design and furniture: Elizabeth de Portzamparc. Artists: François Morellet, Georges Noël, François Rouan, Niele Toroni, Martin Wallace, Zao Wou-Ki. Landscape: Régis Guignard, Méristème. Acoustic: Jean-Paul Lamoureux. Date: Winning entry of design competition, 1997; completion, 2003

Two pencil sketches of the French Embassy, 1996

above: The multi-level interior garden. opposite page: The diplomatic promenade dominates the garden and the courtyard all along the site.

Entrance Hall. The stairway of Honor

A view of the garden from the Room of Honor

opposite page: Hall leading from entrance on Parizer Platz to reception area

opposite page: Two rooms in the central building

Les Champes Libres, Rennes, France, 1993

Chapter 3
Composites Objects: The 1990s

From the 1970s to the 1980s, with my designs for the Water Tower, La Roquette, École de danse and La Cité de la musique, as an architect I reexamined different periods in history, following in the footsteps of our masters in this art, Picasso and Stravinsky, who in a given period revisited history through painting and music. I reinterpreted archetypes to test their permanence in today's world and to explore what we had lost to Modernist principles. The urban planning projects of the years 1988–1990 introduced me to other architectural themes through the rather curious Port de la Lune in Bordeaux and the Place Coislin in Metz. With the Café Beaubourg, Fukuoka and the hotel for Disney, I focused more on the "pictorial" and textural. I put my white period behind me, I did not want to get stuck in a rut. I had learn to build in concrete, to master the lines, numbers, rhythms, proportions and dimensions, but I needed to approach new territories.

The École de Danse and the Cité de la musique gave me a grounding in programs for major public institutions.

In the early 1990s, I built up a variety of experience, by completing fifteen studies and competitions in three years. There was something new about each project, that I welcomed as an element of luck. Overseas projects in Fukuoka, Tokyo and Seoul brought us into contact with different clients and alternative working practices. The situations and programs were so different, each requiring different ways of thinking, that there was no chance of falling into a routine. They added a lot to my intellectual experience and I moved slowly from the fragmented composition of series of objects to composite objects.

As an exemple, in 1990s, with the Tour de Lille, the pleasure of working on a bridge "terrain" on the Euralille audacious plane designed by Rem Koolhaas, pushed me to search for a new, unitary forms, guided necessarily by structure, economy and the orientation of the offices toward the city.

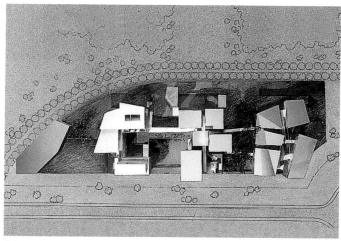

School of Architecture, Marne-la-Vallée, France, 1995

International Convention Hall, Nara, Japan, 1992

In Nara, Japan, I still worked in a fragmented strategy. The program of the future International Convention Hall was going to be located in the new city, close to its most ancient temples in the gardens of the old town. I created an ensemble of three main sculptural sections housing the respective conference rooms, which interact on a dark stone base surrounded by grass, slabs and water. At the bottom, the fourth section is like a long green sandstone rock and houses the common areas while linking the three conference rooms. An interior courtyard opens into the base. Arata Isozaki won with a beautiful unified project.

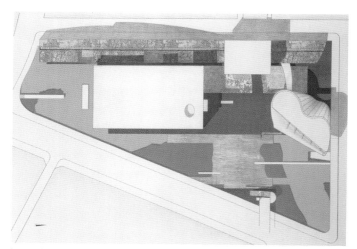

International Convention Hall, Nara, Japan, 1992

National Museum of Korea, Seoul, 1995

Situated in a large park surrounded by the river Han in the center of Seoul, the museum was intended to be a symbol of national identity and to provide an insight into the country's history. To avoid the water in the museum and storages and to meet the symbolique requirement, I conceived the museum as a pure, floating volume detached from the park's uneven surface. This white entablature houses the galleries. It is supported by four dark pillars containing the flood reserves. The complex forms an island surrounded by water.

The park, lake, island, piers and entablature form a whole; the museum unifies and underpins the park.

A stone avenue crosses the museum and opens a footbridge on to the park, linking the river Han in the south to the view of Mount Nam Sam in the north.

Within the rectangular volume, several free solids house entrances and reception areas, amphitheaters, facilities for children, waterside restaurants, stores, walks and a garden around the hall of large pagodas. In a Korean way, kiosks scattered around the island provide shelters within the park.

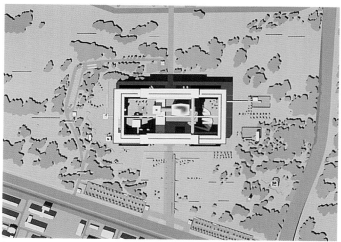

National Museum of Korea, Seoul, South Korea, 1995

Model of the School of Architecture, Marne-la-Vallée, France, 1995

Model of the International Convention Hall, Nara, Japan, 1992

Alternate model of the National Museum of Korea, Seoul, South Korea, 1995

Composites Objects

Despite the east wing of the city of music, the activity in Japan and the Lille tower, my practice was endangered by the fact that I lost 15 competitions in the first three years of the nineties. I was beginning to work on whole objects, assembling several main sections forming unified assemblages. "Object systems" gave way to "composite objects."

In the following years, towers like Bandai in Tokyo and LVMH in New York present a dominating unity reached through a process of assembling different pieces. The plural aspect is still there, but not composed of separate objects.

I found a note from 1996 that described this variety of experiences: "I'm not worried about evolution, or strategy, or marketing. I always get the impression that I'm responding to situations and intervening in them: fragmented in the Cité de la musique, prismatic in Lille, elliptical in Grasse, shell-shaped for Bandaï, rectangular in Seoul then prismatic in New York for LVMH . . . Eclectic? Dual? Triple?"

Since these years in the nineties, I do not build in the same "style" from one project to another. The extension of the Palais des Congrès at Porte Maillot in Paris and the Philharmonie Luxembourg are examples of composite objects formed by a principal volume and the addition or apparition of secondary volumes contrasting with a pure, oblique and solid wall in Paris, and a cylindrical and filtering wall in Luxembourg.

Tadao Ando once said, as he was introducing me at a conference in Osaka, that he saw an enviable feature in this renewal, but I don't see these variations between my projects as a quality in itself, but rather a desire to reject, in my approach to design, formal concepts that could become mannerisms, blinding thoughts. As every situation is unique, it is a pleasure to be presented with new demands and introduced to new compositional or construction methods. Then, you always need to know how to overcome them in order to find the best response to an economic, technical and climatic context, to needs arising from an activity, or to a demand.

Although globalization has tended to gradually standardize technical cultures, programs and esthetic modes, each country has its own geography, its own climate, its own economy, lifestyles, specific traditions and work organization. For each country used materials and construction expertise all vary.

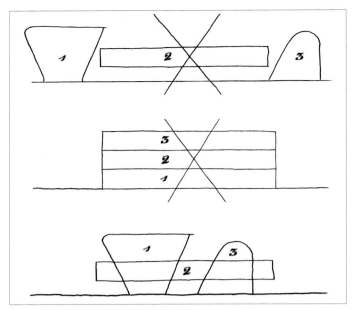

Les Champes Libres, Rennes, France, 1993–2006. Neither fragmented nor unified, the Champes Libres is composite. Three in one.

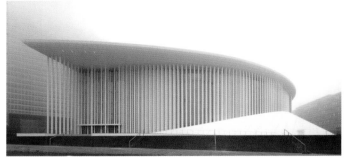

Luxembourg Philharmonic, Grand Duchy of Luxembourg, 1997–2005

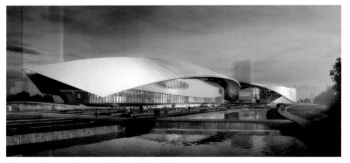

Cultural Center, Suzhou, China, 2013–2019

Casarts, Casablanca, Morocco, 2009–2019

The challenges

Yet for each project, we always act out the same scene: you need to understand the "client," the mayor, and imagine how, in the allotted space, life might "take root." And you almost always hit an obstacle. Something just does not work. You discover that building a residence or an institution in an intended location is going to cause problems. The program hides an unexpected difficulty, a regulatory, quantitative or budgetary limitation. The response should reach outside the program, transform it and use cunning to overcome the obstacle.

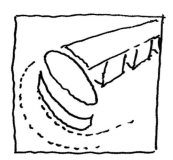

To get a clear understanding of the problem I learnt to formulate to me and the team the simple question or the main "trigger" challenge presented by the commission, the overriding necessity that I had to creatively overcome and work around in order to create an "obvious" or at least understandable building that would erase the memory of how the problem was overcome. This formulation is what triggers this search. That's the point at which the study can really start.

And I think I've got the project right when I feel—and soon after have the conviction—that the forms, orientations, dimensions, materials and the modes of building the assembled volumes respond to this question and challenge and provide a lot more unexpected advantages. At the same time, I try not to be blind to the latent idiosyncrasy and subjectivity lying in the drawings and the spatial or architectural choices, I try instead to spy if I have to respect their unexpected way to give more utility or a unexplicable beauty.

This is how the development of each project was driven from the start by the formulation of its main "trigger" challenge.

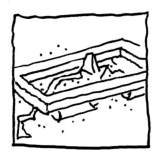

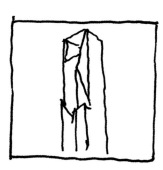

Composite objects

"Les Champs Libres," Rennes, France, 1993–2006

In Rennes, the program presented us with a very specific challenge, although it was not obvious from the start. There were three programs: the library, the museum and the science center. Respecting the identities of each institution which already fronted the city street was self-evident to me, I initially favored a fragmentation approach with three separate and adjoining volumes. But I soon realized that the mayor of Rennes, Edmond Hervé, wanted one cultural center, not three. More than a series of learning places, he wanted to forge a synergy between the three institutions to encourage learning. It was the source of its innovative quality of the project, and precisely what was challenging. So set for myself one golden rule: the building should be neither three nor one, but three-in-one. The institutions needed the junction of this trilogy both from inside for the public perception and from outside for its presence in the city. To see and cross each program was the key to the project and the institutions needed to see and cross each other. I took a calculated risk and started to design three intersecting objects in three dimensions.

The Musée de Bretagne needed a horizontal platform occupying the entire area, whereas the library and science center could be spread over several themed levels. This led me to cross the museum's horizontal platform through both of them as a pure pre-cast concrete parallelepiped, designed with Martin Wallace in granite relief. The library may only have limited reception area on the ground floor, but needed to open out in the upper floors. An upside-down pyramid placed the reading rooms above the museum in the light. In contrast, the science center's expanded exhibition rooms below are enclosed in a conic shape with its spherical planetarium with a dome on top pierces the museum block upwards.

In the 1993 competition, I showed that the lines of the rectangle museum were providing the beginning of a perceivable shape to the huge square in the other side of the street, and later on we were called to built, on the other side of the street, a movie theater, completed in November 2008 for Gaumont, which picks up the horizontality of the "Champs Libres" cultural complex and constitutes one of the sides of the esplanade. It uses the same materials: colored concrete, white aluminum and dark roofing.

Les Champs Libres, 10 Cours des Alliés, Boulevard Magenta, Rennes, France Program: Public facility regrouping three main institutions: the municipal library, the scientific technical and industrial cultural center, and the Brittany Museum, accompanied by a 500-person conference room, general adminstration and staff parking. Surface area: 36,600 square meters. Client: Rennes Métropole. Museography project manager: Elizabeth de Portzamparc. Acoustics: Xu Acoustique. Scenography: Changement à vue. Date: International design competition, 1993; completion,2006

Les Champs Libres and, across the street, a movie theater for Gaumont (2008)

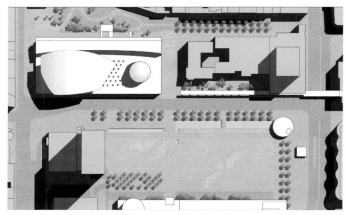
Mass Plan

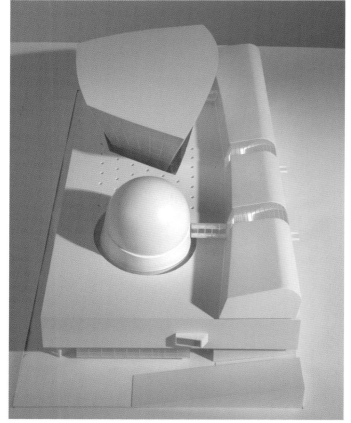
Model

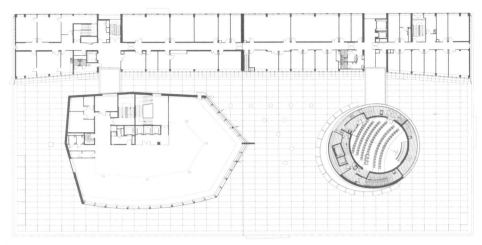

Seventh Floor Plan

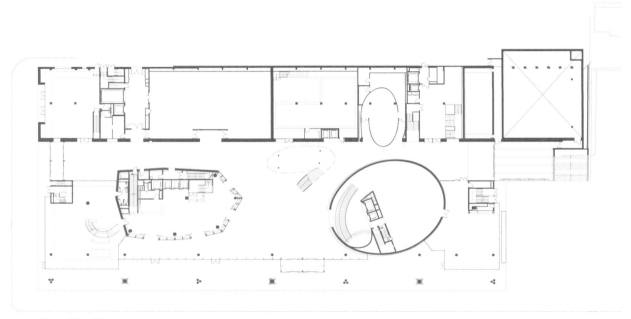

Ground Floor Plan

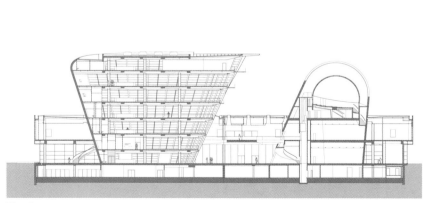

Elevation

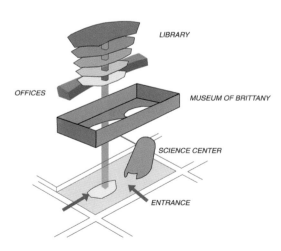

LIBRARY

OFFICES

MUSEUM OF BRITTANY

SCIENCE CENTER

ENTRANCE

Multimedia library façade

opposite page: The multimedia library interior, with view of town beyond

Suspended walkways in the Entrance Hall

Law Courts, Grasse, France, 1993–1999

In Grasse, the site was immediately the biggest challenge, it was totally unsuited to the presentation of a judicial institution.

In the city, we think justice should be visible, balanced, even symmetrical and stable. In this site, everything is on a slope and the plot was a terrace accessed via a head of land on a hairpin bend, the only place in the city where the institution would have a presence. To give the law courts a stable visibility, I conceived this bend as the linchpin with the commercial court at the center of it. It is the visible part of the law courts, like a metonymy, a part representing the whole, around which the public traffic moves, along the bend of the beautiful base wall that consolidates the city.

The commercial court is an ellipsis, the low enclosure of which contains the rooms; the façade of the office floors above is fitted with large white mobile sun breaks that offer both shade and broad views over the valley.

The complex is then laid out along the terrace, divided into three courts (commercial, criminal and civil). They are distributed around a long waiting hall, which forms a gallery open on to the garden and view from the terrace.

Elizabeth de Portzamparc designed the interiors of the audience rooms.

The need for an environmentally friendly, energy-saving design suited to a sunny climate was a decisive architectural factor in my 1993 competition entry, which featured mobile and static sun breaks, interior courtyards, continuous ventilated double roofing allowing for air circulation, sun protection and technical equipment facilities. With its curved red concrete slabs housing the technical facilities, this over-roofing is the fifth façade visible from the whole of the upper town.

Law Courts, 1-23, avenue Pierre Semard, Grasse, France. Program: Public facility grouping together the County Court, the Commercial Court, the Industrial Tribunal and first degree courts of law; surface area: 15,400 square meters. In association with Elizabeth de Portzamparc Agency for the interiors and Martin Wallace for the sun screens. Client: French Ministry of Justice. Interior Design: Elizabeth de Portzamparc (auditoriums). Acoustic: Xu Acoustique, Xu Ya Ying. Date: Competition entry, 1993; completion, 1999

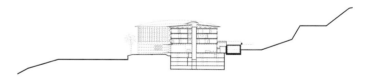

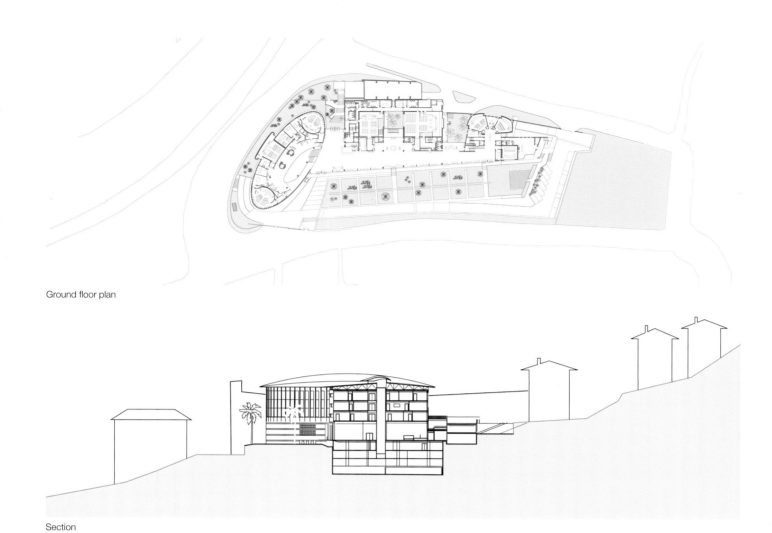

Ground floor plan

Section

"La salle des pas perdus," the Public Lobby with a view on the garden and the valley

The ellipsoidal gallery in the Commercial Court

Palais des Congrès de Paris, France, 1994–1999

In 1994, an other challenging competition was organized to extend the Palais des Congrès de Paris in front of its façade in order to enlarge the exhibition spaces for congress. The site, limited by the existing traffic circle, made the public space left at the entrance very narrow and squeezed between cars. And inside, due to the existing theater hall of 2,000 seats, half of the surface to be added would be occupied by additional evacuation closed staircases. To avoid tightening the parvis at street level, I decided to slope the façade to gain exhibition space in upper levels. To avoid many interior staircases, I create a huge balcony at ten-meters-high, as an emergy issue where the public arrived is no longer considered to be exposed to smoke. Exhibition spaces needing no openings, the slope is a simple plane opened by a tangent cone containing the new hall and marking the entrance.

Palais des Congrès, International Paris Convention Center Extension, 2, place de la Porte de Maillot, Paris, 17th District, France. Program: Extension of the Paris Convention Center, with exhibition spaces, offices, 650-seat conference hall; redeveloped surface area: 13,606 square meters; new surface area: 46,915 square meters. Client: Société Immobilière du Palais des Congrès (SIPAC). Date: Competition entry, 1994; completion, 1999

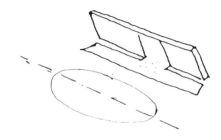

la porte
la parvis

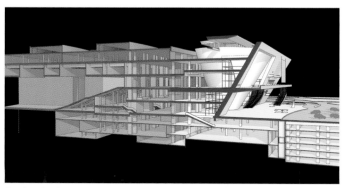

Section drawing showing the new extension

Front façade of the Palais des Congrès building

Philharmonie Luxembourg, Grand Duchy of Luxembourg, 1997–2005

In the middle of a public piazza, how to design a theater that is open in all directions, given that the rear area is always used for backstage scenic functions? This was the challenge we faced in Luxembourg.

At the competition stage, before I visited the site, I looked at photos of this neighborhood of Luxembourg and, seeing the sad, gray office buildings that surrounded the future Philharmonie, I had the idea of creating a ring of tall trees to separate the concert hall from the new city. The public would need to cross through this initiatory filter to enter into the musical field.

After visiting the site, I realized that there wasn't enough room to plant trees, also understanding that the basement was going to be a huge car park. I kept the idea of a façade filter, but rather than plants I designed crossed stems: this weave, neither opaque nor transparent, would form a shell of light at the center of which would stand the concert hall. Then I removed the oblique forms to give these elliptical rows of vertical and parallel stems a mathematical and musical rhythm.

This filter lets light through while creating an exceptional space that neither looks outwards nor gives visitors the feeling of being confined, since it is possible to look between the column stems. The peristyle of light surrounding the building became a circular lobby around the main hall.

To make this possible, and in order to avoid a technical zone behind the stage, the floor of this lobby is slightly inclined, from the entrance to the opposite angle of the almond shape. There it provides enough space below to open the connection between back stage and the ochestra stage.

The large concert hall stands at the middle of this foyer. A concert hall is a musical instrument on a collective scale and, you might even say, a "space instrument". Inside the Philharmonie, the audience "inhabits" the walls of the hall in tiered balcony-towers which surround the stalls like buildings around a public square at night. I wanted the musicians and the audience to be aware of one another, close together, and to feel a sense of grandeur and intimacy, and to free the imagination. I worked, as I always do, with the acoustician Xu Ya Ying to use these balcony-towers for the opportunity they provided us to install these highly absorbent and reflective materials. They each face in different directions to avoid alignment with the walls of the hall, which would have caused floating echoes.

I like the contrast between the radiant, snow-cover feel of the peristyle and the sudden shade you can find yourself in when you enter the concert hall, crossing through the exterior wall of the outer space.It is designed like a prismatic casing or cliff with hollowed out rifts to indicate the entrances. A walkway winds around the building and floats midway, giving access to the hall's upper seats. These large

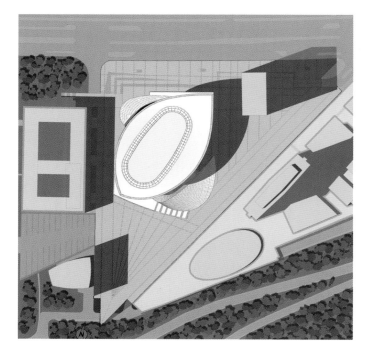

rifts play with the light, since the color spectrum changes during the day and night, using a system I developed with colored niches for the concert hall at La Villette, which I experimented with twenty years ago. These large rifts in Luxembourg are altogether more subtle chromatically since the geometry of the sides breaks up the colors according to the angles at which they are projected onto the facets and over a height of twenty meters.

I still had to find a place for the chamber music hall. In the pentagon-shaped area allocated to built, the main hall occupied a position which left a space beside the almond-shaped façade filter. This was a perfect chance. I put the chamber music room, like a petal curling up from the ground and resting against the peristyle. This small room is an interior

opposite page: Each tube, empty or full, responds to a use; some support the roof, others the glass, others are conductors of air or serve as downspouts for rainwater.

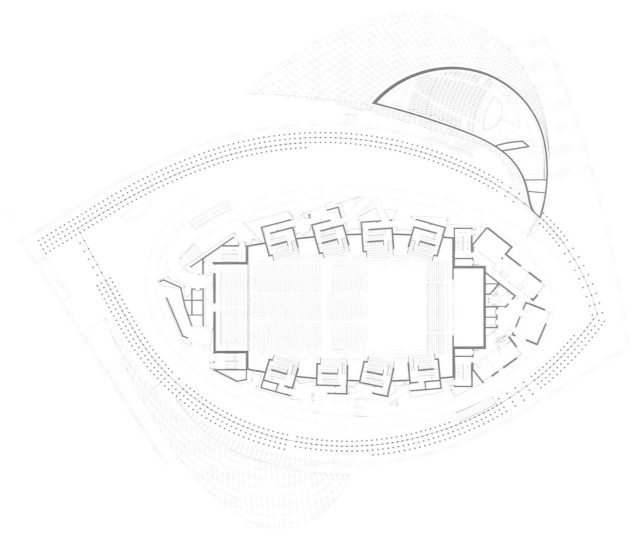

Plan of the Grand Auditorium and the Chamber Music Room

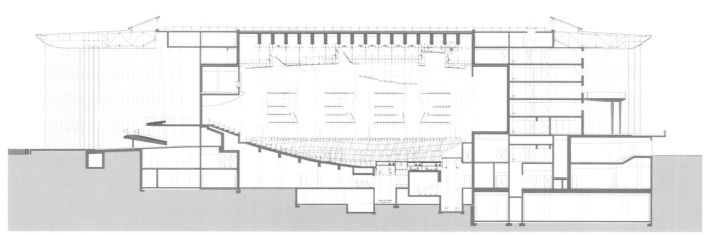

Section drawing of the Grand Auditorium

shell, contained within a fragment of twisting surface, a form based on our experience of working on the Möbius strip begun in 1993 for the Nara competition in Japan.

This full twisted petal interacts on the outside as a contrast with the filter by masking it diagonally, and on the other side, we find the same volume, but smaller in dimension, which allows people to enter from the car park basement.

This contrasting interaction between opaque and transparent, filter and petals, grounds the unity of the design for me. That's the moment at which it felt perfectly complete and I wouldn't have been happy with a single almond-shaped object.

The Philharmonie Luxembourg, 1, Place de l'Europe, Plateau de Kirchberg, Luxembourg, Grand Duchy of Luxembourg. Program: Cultural facilities accommodating a Grand Auditorium (1,500 seats), a Chamber Music Hall (300 seats), and an electro-acoustic hall (120 seats) ; surface area: 20,000 square meters. Client: Ministry of Public Works, Administration of Public Works, Grand Duchy of Luxembourg. Architect of Record: Christian Bauer & associés. Acoustic: Xu Acoustique, Xu Ya Ying; AVEL Acoustique, Jean-Paul Lamoureux. Scenography: Changement à vue. Lighting: L'observatoire 1. Artist: Roberto Cabot. Date: International competition entry, 1997; completion, 2005. Awards: Luxembourg Architecture Prize 2007 Golden Awards by Foundation Architecture and Engineering; 2008 International Architecture Award for the best new global design given by The Chicago Athenaeum

Forest of Columns

A series of 823 slim steel columns form a forest around the hall and lobby. An oscillating oil-immersed pendulum is built into each column to prevent the tubes from vibrating.

Apart from their appearance, the columns, which measure between 17 and 20 meters high and around 32 centimeters in diameter and which are fitted with integrated shock absorbers to prevent vibration, perform different functions. The inner columns only carry their own weight (around 700 kilograms: the steel is 5mm thick) and function as shafts for ventilation and other fluids. The next row exclusively carry the weight of the glass façades and is composed of composite shafts with a square core in solid steel to support the load. Each weighs between 3.5 and 4 tons. The outer columns support the roof and therefore have a static function, requiring a steel thickness of between 5.6 and 14.2 mm. The integrated shock absorbers are oscillating pendulae inside an oil bath. Lastly, most of the final row of outer columns are not load-bearing, although they can provide load transfer from the roof. In this complex structure with an apparently simple form, the stress remains hidden. —Genael Querrien, "La Philharmonie de Luxembourg," Archiscopie*, no. 52, Oct. 2008.*

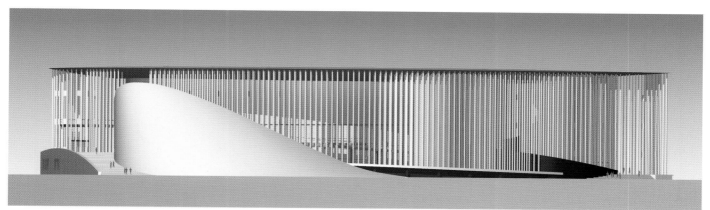

East elevation

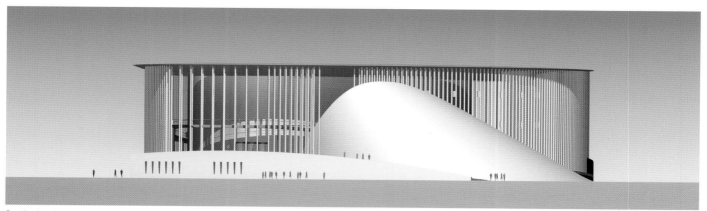

South elevation

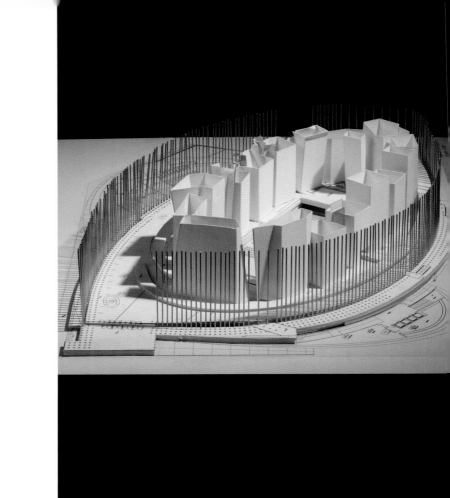

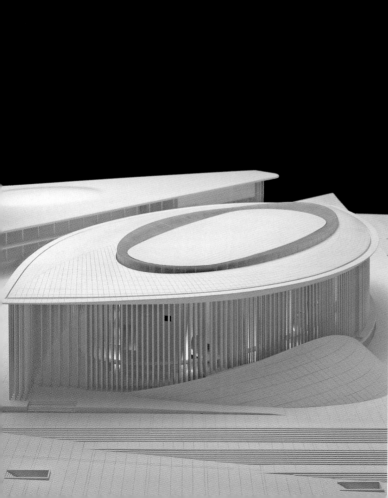

In the foyer of the Main Concert Hall of the Philharmonie, evolving slowly, changing colored lights emphasize the various geometric shapes of the structure and interior spaces.

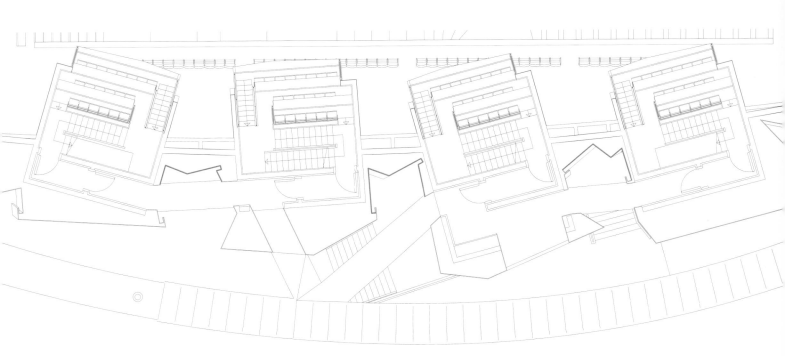

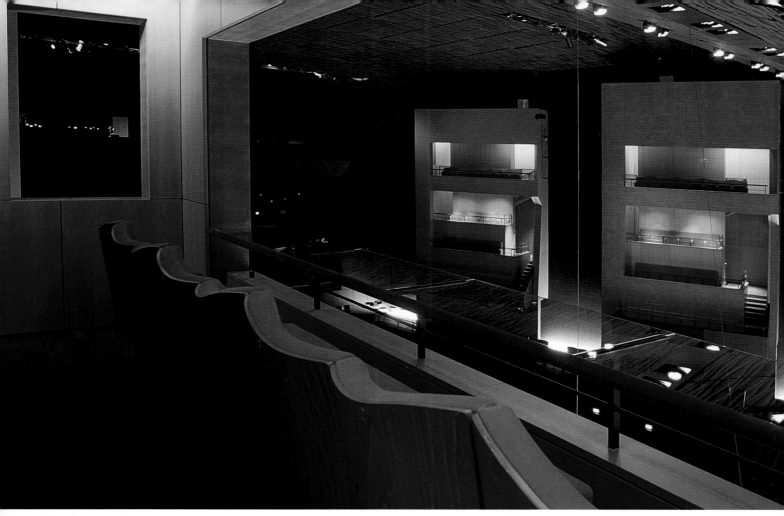

The Main Concert Hall. A "shoebox" was requested by the client; here this was interpreted as a public square with towers of lodges all around.

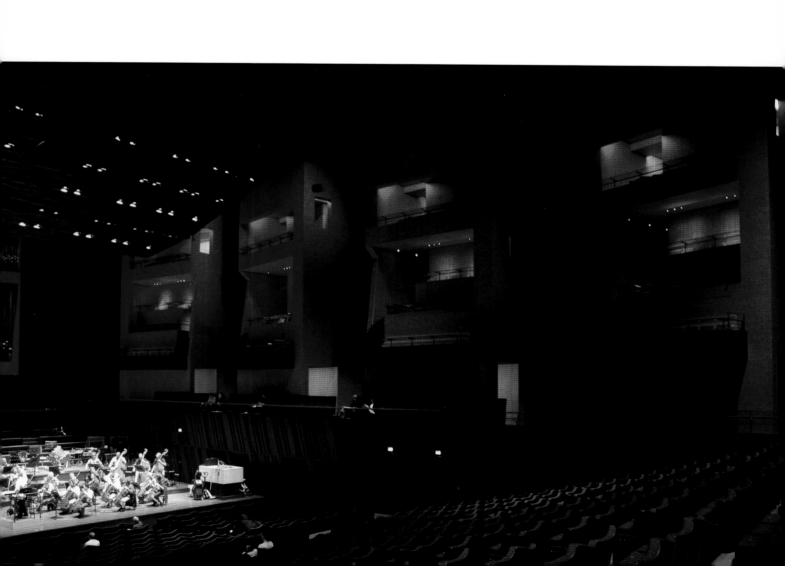

above: Chamber Music Hall stage. opposite: access hall of the Chamber Music Hall

Architecture as Music

There are some parallels between architecture and music which have been over used, rhythm, harmony and proportion, "architecture as petrified music converted in stone" (Goethe).

I feel that the perception of space in a timeline, through motion, brings the true correspondence with music. I like architecture as discovery and movement. On the contrary, Sebastiano Serlio said: "The most beautiful building is one whose layout you understand immediately just by looking at the outside." when he described the château d'Ancy-le-Franc summed up a classical ideal in the fixity of a suspended time. It's precisely the opposite what interests me about the Cité de la musique in Paris, the Philharmonie in Luxembourg, and the Cidade das Artes in Rio de Janeiro. You need to achieve a balance between the things people recognize and surprises, and to provide a succession of distinctive experiences which, in the way we perceive them, appear one after the other, and communicate a real excitement about life inside the building. The notions of approach, length, space and contrasting emotional experiences are fundamental in my eyes, and naturally make me think of music. Music is a concentration of a sort of impressive primitive energy. It's no accident that the word "inspiration" refers to the act of drawing breath and, therefore, singing.

For a long time, I thought that music had an emotional power that goes beyond architecture or the other arts. Now I know that places and spaces have an emotional impact on human beings that's just as great as music: our lives are intimately tied up with the many places that haunt our memories; they build our present and help us think about the future—our childhood home, school, garden, the apartment where we live, or lived, our workplaces, etcetera. All biographies are architectures, if we extend the idea of architecture to include, more generally, space and landscape. Considered from this angle, it's obvious that the emotional power of place has a power that's akin to music. But music can be like a burn, a one-off event that you feel deeply, whereas we have a more everyday, calmer relationship with space.

Philharmonie de Paris, France, competition drawing (2007)

1. Opera House, Suzhou, China, 2013
2. Congress Hall, Palais des Congrès Paris, France, 1994
3. Philharmonic Hall, Philharmonie de Paris, France, 2007
4. Concert Hall, Philharmonie Luxembourg, 1997
5. Multi-purpose Hall, Casarts, Morocco, 2009
6. Concert Hall, Cité de la Musique, Paris, France, 1984
7. Concert Hall, Music Conservatory, Shanghai, China, 2013

Casarts, Casablanca, Morocco, 2009–2018

The vast Place Mohammed V in Casablanca is a classic rectangular 1920s composition inherited from Maréchal Hubert Lyautey and urban planner Henri Prost, and is lined at the north side by beautiful buildings representing the power, the Charles Boyer's wilaya, the Courts of Justice and at the southern side by two long administrative buildings facing each other. On the square's last free side, the city decided to install a major cultural building, CasArts, set to be the biggest theatre in Africa.

This beautiful place is popular among Casawis who gather every day around its central fountain.

The classical, strictly symmetric and highly centered composition would lend itself to a neoclassical response. Making it contemporary was a real brainteaser to me and probably to all the five other architects entering this international competition in 2009: Franck Gerhy, Zaha Hadid, Rem Koolhaas, Aziz Lazrak and Mecanoo. The cultural program was a way to breathe a renewed public life into this vast institutional square.

I begun to imagine an autonomous, univocal architectural object, but if symmetrical it was too strongly centered and if not it was strangely out of the game.

My solution arose when I conceived several "pavilions" like an inner city in the city.

The central pavilion is a giant door that may be set out as an outside stage for an audience of 6,000 in the place. The façade is already framing a stage in itself. Then the ensemble does not break up the symmetry, it interacts strongly with by its built frame more than by the lines, without breaking it up. This vision of the theater invites visitors to penetrate into the shade of an inner world by opening several rifts and entrances into a large and high public gallery that crosses the ensemble as an urban passageway, formed from curved red staff pillars. A place where you can sit and enjoy a coffee, the air refreshed by natural ventilation. It's also the stage of an open-air theater: the doors part, the stage appears and the square welcomes the audience. CasArts is a transformable urban scenographic device.

The main hall is a1,800-seat theater conceived to be used for acoustic concerts, classical theater and large-scale productions.

In this hall, a "fan" of balconies is supported by the same curved supports along which visitors walk in the large entrance gallery. It revisits the opera format, with its horseshoe shape, while reflecting the qualities of a frontal view and catering for a larger number of audience members.

Casarts, Place Mohammed V, Casablanca, Morocco. Program: Africa's largest theater and arts space; multi-purpose hall with 1,800 seats, flexible theater with 600 seats, amplified-music hall, public rehearsal rooms opened to the public, special events rooms and "cultural intensity" place, shops, restaurant, café, cyberspace, reading area, library, showroom and art gallery; surface area: 20,245 square meters. Architect of record: Rachid Andaloussi. Client: Casablanca Aménagement S.A.; Egis Bâtiments International. Scenography: Theatre Projects Consultants. Acoustic: Xu Acoustique, Xu Ya Ying; Acoustique & Architecture. Landscape design: Régis Guignard, Méristème. Date: International Competition laureat, 2009; opening planned for 2018

Casarts, on the square of Mohammed V

On the square, the front façade of Casarts can become an outdoor theater stage.

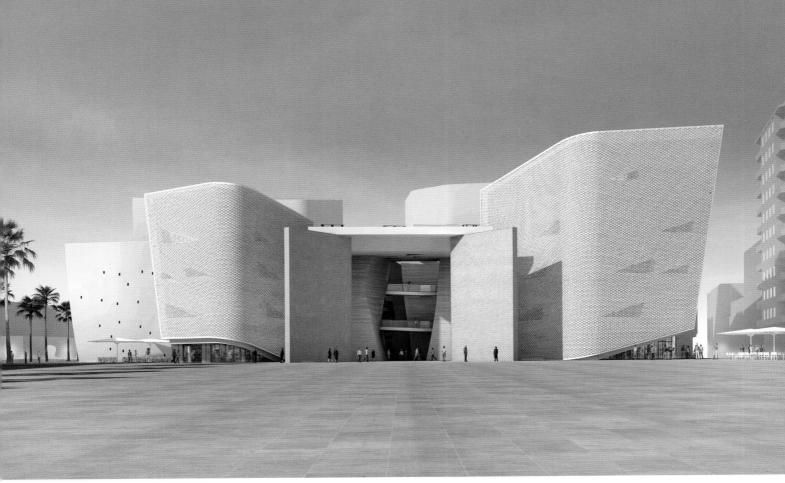

The main façade, as seen from the square of Mohammad V

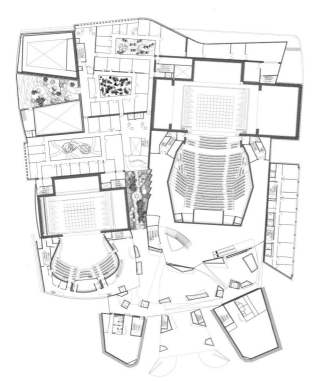

Plan showing the two theater halls, level 2.

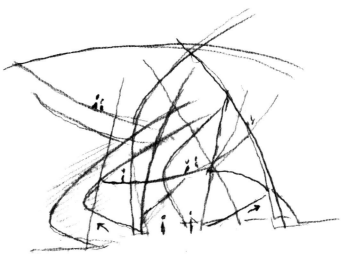

A large urban passage makes its way through the theater, from one side to the other.

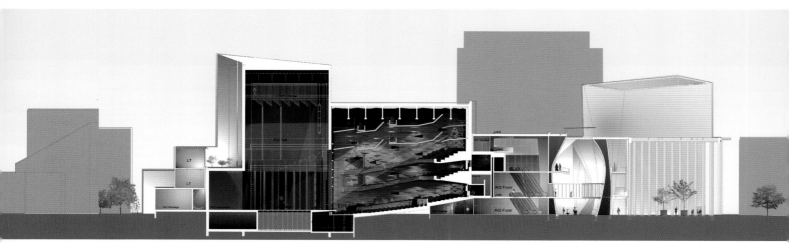

The Main Hall, a horseshoe shaped traditional opera with multiple balconies

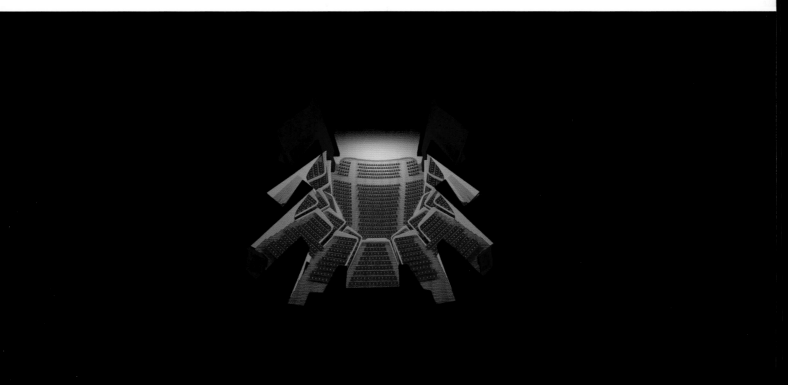

U Arena Stadium, Nanterre, France, 2010–2017

Situated close to the Arche de La Défense, U Arena is both a performance hall and an indoor rugby stadium incorporated into the dense, rectangular urban fabric which forms now a new neighborhood linked to La Défense in the territory of Nanterre. Jacky Lorenzetti, President of Racing Métro, the rugby club of the Hauts-de-Seine, organized first a competition of architect for the stadium of his club, but the program slightly evolved into a performance hall with a capacity for 10,000 to 37,000 people in which "we're going to play rugby," said its developer. It has a horseshoe layout, with one side given over to the offices of the Conseil Général des Hauts-de-Seine.

To express its identity as a performance space, I added a main entrance on the core axis of La Défense, but as in all major stadia, the access points are on the three sides of the U shape.

Under the seating, the space is totally occupied by reception areas, dressing rooms and refreshment areas, to give them light and to create address along the street. I surrounded the lower part of the seating with a "necklace" of glass scales forming a regular series of shells in white and gray aluminum and lightly serigraphed glass. This necklace illuminates the lobbies and dressing rooms.

U Arena Stadium, Grand Axe de La Défense, Nanterre, France. Program: Rugby stadium (32,000 seats; variable capacity, 10,000 to 40,000 seats); entertainment hall and offices; surface area: 117,000 square meters. Client: Racing Arena. Acoustic: Avel Acoustique. Date: Competition entry, 2010; completion, October 2017

Mass Plan

Section showing configuration for a rugby competition

Section showing configuration for concerts/shows

opposite: The stadium under construction

Suzhou Cultural Center, China, 2013–2019

The Suzhou Cultural Center is under construction as one of a series of projects launched by the city within the Wujiang Lakefront Masterplan. The site is spectacular. By the most beautiful lake of China, between the water, the sky and a new emerging city, the project to build for the competition consisted of an opera house on one side and two museums on the other. Additional element came later.

Here is the meeting point where the large urban axis of the new city meets the lakeshore. I wanted to focus the perspective of this axis through a large opening. An urban arche is formed toward the lake by a long metallic band that joins the opera to the museum.

Linking up the two facilities, this band, part-roof and part-façade, brings together musical and museum spaces on either side of the large pedestrian axis. The band's movements in curves and counter-curves shelter the crossing. Its lines rise and frame the sky. Visible from everywhere it provides a promenade at 37 meters high as a belvedere from the top of which people can admire lake and city. The building interacts with the landscape by linking the water and the sky in an interplay of iridescent reflections created by the band and façades. This prow announces the new neighborhood at this exceptional site covering more than 100,000 square meters in a movement from north to south which generates an infinite figure.

This approach of the endless curve is similar to the one taken on the Nara (International Conventional Hall, Japan), Luanda (Uganda Cultural Center) and Nankin (Jiangsu Theater, China) projects.

The complex is composed on one side of a 1,600-seat opera house, a modular 600-seat performance space, and on the other of a museum (24,000 square meters), an exhibition center (18,000 square meters), a convention center (14,000 square meters), cafés, restaurants, movie theaters, and 14,000 square meters of shopping malls, for a total surface area of 202,000 square meters divided between the north and south of the urban axis.

Suzhou Cultural Center, Taihu Lake, Suzhou, China. Program: Cultural facilities including an Opera House (1,600 seats), a modular room (600 seats), a museum, an exhibition center, a conference center, cinemas, cafés, restaurants, shopping malls; surface areas: 202,000 square meters (museum: 24,000 square meters; exhibition center: 18,000 square meters; conference center: 14,000 square meters; shopping malls: 14,000 square meters. Client: Suzhou City. Acoustic: Xu Acoustique, Xu Ya Ying. Scenography: Theatre Projects Consultants, Ltd. Date: Competition laureat, 2013 (Under Study); completion planned for 2019

The cultural center is at the end of the great pedestrian axis of the new town, on the lake. At one side of the building is the Opera School of Music; on the other side is the museum and congress hall.

All projects involving cultural institutions combine unity and plurality, they are often composite objects. This was present in the precedent projects but also in studies that didn't get to be constructed.

Academy Museum of Motion Pictures, Hollywood, Los Angeles, USA, 2007

Over two years, we worked on two successive different programs for the conception of the building (the institution which awards the Oscars), for which we had been chosen in 2007. It contained a museum and a movie theater hall.

The entrance was a mysterious pavilion, a high, dark room accessible from the piazza and situated in front of the ticket office, which operated as an immersion in projected light. This was an idea thought up by Steven Spielberg which said "the motion picture art began when man moved the shadow of his hand over a rock, it's all about light and shade."

The two parts of the project created a piazza, an entry square close to the existing Pickford Center, where ceremonies like major premières are held. The building addressed the city through an architectural screen, showing movies sequences. After the financial crisis of 2008, the fund raising stopped and the project was abandoned.

Academy Museum of Motion Pictures, Corner of Sunset Boulevard and Vine Street, Hollywood, Los Angeles, U.S.A. Date: Prize-winning entry of international competition, 2007; project abandoned, 2012

Seat of the Algerian Parliament, Algiers, Algeria, 2014

Fifty years after gaining its independence, Algeria began the planning to build a new seat for its parliament, which is currently spread over several sites in the city. It is a major national building project. Situated in the Bay of Algiers, alongside the new museum and the main mosque, the parliament will be a landmark in the city's urban transformation.

In partnership with Salah-Eddine Saidoune and Tom Sheeman, we won the competition for this project.

Bordering the classic center, the site is characteristic of Algiers, with its slope down to the sea, and the project is fully inspired by this splendid city. The program consists of two chambers, the National Council and the People's Assembly, along with residences, the plenary room, and shared facilities. We have designed a parliamentary district inspired by a Mediterranean conception of the city, in which we sought to create shade, passageways, patios and courtyards. After designing the general plan as a team, I focused on the square's architecture and its two chambers and offices, while Salah-Eddine and Tom designed the documentation, administration, social

and hotel buildings. The two chambers are situated on a public square with a diagonal layout, continuing into the courtyards of the parliament and their buildings.

The National Council building and the People's Assembly building convey the idea of stability through the balance and symmetry of the shear wall structures. Each contains a large assembly room. The National Council is an upside-down cone placed on the ground; the People's Assembly chamber is a large circular suspension supported at four load-beating points by shear walls.

The project as a whole has been approved unanimously by both chambers, following the jury statement of the competition.

Seat of The Algerian Parliament, Boulevard des Fusillés, Algiers, Algeria. Program: Institutional and administrative facility; 208,370 square meters, total floor surface; 172,000 square meters, usable surface. In association with architecture agency ATSP, Tom Sheehan and Salah Saidoune. Client: Algerian Government. Acoustic: Xu Acoustique, Xu Ya Ying. Construction: CSCEC (China State Construction Engineering Corporation Limited). Date: Competition entry, 2014

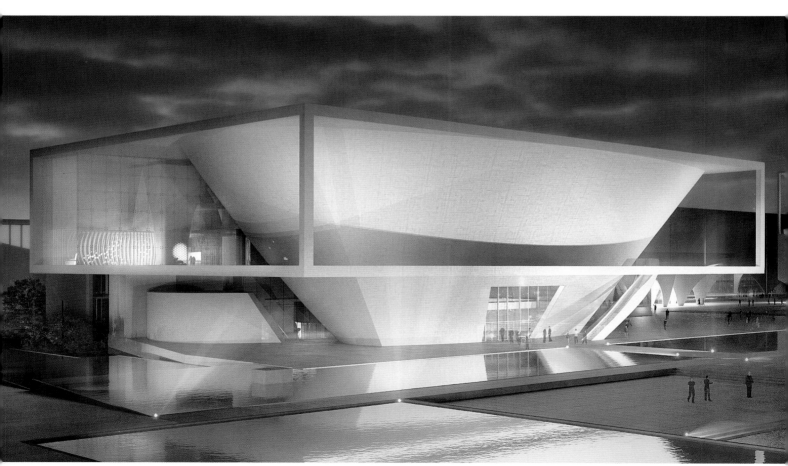

The Council of the Nation and the People's National Assembly on the Institutional Place

The landscape slopes gently toward the sea.

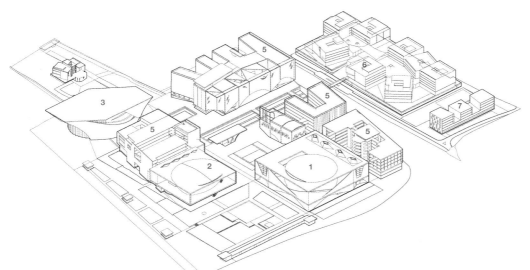

1. The People's National Assembly
2. The Council of the Nation
3. The Plenary Room
4. The President's Pavilion
5. Offices
6. Hotel
7. Housing

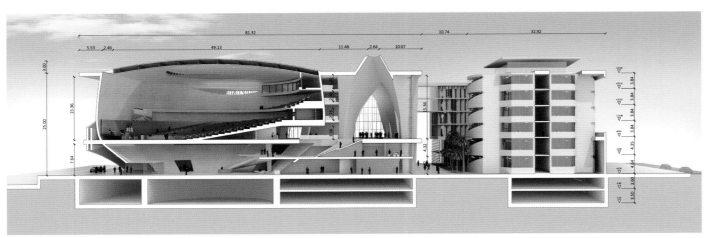

bottom: Council of the Nation chamber

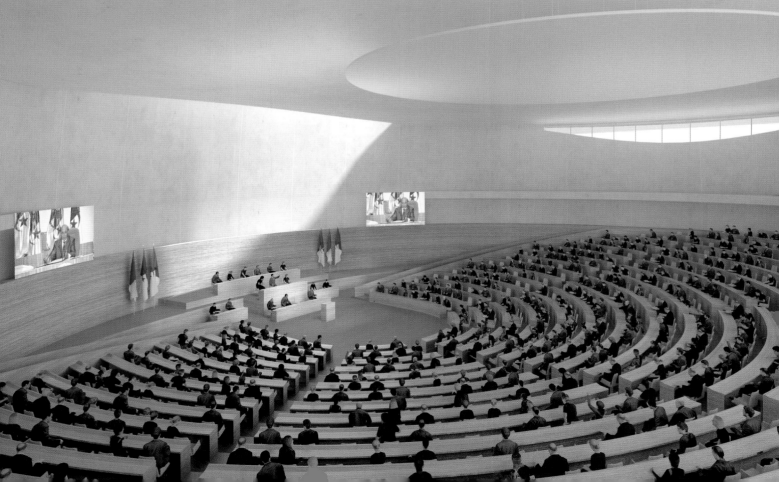

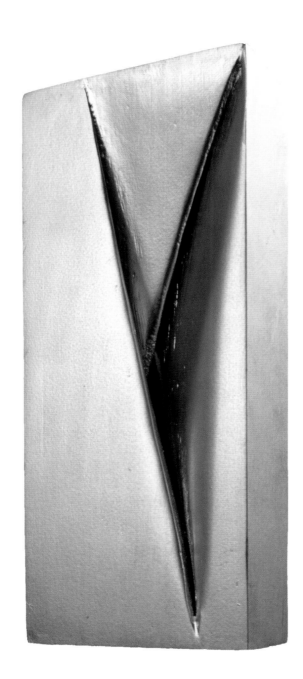

Chapter 4
Carved Blocks: The 2000s

From the 2000s on, several programs led me to design large public atriums. As part
of the competition for the library in Montreal (the construction of a large library for the
Catholic University of Montreal), we were asked to create a meeting point between
cultures, open night and day, which we understood as a large public agora,
a requirement for this winter climate where "outdoor piazzas" are an impossibility.
Elizabeth worked on the outdoor and indoor public space and I concentrated on
organizing the rooms in the large enclosed volume based on a geometric form
within the space where four "fish" appear to swim in an aquarium.

We interpreted the large library as a reception area and a meeting point set around these cultural resources, inviting visitors to discover knowledge, and as a place for research and reading—a sort of public forum. We expanded and extended the reception space into a vast, light-filled nave that broadly opens up panoramic views over the city. It's an air-conditioned glass shell that's high enough to allow the side light to penetrate the building.

The project was judged to be ten percent too expensive, but its concept of a tridimensional open block interested me. Its impact is felt in Rio and on other projects such as the New York City Opera, the Musée Hergé, and in the building for the Rhône Alpes region's headquarters.

In these projects, a block is open, the external volumes were a pure straight parallelepiped block hollowed out from irregular interiors. In the Rio's building, the notion of envelope is more virtual and play with long flat cylinder veil of concrete. I called these projects perforated bricks because, with this technique, I was returning to the sculptures I used to do as a teenager in Rennes, when I hollowed out non-fired bricks with six tubular voids, by carving out their interiors and observing the opposition between the geometry, the shell of the parallelepiped block and the curved, irregular crannies of the interior cavities that I expanded using a knife. This opposition between straight and curvaceous, between geometry and irregular randomness has always interested me and you can see it in the watercolors I painted at that time.

Contrasting the Platonic purity of geometry and its opposite, the more or less random irregularity of surfaces and volumes, has interested me a lot since the 1960s. This three-dimensional open block project synthetized a vision of the interaction between solids and voids, space and object, which I went on to develop. It sublimated form of the open block.

Nature everywhere provides us with an infinitely irregular spectacle. Sigfried Giedion saw the mastery of the surface plane as the birth of architecture, the first "conquest". When compared with geological, animal and vegetal forms, geometry is anti-nature, a sign of the presence of man as an exception on Earth. The fate would be law. Since it first appeared, geometry has been a sign of mastery. First as game of decoration, geometric forms appear like exceptions in the landscape, an ambition, a determinism. To assert an architectural ambition is to assert man against nature. A method for surveying, cutting and assembling, initially geometry exceeded this technical utility to become a gateway to rational thinking, and the concept, when Euclid wrote its first laws. With architecture, geometry became a symbolic form. From Plato to Descartes, it represents the program of man mastering nature.

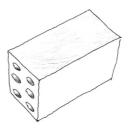

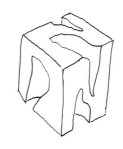

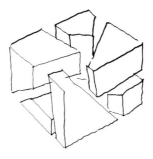

Drawings of the "hollow brick"

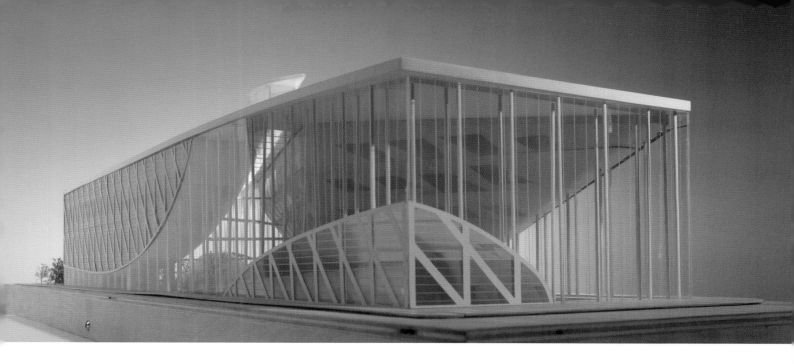

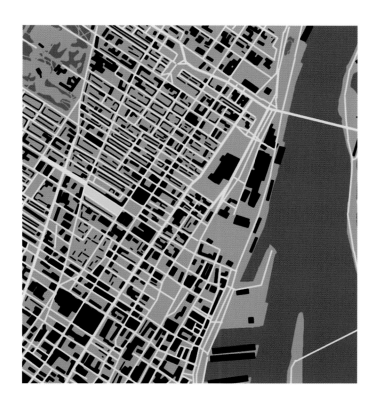

Drawings for the Great Library of Quebec (competition), Boulevard de Maisonneuve Est, Montreal, Canada, 2000

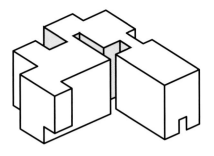

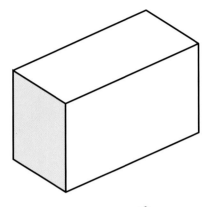

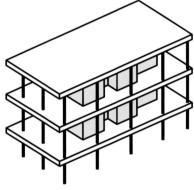

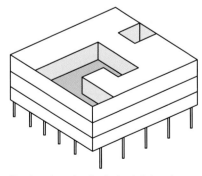

Drawings based on Le Corbusier's *Les 4 Compositions*; extract from *La Ville Radieuse*

Geometry

When Le Corbusier wrote about the different compositional modes for his houses, he distinguished between the four layout principles he had used. Writing about the model of the Villa Savoye, he explained: "Of the highly generous proportions, the exterior is conceived from an architectural ambition, while the interior satisfies functional needs (insulation, proximity, circulation)." To assert an "exterior conceived from an architectural ambition" was for Le Corbusier emphasizing the contrast between the simple Platonic geometry of the exterior shell and the free unregular nature outside. This meant celebrating through architecture the statement of man against nature. But it provided also a contrast between geometry of the exterior and of the interior. The terrace space appears to have been unregularly hollowed out from the interior of the parallelepipedic shell.

What Le Corbusier calls an "exterior conceived from an architectural ambition" is a demonstration of simple, Platonic geometry. To assert an architectural ambition is to assert man against nature.

The week of intense emotion felt by Pierre Jeanneret, the future Le Corbusier, on the Parthenon hill in 1911, was therefore a founding moment. "This is a machine for moving, we enter into the implacability of the mechanical," he states. Confronted with the mastery of geometry that dominates, reveals and sublimates the natural site, Le Corbusier rid himself of Art Nouveau, a tendency to imitate nature in order to counter the tightening grip of industry over form and to resist the geometrization of the world through the metaphor of a union with nature. The young man took up the torch of the antique world and, ten years later formulated the Modern project, applying the same enlightened, visionary eye to the airplane and cruise liner, wheat silo and Citroën car. It was a meeting between the assertion of plainness and the rationalism of construction.

The initial energy of modern architecture in the twentieth century emerged from this rejection of the softening of forms found in Art Nouveau.

I was drawn to the idea of a non-Platonic Euclidian geometry early as a student. I went to see works by Hans Sharoun and I abandoned the set square for a while. Georges Candilis brought me back into line when he asked me to explain my non-square angles! Later, on looking at the city and the conditions in which we perceive urban space, I sought to achieve the most clear and legible perception of space possible and, to do this, respect the markers of geometry and its perspectives. From then on, I steadily evolved between geometry and anti-geometry. An important aspect of current international modernity in architecture is moving in that direction. For more than twenty years we have seen a silent evolution in everyday façades. They used to be formed in repetitive grids, but everywhere regularity

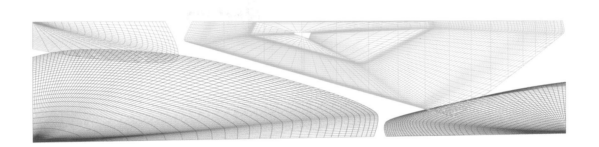

Grande Bibliothèque du Québec, Montreal, Canada, 2000

have given way to façades in which windows and lines are off-set according to an approach based on randomness and irregularity. The repetitive serial esthetic no longer gives a "good image" to a housing project. Equality within a multitude of masses has been replaced by the pluralism of individuals where "everyone is unique." And to be iconic and unique is sometimes the only program given by a client to the architect. The quest for visibility often leads architects to depart from right angles and repetition. Formless and complex geometry is competing with Platonic isometry.

Lastly, we have entered a period where our drawing tools and calculations offer us forms with geometries that are far more complex, facet by facet, pixel by pixel. We visualize, generate and calculate surfaces that no longer take Platonic geometric ideals, as their reference point. Digital technology has enabled us to use non-symmetrical geometries to design and build, and allowed businesses to produce small series, specific cases, and to free them from the repetition that was previously the rule in industry. It provided engineers with the means to calculate structures with highly irregular asymmetric forms that would have required years to calculate just 15 years ago, and which, for the last 15 years, have enabled us to build forms that were not possible before.

Since then, our formal culture has often been an interaction between geometry and anti-geometry, regularity and randomness. It has produced sculptural masterpieces and sometimes an excess of ostentatious forms that are "meaningless", extravagant and sometimes hostile to their environment. The rejection of geometry would appear to expose us to the abuse of individual arbitrariness, whereas all architecture in a public space is duty bound (nothing less!) to represent a sort of legitimacy that drives civilization, a legitimacy that no text or theory has defined today. However, for better or worse, and perhaps unknown to those who produce these irregular forms, what it seeks to do is not meaningless. In these random façades, the society of the greatest number promotes the individual, and the cybernetic and digital program allows us to talk to the individual and not the masses. But above all, the heroic assertion of the domination of Promethean man over nature has ceased to be the "ultimate" ideal that it was. Geometry is not anymore the unique metaphor to represent human versus nature as it was from the ancient Greeks to Descartes, Mies Van der Rohe and Le Corbusier. The planet is no longer there to be conquered. Virgin nature untouched by man no longer exists; he transforms it at every turn.

And a new, sometimes naive architectural metaphor is being sought in this relationship to natural irregularity. It occasionally tends toward a symbiosis that echoes the reversal experienced since the 1970s.

New York City Opera, USA, 2005

In 2005, the New York City Opera decided to move its premises to a plot of land of the site of the Red Cross just next to the Lincoln Center. The site had been bought by Albert Kalimian, our client for the 2002 Prism tower project. We worked two years on this join effort between the promoter and Lincoln center to accommodate the new opera house, its services and housing units.

The size of the block presented the project's main challenge: it was just about big enough for the opera house and the housing above it. However, the "non-profit building" quality obtained upper "air rights"

I approached this dual program as a meeting between the residential towers and the presence of the opera house in a series of geometric collisions within the carved block concept whose façade is defined by a filter of slim columns.

The arrows of the residential towers shooting upwards from the filter magnify the presence of this performance space at the heart of New York while the curved auditorium floats in a square volume defined by the street alignment. Between the façade's plane and the bulb of the opera house, the lobbies hover amid the slopes and footbridges that distribute the building's various functions. The Project stopped with the 2008 crisis.

Project for the New York City Opera, 150 Amsterdam Avenue, New York, NY, U.S.A., commissioned in 2005; project abandoned

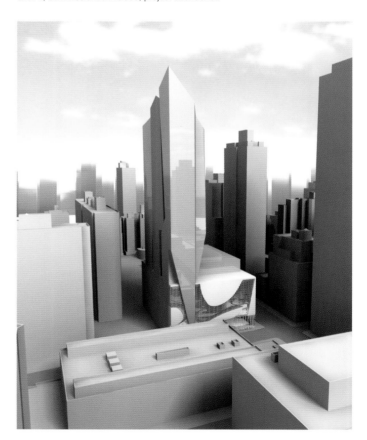

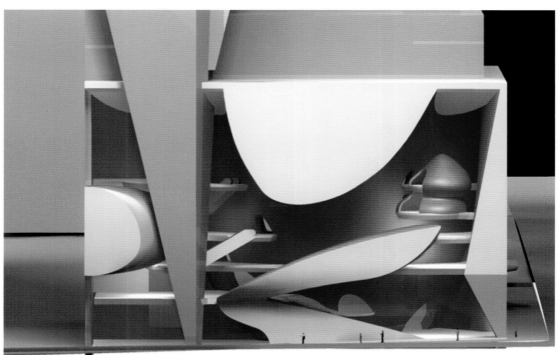

Cidade das Artes, Rio de Janeiro, Brazil, 2002–2013

History of a project

I like Rio. In old premonitory dreams, I was in Rio with its mist and oceanfront. I like the unique alliance between geology and architecture. I've been going there often, for many years. It's Elizabeth de Portzamparc's city.

In 2002, the municipality of Rio visited the City of music in Paris and Cesar Maia, the mayor of Rio de Janeiro commissioned me to design a similar complex of facilities for Rio including concert hall movable in a theater.

Bertrand Beau and I were flown over the city in a helicopter, starting with the laguna, around Corcovado, then over the northern zone to Barra da Tijuca, the vast urban plane constructed, within the space of thirty years, along the fifteen-kilometer-Long Beach. In the center, at the junction of two roads choked with traffic, was the site proposed by the mayor, an empty triangle 400-meters-long called "Cebolão", the big onion.

My first reaction was "no," the site was isolated as an island in a sea of cars. However, Cesar Maia explained to me how the neighborhood was lacking of anything other than shopping malls along highways, offices and housing units, that it was without public buildings, streets or squares. He wanted to bring there a public symbol which would be cultural, not a bureaucratic ensemble. The demand had a civic consistency.

I remembered this vast, empty plain, and its lakes, in the early 1980s, the beach and the mountain dance in the horizon. Yet the two high speed avenues were there and I realized that they contained Lúcio Costa's vision planned when he designed them in the '60s: one day Greater Rio would run all the way around the Corcovado, and that's effectively what's happened since. This crossing was crucial: Central and free for the city, the place was symbolic by itself, visible in the center of the traffic jam at the geometric heart of Barra. But the two highways stretched along kilometers of condos, housing blocks, offices and shopping malls, without any public places made of this vast new Rio a series of forbidden cities, closed enclaves without streets. Then I felt that the idea to invite public life here was spot on.

A complete redevelopment was about to start in this suburb that has since played host to the Olympic Games.

The mayor of Rio also explained that the city needed a concert hall for the OSB, the Brazilian Symphony Orchestra. A major orchestra has to have a large concert hall with excellent acoustics, because that's the only way they'll get a quality sound experience. The concert hall is the orchestra's instrument. He wanted a concert hall that could be converted into an opera house, with a fly loft and orchestra pit. The existing opera house, the Teatro Municipal in the city center is not well suitable for opera productions because the wings and backstage are too tight.

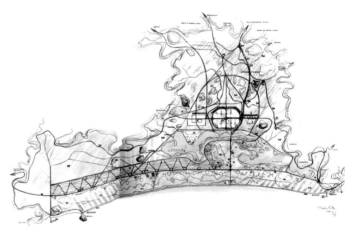

Lucio Costa Master Plan, Barra de Tijuca, 1970

The site for the Cidade das Artes, 2002

opposite page: West corner of the Cidade das Artes, 2009

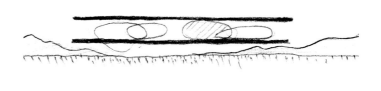

Every big city needs its major landmarks, its points of reference, to help people understand "a mental image of their space" and organize their lives around them.

The traditional part of Rio is exceptionally blessed by nature, with its central districts and "glamorous" heart, whereas in Barra, the landscape spreads out and the mountains are far off. To create something striking here, an urban landmark, sends out a strong signal about the development of the new West Rio.

But on the ground, on a patch of grass, surrounded by cars, in the middle of this vast space, all we could see were the tops of a few towers, shopping malls, and traffic jams stretching monotonously into the distance.

Quite by chance, there was a sort of amphitheater, a mound of earth that had been raised there, ten meters above the ground. When we climbed up the mound, everything suddenly become clear; you could suddenly see things in the distance; the plain, the sea, and the dancing lines of the mountains all appeared: the city became beautiful. That's when it became obvious to me that we needed to be up there, to occupy the big site, but also to feel still being in Rio. You needed to discover the entire city, the mountains and the sea from the building. And the building also needed to be seen from a distance to provide a strong landmark, and to stop the neighboring shopping mall from dominating it. On the ground, the Cidade would have disappeared into everything else.

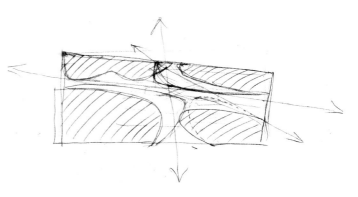

I came up with the idea of a very large belvedere— a public space with a garden. It gave the concert hall program another dimension.

After the visit, we talked things over with Bertrand Beau. The construction costs in France, and the cost of our team in Paris were three times higher than those in Brazil at the time. So we couldn't take responsibility for the whole project. We'd do an advanced preliminary design in Paris, and then we'd need to set up an architecture firm in Rio fairly quickly, along with a team of engineers on the ground. Several of us would travel from Paris on a regular basis.

Nanda Eskes, who had worked for our firm in Paris, joined Ana Paula Pontes and Clovis Cunha. They formed the core of our practice in Rio.

Mass Plan

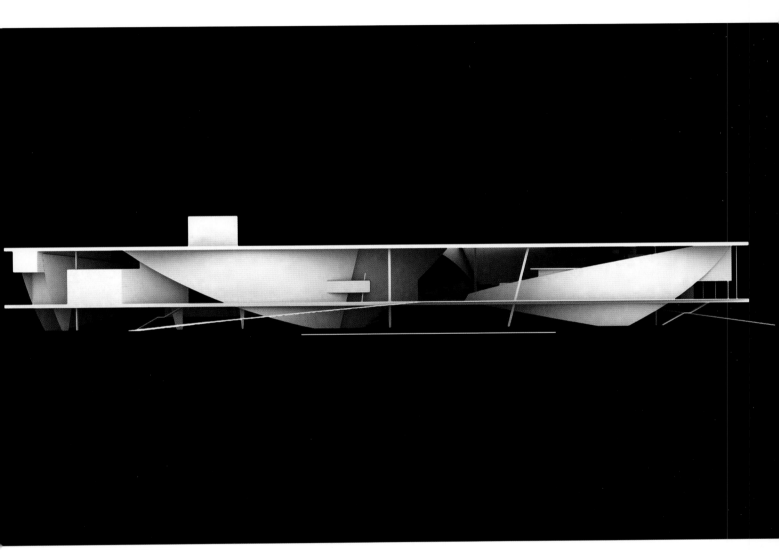

Conception model, January, 2003

We accepted the challenge.

The next day, early in the morning, I looked out of the window of my hotel in Leblon and saw an extraordinary sunrise. To the north were black clouds. Night still reigned over the Corcovado. Below, to the right, the beach was a path of light leading to the sun and the mist above the waves filtered the early morning colors. Rio was giving me this wonderful dawn serenade and you'd have had to have a heart of stone not to feel something!

The Brazilian Symphony Orchestra provided us with the program, covering all the facilities for rehearsal and back-stage of an international standard and that was overseen by an expert and the director of the BSO, Yeruam Scharovsky, who had some very clear ideas. Movies theater, restaurants and library were then added to the initial demand.

The Cidade would be composed of a 1800-seat philharmonic hall that could be transformed into an end-stage opera house seating 1,300. this is this very particular program which drove me to work with the principle of the balcony towers, with four of them mobile on air cushing, in a similar layout to the concert hall in Luxembourg. The 500-seat chamber music hall with a swiveled stage offering two possible layouts is a curved and asymmetrical room.

We had to design also ten rehearsal rooms for choirs, string instruments and percussion, and dressing rooms, dance practice rooms and everything you needed for set storage and wardrobes, along with spaces and studios where the musician would give lessons to students on-site as they were doing in the city. The program also included movie theaters, a media library, and an electro-acoustic space with 180 seats.

We needed to take a simple constructive approach to the building, adapted to Brazil. It had to compete with the shopping malls in terms of visibility, but I also wanted the diversity of the program's different areas and rooms to be perceptible in order to create a symbol of a permanent and open public space. What response should the design give to the line of the mountains and their sinuous shapes? It would have been unforgivable not to create that dialogue.

I developed the concept of an outdoor terrace veranda that would distribute all of the activities, a sort of internalized landscape contained between two large horizontal planes: a terrace ten meters high and a roof plane thirty meters high. The solid volumes of the rooms occupy this empty volume. Like the Montreal library project, it's a block that's crossed by transparencies. The veranda is a typical Brazilian feature. It reflects the climate. The idea was to create an open reception area, a physical striking space, something enjoyably monumental that you and the children want to climb up to via gentle slopes, and to pass between the closed volumes of the concert halls, which would respond to the magnitude of the Baixada, the urban plain. The project would be in the middle of a mangrove garden that we commissioned from landscape designer Fernando Chacel, a follower of Burle Marx.

The last month of 2002, the municipality came to Paris to see the process. I was working with the concept of the "hollowed out brick," the upper structure was interesting and they loved it but I didn't. The slab elevated at ten meters was supported by a lot of pillars and that was ugly as a parking building. It is in January, flying between Luxembourg and Berlin that I designed concrete triangular shear walls rising up from the ground to hold up the roof slab to contain the halls. These walls were enlarging from ground to sky to support the slabs, the drawing was a solution unifying aesthetic and technical question in one static thought.

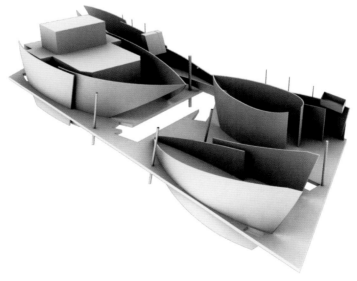

Drawing that shows the structural curved shear walls of the Cidade das Artes

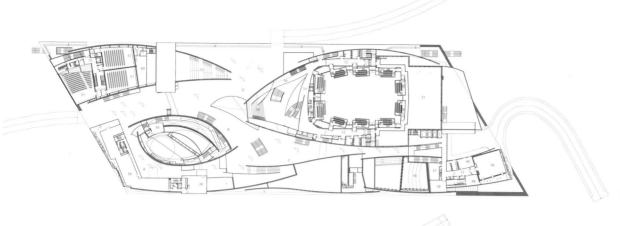

Level N4: 22.96

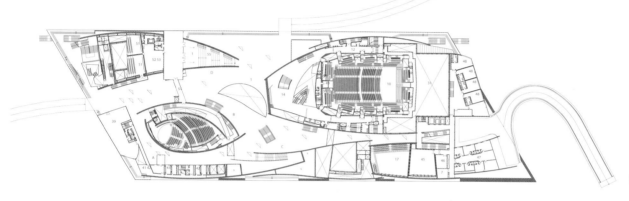

Level N3: 17.64

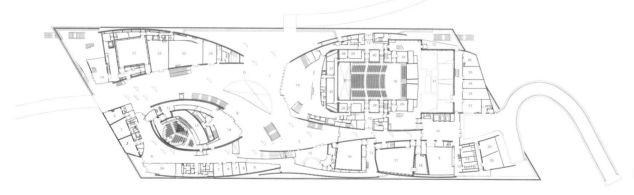

Level N1 : 10.00

A. OSB (Brazilian Symphony Orchestra)	6. Deposit piano	Orchestra	41. Hall	53. Restaurant
B. Chamber Music	7. Instrumentas deposit	18. Rehearsal Room for percussion	42. Meeting	54. Catwalk
C. Rehearsals	8. Deposit	19. Toilets and changing rooms	43. Balcony	55. Bleachers
D. Cinemas,	9. Library		44. Classrooms	56. Cabin Audio
E. Main Hall	10. Scenery	20. Reheasal room	45. Choir Rehearsal	57. Extension area
	11. Stalls	21. Room electroacoustic	46. Deposit Dressing Room	58. Dance rehearsal
1. Terrace	12. Circulation	22. Shop	47. Individual Dressing Rooms	59. Topper Booth
2. Rehearsal room, dressing room	13. Ventilation	23. Gallery	48. Dressing Rooms	60. Technical Area
3. Cafeteria	14. Foyer	24. Cafe	49. Light Booth	
4. Cuisine and storage	15. Reception, information and ticketing	25. Video Booth	50. Loges	
5. Depositing scenery	16. Multi-function Room	26. Annex booth	51. Cinema	
	17. Rehearsal Room for	27. Recording booth	52. Cuisine	

Legend items:

A. OSB (Brazilian Symphony Orchestra)
B. Chamber Music
C. Rehearsals
D. Cinemas,
E. Main Hall

1. Terrace
2. Rehearsal room, dressing room
3. Cafeteria
4. Cuisine and storage
5. Depositing scenery
6. Deposit piano
7. Instrumentas deposit
8. Deposit
9. Library
10. Scenery
11. Stalls
12. Circulation
13. Ventilation
14. Foyer
15. Reception, information and ticketing
16. Multi-function Room
17. Rehearsal Room for Orchestra
18. Rehearsal Room for percussion
19. Toilets and changing rooms
20. Reheasal room
21. Room electroacoustic
22. Shop
23. Gallery
24. Cafe
25. Video Booth
26. Annex booth
27. Recording booth
28. Scenery room
29. Cloakroom
30. Ventilation
31. Backstage
32. Maintenance deposit
33. Lighting Deposit
34. Installations deposit
35. Scenic deposit
36. Furniture Deposit
37. Broadcast video
38. Deposit Audio and Video
39. Offices
40. Deposit chairs
41. Hall
42. Meeting
43. Balcony
44. Classrooms
45. Choir Rehearsal
46. Deposit Dressing Room
47. Individual Dressing Rooms
48. Dressing Rooms
49. Light Booth
50. Loges
51. Cinema
52. Cuisine
53. Restaurant
54. Catwalk
55. Bleachers
56. Cabin Audio
57. Extension area
58. Dance rehearsal
59. Topper Booth
60. Technical Area

Then in Paris, in my discussions with Joseph Attias, I thought about post-stressed concrete because it was the technic which would permit to have not more than 150 centimeters' thickness for the beams that would overpass the 40-meter span that I designed for the slab of the terrace and roof. Conventional concrete would have required slab-coffers three to four times thicker, and that would have been very ugly. Leading Brazilian companies have mastered this technique, used in engineering structures when, after the war, its inventor, French engineer Eugene Freyssinet, came to Brazil to create a building company.

And these jagged but cylindrical and vertical walls transfer the load to the ground and could be constructed on-site, which would not be too complicated.

As soon as we'd completed the first drawings and small models, we produced straightforward, effective 3D models of the project. So I presented these initial images and plans, along with a small cardboard model to the mayor and the press in Rio in February 2003. The mayor and the audience apparently immediately understood the importance of raising the building on the site of the Barra da Tijuca plain. After this quick approval, I worked with the structural engineers Carlos Fragelli and Bruno Cantarini. They adopted the project, a few columns of my model were expanded, but the thickness of the slabs remained less than one meter and fifty centimeters.

Cesar Maia wanted us to go ahead very quickly, but there was a lot of work. We prepared the concrete work bidding first. Such sculpture-structures could not have been built ten years before, because the walls are not in ordered and symmetrical situations, as in conventional structures where you repeat an arch or a base portico. For an irregular and asymmetrical structure, you need to calculate all of the bending moments in every respect and that would have taken far too long to the engineers to calculate without a computer.

We launched the invitation to tender for the rough work in 2003. We had to outline our design straightaway, whereas the program would change given how much was at stake. That's why I saw the composition of the Cidade das Artes as a puzzle with the key elements, but with spaces left between the pieces. We were able to develop each piece in the

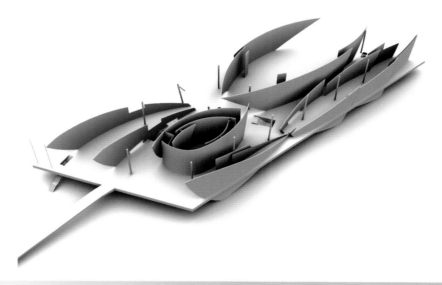

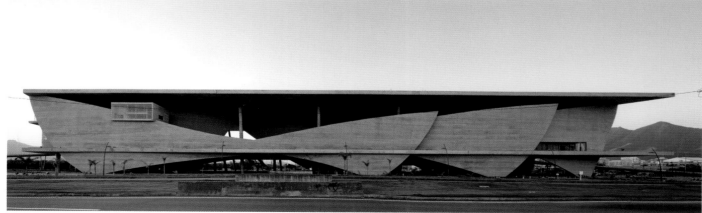

The Cidade das Artes features a large Brazilian veranda raised ten meters above the ground. A roof that seems to float allows for volumes beneath dedicated to music, dance, theater, and cinema.

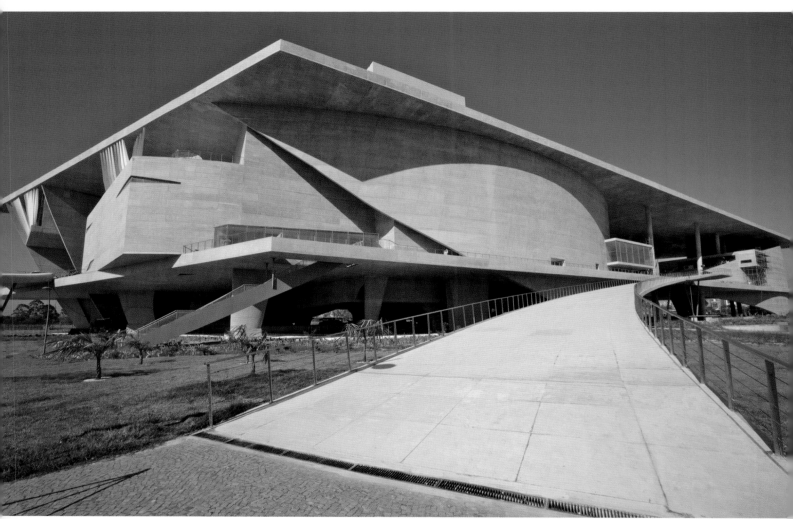

From the west side, the entrance to the movie theater and offices are protected by the oblique lines of the brise-soleil.

Garden of shadows. bottom: Under the main public floor, a fresh public place in the middle of the garden. opposite page: The view from below, looking upward

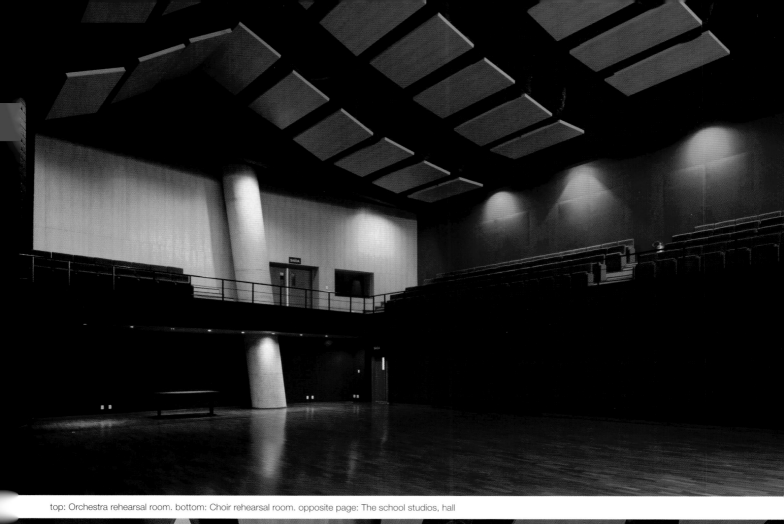

top: Orchestra rehearsal room. bottom: Choir rehearsal room. opposite page: The school studios, hall

architectural study, without impacting on its neighbors. Like the Cité de la musique Est, the sculptural plan was also open to development. It was more flexible than a collection of rectangles stuck one to the other. Each piece of the puzzle was able to change during the development of the design plans, like boats in a port that might glide a meter or two either way. We were able to change, move and increase the size of the angles and release more space.

For the music performance spaces, everyone needs to be physically and visually aware of the audience, but at the same time, everyone should feel being the only one listening. I knew the exceptional acoustics qualities that I obtained with the balcony towers in Luxembourg Philharmonie hall. Here the ten towers have four levels of balconies, and the audience surrounds closely the musicians. From seats in these vertical towers, people really have the best sound and feel being in the front, without nobody between them and orchestra. Having these volumes on the walls help to optimize the distribution of the diffusion, reflection and absorption of the sound.

We needed to allow for the metamorphosis of a 1,800-seat philharmonic concert hall into an endstage opera house seating 1,300, in other words, to go from a concert hall where the audience completely surrounds the orchestra, to an Italian-style opera theatre with a front-framed stage, wings on each side and a backstage area. Four of these towers are mobile to allow for the opera layout.

When the building process begun in spring 2004 we were continuing the study of the plans for the inside spaces. But in 2005, the schedule of the building process lost two years because the city of Rio had to built stadiums to welcome the Pan American Games in 2007. We had time to make perfect plans and many tests for a very particular method for concrete shuttering of the walls.

At the end of 2007, the money came again and in one year 3000 workers finished week the shells roof and core. Then a new mayor arrived, contesting the principle of such a project on such a site. He didn't give order to continue the building inside for three years and didn't provided the resources for the Cidade to function fully. Its director worked courageously and with talent to help it survive. In 2017, a new mayor has taken the Cidade again with a new director. In recent years, the concert hall is not used for philharmonic performances, its primary program, but as a theater, its secondary program.

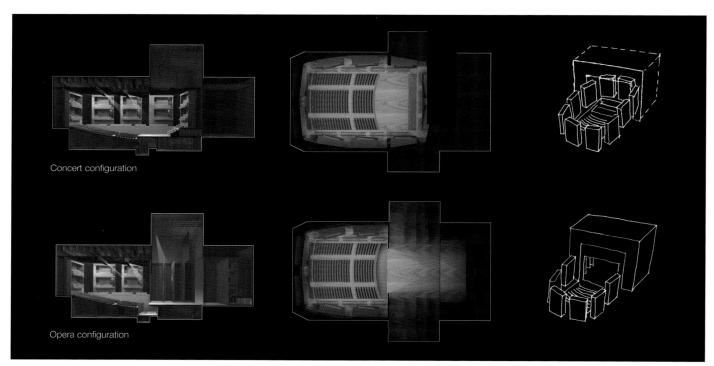

Concert configuration

Opera configuration

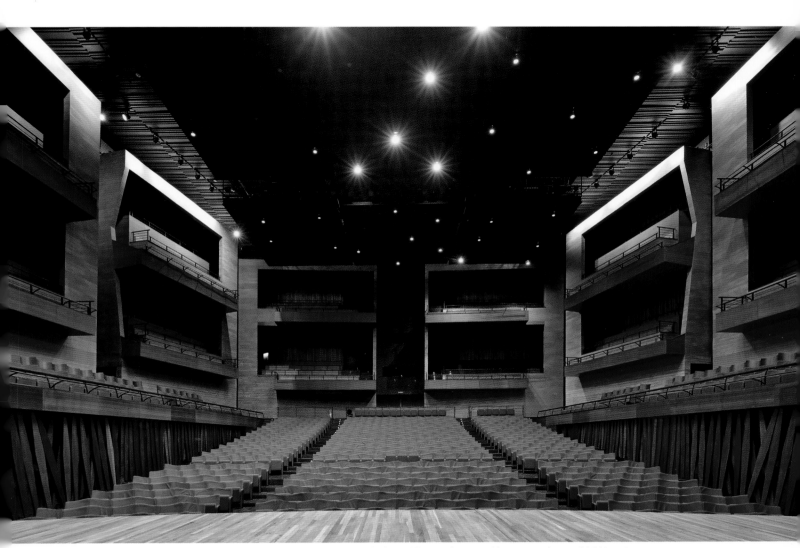

Two configurations for the large interior space are possible, one for a concert hall with 1,800 seats, the second for an opera house of 1,300 seats.

The transformation of the concert hall begins with the creation of an area at the back of the stage, by moving four of these ten box towers. The pneumatic system, as used in several theaters around the world, allows the towers to be moved using air cushions, and they can easily be transported to the back of the concert hall. Next, the front of the stage is lowered, the frame appears like a diaphragm and the orchestra pit is opened. The detachable ceilings are removed to make space for the fly loft, the grid and suspended scenery.

The lobby of the Great hall, where you come during the interval, where people see each other and meet, is a space that moves upwards in all directions. It's full of footbridges, footbridge stairs, staircases, bridges and windows. It is a walk through space, a three-dimensional theater in which the members of the public are the actors.

The Cidade is thought to give access to a public park around it, to be a belvedere and to gather different public for all kind of music and dance, as well as for the movie theaters, cafés, a restaurant. It is also supposed to be the "siège" place of the Orchestra and to be a school. For the whole neighborhood, it's a place where people should be able to come to walk, enjoy the shade of the gardens, with kids for example.

When I was working on this project, I never for one moment said that I was doing a Brazilian design! There's no "stylistic" effort! It was a natural process, following my other designs, accorded with the climate logic in its structure, taking into consideration the cost and concrete technology.

But I had early on a dream of Brazil, learned through the images I had seen of Brasilia. I discovered the real Brazil in the 1980s with Elizabeth. It was with her that I learned more about the vital importance of Brazilian architecture of the post-war years—the '40s, '50s and '60s—around the world. We've often discussed this heritage with Brazilian architects—Niemeyer, of course, and Lucio Costa, Serge Bernards, Reidy and the São Paolo school. Designers often claim to be pure inventors, without predecessors, but they all have a heritage in which they are rooted, and of which they are more or less aware. And I only felt that this project was inherited from this Brazilian culture once we'd completed it. Part of me had become Brazilian.

Cidade das Artes, Intersection of Avenue of the Americas and Ayrton Senna Avenue, Barra Da Tijuca, Rio de Janeiro, Brazil. Program: Cultural venue with philharmonic hall (1,800 seats) transformable into an opera hall (1,300 seats), chamber music hall (500 seats), electroacoustic room (180 seats), headquarters of the Brazilian Symphonic Orchestra, music school, 10 rehearsal rooms, media library, 3 movie theaters, restaurant, shops, administration offices, technical spaces and parking lots; surface area: 46,000 square meters; Gross Total Area: 90,000 square meters. Client: City Hall of Rio de Janeiro, Secretaria Municipal das Culturas. Acoustic in France: Xu Acoustique, Xu Ya Ying; Acoustic in Brazil: Acùstica & sònica, Ze Augusto Nepomucen. Scenography in France: Changement à Vue, Jacques Dubreuil; Scenography in Brazil: Solé e Associados. Structural engineering: Beton Engenharia, Carlos Fragelli, Bruno Cantarini. Landscape design: CAP, Fernando Chancel. Date: Commission, 2002; completion, 2013. Awards: Grand Prix Afex for French Architecture in the World, given by the Association French Architects Overseas, 2014; First Pini Prize, Category "Building," awarded by the Brazilian specialized press group Editora Pini, 2012; International Architecture Awards for "The Best New Global Design" awarded by The Chicago Athenaeum, 2008

top: Living theater/chamber music hall with revolving stage for jazz and Brazilian popular music. bottom: Exterior of living theater/chamber music hall

Interior and exterior views of the dance rooms

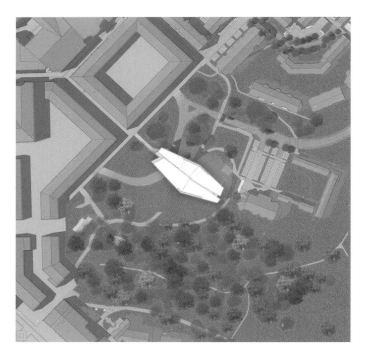

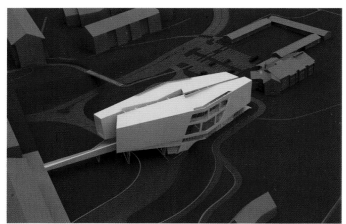

Hergé Museum, Louvain-la-Neuve, Belgium, 2001–2009

Fanny Rodwell, the widow of Hergé, the Belgian author of the Adventures of Tintin and other works, chose me to design a museum dedicated to her husband's work.

The site is on the edge of Louvain-la-Neuve, a university town without cars, on top of a plinth of parking spaces. I saw the museum as an elongated prism that seems to float above a forest of ancient oaks, like a ship stranded among the trees, linked by a long gangway to the quayside of the city. Looking into the museum through large plate-glass windows we see an interior made out of simple volumes. A reminder, perhaps, of the squares of cartoon strips into which we might enter by penetrating the lobby, as you might enter into a drawing (Lewis Carroll comes to mind), where the illusion becomes reality and the drawing seen from outside is shown in relief, revealing an interior-exterior world designed to be explored on foot in three dimensions (ramps, walkways and double heights). The museum is a narrative sequence of events in shapes and colors. The visitor crosses through large solid volumes that I designed to protect Hergé's drawings from the light, in rooms where Joost Swarte has displayed them by theme, not presented here. From the lobby, a black-and-white checkered lift tower rises through the floors of the museum's four opaque volumes. This building is based again on the idea of the hollow sculpted brick: a simple volume hollowed out with several alcoves.

Hergé Museum, 26, rue du Labrador, Anneau Central, Louvain-La-Neuve, Belgium. Program: Cultural facilities accommodating a museum dedicated to Hergé, as well as permanent and temporary exhibitions areas, a video projection room, a cafeteria, shops, studios, storehouses and administrative premises; surface area: 3,600 square meters. Client: La Croix de l'Aigle SA, Fanny et Nick Rodwell, Studios Hergé. Client representatives: INCA, Walter de Toffol. Architect of record: Pierre Accarain, Thierno Dumbuya. Museography: Joost Swarte. Scenographer: Winston Spriet. Landscape design: Jacques Wirtz. Lighting: Suzanne Fleischer-Harchaoui. Acoustic: AVEL. Date: Commission, 2001; completion, 2009. Award: Belgian Building Awards, 2010

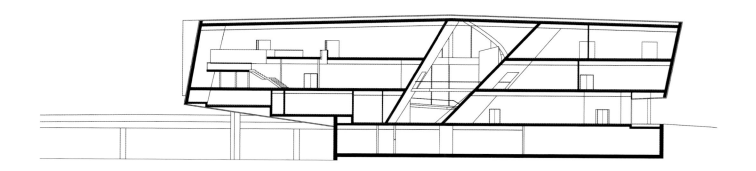

Plan and elevation of Hergé Museum showing exhibition level

The multicolored universe created by the father of Tintin is brought to life at the museum in Louvain-la-Neuve: a prism built around four exhibition spaces.

The evidence is there before you, straight away; you can't miss it. The long front of the Hergé Museum reveals itself as a comic strip, punctuated by panels of different sizes. A seemingly neutral, neutralized picture brings out, in the middle distance, the multicolored world created by the father of Tintin, Jo and Zette, Quick and Flupke, the master of the "clear line."

"I have always been passionate about space as it was before the invention of perspective: that pre-Renaissance space where distances were indicated by one plane in front of another, by that minimum indication of depth," confides Christian de Portzamparc.

As you approach the museum on this sort of walkway across the route below, it begins to look like a large ship stranded on the edge of Louvain-la-Neuve. You are reminded, then, of the ships, the clippers and junks, the dhows and cargo boats that accompany the long voyages undertaken by Tintin, Milou (Snowy) and Captain Haddock. And this detachment, this sort of extraterritoriality, gives it all a sense of levitation. Little by little, the colors you only half noticed from a distance begin to take shape.

And behind the museum one glimpses a backdrop of centuries-old oak trees that seem to unify the different panels and pictures. Upon entering the museum, you notice the cornerstones of Portzamparc's architecture: fragmentation, overlappings and displacements, ubiquity.

Not a museum, but a universe: Hergé's still more than Portzamparc's. Five "landscape objects" spell out the space, each with its own personality and peculiar sculptural form. Each with its own color and graphism, and bearing a vastly enlarged extract from a Hergé scene. Each exuding one of the famous little reporter's remarkable adventures, against a mixed background of towns and wide-open spaces.

We are therefore presented with an organized assemblage of frames, rhythms, breaks and cuttings-out which make this space, these spaces, much more than just architecture. A multiple place is created, whose crossings, passages and walkways over the void in their turn multiply to infinity the angles of view, with sensations, discoveries and emotions to stir the imagination.

Meanwhile, Joost Swarte's scenic design of the exhibited works is admirably discreet and restrained. In a classic museum, the route takes the form of a progressive itinerary, from room to room and period to period, episode to episode.

Here it is the space itself that composes the route. Almost more cinematographic than architectural, it fades in and out of sequence, screen and counter-screenshots, travelling shots and perspectives . . . in a playful use of solids and voids that is also a game of lines. This apparent displacement expands the space and opens up views. And then, a phenomenon of reversal in the shape of performance: when the comic strip, a two-dimensional territory, never ceases to conjure up and depict the three dimensions. In these, the architect has succeeded here in evoking, or representing, the two-dimensional.

—Gilles de Bure, Domus, September, 2009

Rhone-Alpes County Council Hall, Lyon, France, 2006–2011

As the French regions grow in power so their influence needs to be felt in the urban space. Formerly located in an almost "rural" setting, the Région Rhône Alpes decided to move its offices to the peninsula of the Confluence district in Lyon.

I organized the 40,000 square meters of offices for 2000 people as a carved block enclosed by glass, in order to create an interior landscape, temperate, light-filled, and planted—forming a series of indoor/outdoor spaces; a succession of atriums and covered gardens would lead to a media library, exhibition rooms, a conference room and a large council chamber. It is a network of bright interior spaces "defined by" the office buildings enveloped and whirled around them like a snake. The daylight is diffused over large areas and offers multiple views. This three-dimensional opened space becomes a forum, a "square," a shared and accessible public center.

Rhone-Alpes County Council Hall, 1, esplanade François Mitterrand, Lyon 2nd District, France. Program: Administrative and public building dedicated to the Rhône-Alpes County and accommodating offices (1,500 employees), a conference room (500 seats), a boardroom, reception halls, a staff restaurant and a car park; surface area: 45,650 square meters. Client: Regional Council Rhône-Alpes. Acoustic: AVEL. Landscape design: Régis Guignard, Méristème. Date: Competition, 2006; completion, 2011

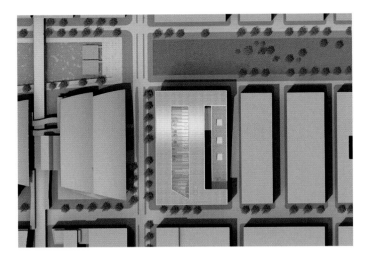

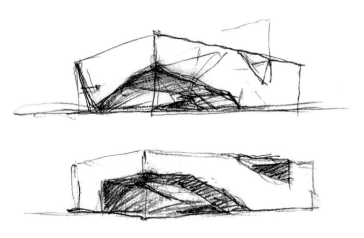

opposit page: A large city hall, accessible to the public

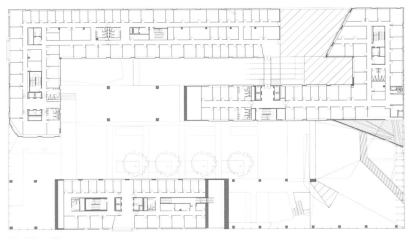

Third Floor Plan

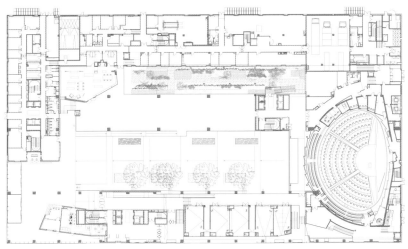

Ground Floor Plan

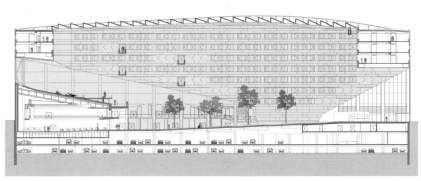

Elevation

2

3

4

5

6

7

Faults

The cross-cutting rifts of light, as seen here, result from th[e]
hollowed out blocks in many projects.

1. Hergé Museum, Louvain-la-Neuve, Belgium, 2001
2. Cité de la musique, Paris, France, 1995
3. Grand Bibliothèque du Québec, Montreal, Canada, 2[...]
4. Hergé Museum, Louvain-la-Neuve, Belgium, 2001
5. Cidade das Artes, Rio de Janeiro, Brazil, 2002
6. Beirut Gate, Beirut, Lebanon, 2006
7. King Abdullah's Equestrian City Central Tower, Riyadh[,]
   Saudi Arabia, 2008
8. Broad Museum, Los Angeles, U.S.A. 2009
9. Cultural Center, Suzhou, China, 2013

Château Cheval Blanc Winery, Saint-Émilion, France, 2006–2011

Chapter 5
Singularities

Constructive Truth and Ornamental Appearance

I kept talking about void and space with the precedent projects although we know that the first thing we have to master is building. In the projects presented previously, void, space context were specific issues and crucial debates of the time. This chapter presents the cases of more isolated buildings in their context. It's the occasion to discuss the constructive thinking which concern in fact every project.

If I say that I think about space, site and uses, I must add that it is soon as walls, construction materials, rocks and trees that this void of space soon exists in my mind: we imagine plain substances, slabs, girders, woodwork, panels and the means we decide to cut, mould, transport, assemble them. Technical effort of construction is obviously generator of buildings and cities transformation. During more than twenty centuries, it was a means, the mean, but it belonged the tools that architecture had to swallow, to incorporate and hide and forget.

A mental revolution happened when technology changed its "status" in the twentieth century, during the industrial age. Technic became a truth. Its assertion in the legitimateness of visibility made it a potential of beauty. This marked the entrance in our new age of architecture. The modern one. We often feel far from it but we will never end to discuss it and work through it.

The rejection of ornament was the credo of modern architecture best adhered to after the publication of *Ornament and Crime* by Adolf Loos. We still cherish the principle that the constructive reality should be visible, whereas previously it was covered in plaster, as in Palladio's buildings. We are familiar with worshipping the union between the beautiful and the useful, as an esthetic of truth that has endured. Through this feeling, we still like the idea that the beautiful does not depend on a gesture, an "artistic" ambition, but on a reason. Behind or beyond this, we like the beauty of architecture, a "natural" beauty, as inevitable as a civilizational reality. We dream that our architecture would be generated naturally. I pretend it, often, and then I have to criticize myself to see what had been obviously logic and what had been personal and idiosyncratic in my process. The non-rational is important.

The technical context that frames contemporary construction is the opposite of a natural "purity." After centuries in which construction methods used stone, wood, the horse and man power, we have known concrete and metal, the elevator and the automobile, plumbing and air-conditioning. The possibilities have become more diverse and extensive. We are now confronted by a tangle of evolving technologies and materials. The conditions in which we implement them, the sustainability of materials, their weight and surface aspect change every year and the need to take the climate into account and to save energy has changed the criteria on which we base our choices. Our buildings have become systems of technical networks and assembled components that we need to fit a body to; they became real machines, not the metaphorical ones of Le Corbusier. This raises the question of their maintenance and "sustainability." Skins, cladding and fluid equipment are becoming more important and our walls have essentially become clothes. Gottfried Semper was right to call them costumes.

Construction has become more complex. We separate the structural function from thermal protection and water-tightness. The demands of insulation, stability, industrial production, transport, storage and assembly determine the schedule and work stages. Maintenance and sustainability often demand that technical machinery and structural purity be hidden. The fact of showing them becomes an intentional presentation of complexity rather than simplicity.

The structure is often covered by several insulating and protective skins. These skins require panels to be laid out; architects are presented with an endless choice of cladding and glazing solutions. These choices require us to make esthetic decisions about transparency, shininess, and the reflective or matt aspect of volumes and their colors—typically ornamental decisions. To achieve calm purity, you sometimes need to conceal, to create unifying lines, to lie.

The search for purity of space and object often ends in designing a body for it. The structure sometimes becomes a complex associated with the "skin," as in the punctured walls of our towers. And we are sometimes happy to be able to see it bared, even magnified and amplified to restore its role in generating plastic reality and beauty as in the Cidade das Artes in Rio de Janeiro where concrete holds everything in place and structures spatial shapes.

For the Renaissance hotel on avenue de Wagram in the 17th arrondissement, near the Arc de Triomphe in Paris, if there is an attempt to provide some beauty, it derives from its skin with its volumetry generated by curved glass. Can we say, then, that this is less linked to the construction and therefore ornamental? That *firmitas* and *venustas* are separate? No. The bow windows are the *utilitas* essential to the rooms, opening them to panoramic views and light specific to their spaces, but also providing them with thermal insulation. Here, the form of the "bodywork" has a purpose that is interior and exterior. In contrast, the horizontal offset of the superposed levels of these sinusoid movements of bow windows is gratuitous. It is sculptural. Is it ornament?

Clearly the concept of ornament or the notion of decor (a word that architects hate, usually without reason), needs to be reviewed in each case Between the structure and the skin's function (insulation, light and views), the partition is a combinatory element to which a lot of possible choices have been added since the construction of walls a century ago in stone, wood or concrete.

At the Philharmonie de Luxembourg, the rhythm of the vertical steel lines dominates our perception of the façade like a giant filter. It's a system designed with relation to the light, to mask the view and protect the interior from UV rays, but it could also be seen as an ornamental device. However, *firmitas*, *utilitas* and *venustas* are all present here: each tube, void or solid, reflects different uses. Some hold up the roof, others are stiffeners or glazing holders, like woodwork supports, others are air conduit tubes, which bring controlled air inside, while others are rain water drains, as it was in the system of cornices molding columns lines in the Greek temple, the construction itself is not separated to the ornamental.

Today, would I say that the LVMH tower in New York is ornamented or not? We would generally say no, because everyone understands ornament as an addition that is not "useful," but used to symbolic purpose. (Ornament is often seen as an accessory, while the rejection of ornament is seen as purity, as the return to an original, essential meaning).

But the trapeze-shaped cut of the glass sandblasting that provides views to the exterior is a pictorial or decorative motif.

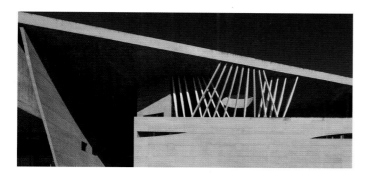
Cidade das Artes, Rio de Janeiro, Brazil, 2002–2013

Les Champes Libres, Rennes, France, 1993–2006

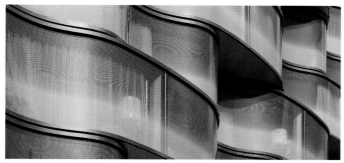
Hotel Renaissance Arc de Triomphe, Paris, France, 2003–2009

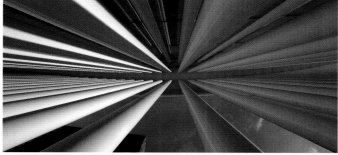
Philharmonie de Luxembourg, Grand Dutchy of Luxembourg, 1997–2005

U Arena Stadium, Nanterre, France, 2010–2017

We no longer talk about ornament when the form models the space, we talk about Baroque culture, but we should talk about ornament whenever there is a "decorative" addition or effect. What was once a crime can now be openly claimed. But where does the limit lie? When we settle on the position of the ventilation grids on the façade, a technical necessity, part of the work is "ornamental," to the same extent as the spacing of holes in the form panels of concrete walls or the layout of aluminum or copper plates.

Every building hides or extols technology, rejects it or deflects it. And architecture shows these varied choices in ways that might be ostentatious or discrete, conventional or bold, brutal or strict, but always in response to this question: how can we transfigure technology into a benefit, into beauty, into social and ecological properties? How do you make technology an esthetic and practical reality?

This is a civilizational challenge: the public, without saying or knowing it, expects from architecture and the architect a sort of "guide" to the contemporary world, the world of technology. A world in which there is more personal and less temporary repercussions for the image of the status of human being on earth than even his choice of car. This choice describes the age in which each person feels to be in and dreams to be in, the future they would like to see and share. As soon as we start talking about taste in architecture, we label it with a date—the eighteenth century, the thirties, the fifties. Time and evolution are at work when we evoke history and the future, progress and its rejection.

Decorative excess is often rejected, and yet it reappears, sometimes in surreal ways, and no doctrine could discuss it without being ridiculed. We can no longer say today: "Here are the rules of architectural legitimacy," as Mies Van der Rohe was understood or believed to be asserting. Is everything allowed then?

This is what we often think when we feel surrounded by ugliness. But we know that a doctrine is out of expectation in the world. We are aware sometimes we can discover unwanted wonders in landscapes of metropolis. We watch the irrational combining with inevitable calculation, waiting absolutely new, unpredictable esthetic experience. And we try to open and disseminate the protected pure oasis that are the effort of architecture.

Creating spaces for a building or for a movie suppose creative and technical efforts, they offer boundless adventure equally important for the mind and senses. Not as important in our economy if we compare the team of a movie and the one of city's urban office. However, if one is entertainment, the other is for real life.

A Transformation
Headquarters of the Newspaper Le Monde, Paris, France, 2001–2005

Here, the ornamental element plays a decisive role in the result, whereas total restructuring of the existing building is a matter of volume and structure.

More and more buildings are being transformed and given a new lease of life. After the metamorphosis of the rue Nationale and the expansion of the Palais des Congrès, I once again shared my vision of this process by transforming the former headquarters of Air France's sales division—a 1960s building in the Paris 13th district. It was a demand of the newspaper Le Monde and for the first time we were working for Bouygues Immobilier who acted as promoter. This basic project turned out proving how much a transformation can be a rebirth.

I approached the existing building as a complex with potential, where we could create workspaces adapted to new working practices. I created a new presence on boulevard Blanqui that would enhance the slightly anonymous and drab area between the Place d'Italie and the Butte aux Cailles, more hidden and unique. This future building would house the headquarters of the newspaper.

I worked with the original building and shaped it by subtracting and adding volumes. I started by removing the three top floors to avoid falling under high-rise buildings rules, and cut the upper profile at an angle sloping from south to north. I horizontally expanded the side wings of the main body to extend the office floors.

Along boulevard Auguste Blanqui, a laminated screen in serigraphed glass featuring the first page of Le Monde, with a text by Victor Hugo on press freedom, was placed along the entire length of the wall like a transparent "double skin" to protect this southern façade. The superposing of three layers of glass filters the sun entering the offices and mitigates, behind an inconspicuous screen of glass, the old building's grid of windows and parapets.

On the east and west wings, I conceived the façade as a mosaic in aluminum and glass that integrates the windows and follows the profile of the new skyline in a chiaroscuro of grey and white.

Journalists wanted a street level atrium where they would meet, leave to outside reports and come back.

This is why a transparent entrance leads to a central atrium, meeting hall that I imagined as a square of two floors high. It is marked out by tall light columns made by Martin Wallace.

When you enter this lobby, you see the sky outside through the glass wall at the end, open and large as if the Paris landscape was a plain! This is a nice, perfect illusion. I installed a sloped mirror turned toward the sky. This feature brings the pure light of the zenith in the entire interior of the hall.

Le Monde Headquarters, 74–84, Boulevard Auguste-Blanqui, Paris 13th District, France. Program: Heavy restructuring of a 1970s building into new headquarters for the newspaper Le Monde; surface area: 18,500 square meters set on over 3 hectares. Client: Bouygues Immobillier. Owner: DB Real Estate. User: Le Monde Newspaper / Interior Architect: Elizabeth de Portzamparc. Landscaper: Méristème, Régis Guignard. Lighting concept in the hall: Martin Wallace. Date: Commission, 2001; completion, 2005. Award: Mipim Award, 2005

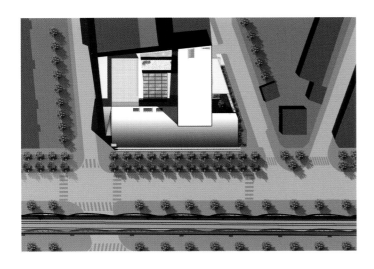

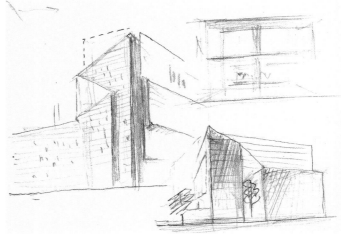

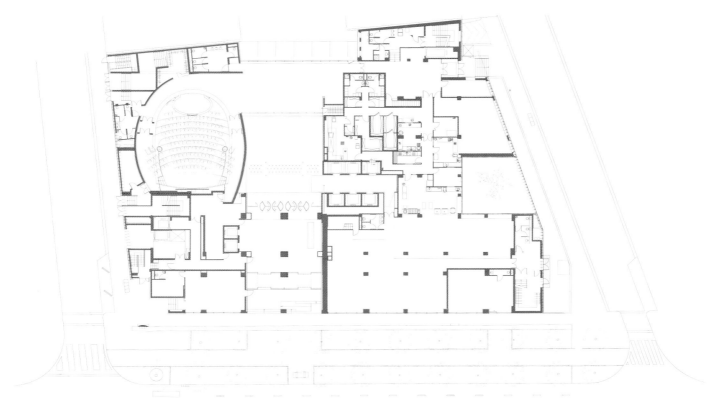

Ground Floor Plan

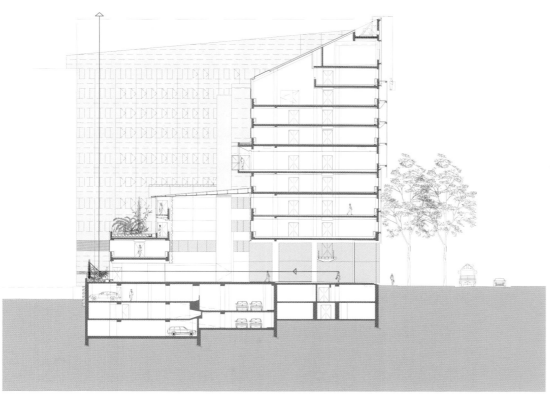

Section

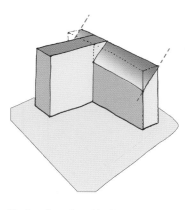

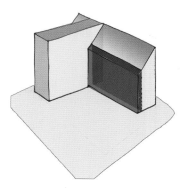

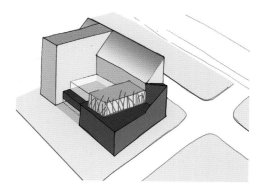

The transformation of La Monde Headquarters included three stages, shown in drawings above. Stage 1 involved modification of the profile of the building by cutting obliquely into the top of it so that the structure is no longer a high-rise building.

Stage 2 involved widening the main building in order to enlarge the office spaces.

Stage 3 involved the addition of an extra volume to the side wings to compensate of the sacrificed upper floors.

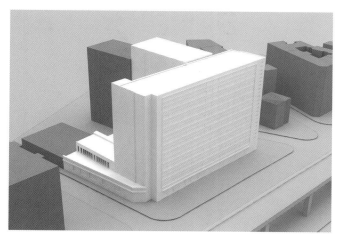

Existing situation, 2000

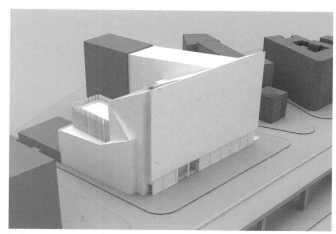

Project as designed, 2000–2005

Two views of Le Monde Headquarters showing the transformation of the building from original structure, at left, to transformed building at right

The lateral volumes of the façades of
the Le Monde Headquarters building
are composed of glass and aluminum
marquetry. On the boulevard, a white
serigraphed "double-skin" with an
inscription from the writings of
Victor Hugo

Auditorium

opposite page: The reception hall, under a lightweight glass roof, is suitable for informal meetings. A wide mirror turned toward the sky creates the illusion of a horizon that enlightens the interior space.

Hotel Renaissance Arc de Triomphe, Paris, France, 2003–2009

Is this hotel's façade ornamental or utilitarian? The rooms it "produces" are, in any case, prized and requested by the hotel's guests.

Located on the avenue de Wagram, less than 500 meters from the Arc de Triomphe, the hotel was supposed to have stone façades. But when Jean-Marc Blanchecotte, Head architect of Bâtiments de France considered the designs in the light of this rule, he accepted the glass façade. He asserted that his role was also to protect contemporary design and not to keep the city frozen in the past.

The hotel commissioned by Alain Taravella gives onto the avenue, but also faces the rear inside the block and gives access via an open entrance on the ground floor to the famous and historic Salle Wagram through a sloping garden.

Bow windows open up views from the hotel's rooms onto the Place des Ternes and the Arc de Triomphe. The windows were designed and produced with a double layer of curved glass cast in one piece by the firm Seele, and its installation was a small technical feat.

The second particularity of the bow windows is the irregular weft pattern. From the study stage, the perfectly offset superposition of horizontal strips produced by the design required that particular attention would be paid to the structure, water-tightness and thermal insulation between bow windows from one floor to the next.

The third characteristic of the façade is the whitened glass. I thought to use the same process of sandblasting of the glass that I used on the LVMH tower in New York, here with serigraphed lines. This weft of horizontal white lines, shaded from the lower portion of the rooms upwards, heightens UV protection. It enhances privacy with a visually streamlined effect, reduces mirror reflections and highlights the glass volumes.

Hotel Renaissance Arc de Triomphe, 39–41, avenue de Wagram, Paris 17th District, France. Program: Hotel situated at the site of the old Empire Theatre, just steps from the Champs-Elysées, the Arc de Triomphe and the Place de l'Étoile, restaurants and shops; surface area: hotel, 8,500 square meters; garden, 450 square meters. Client: Groupe Altarea-Cogedim. Operator: Marriott. Head of Project Design: Urban Stirnberg. Landscaper: Méristème, Régis Guignard. Head of Technical and Implementation: HPM. Interior Design: Era (design), Studios Desseins (execution). Date: Commission, 2003; completion, 2009

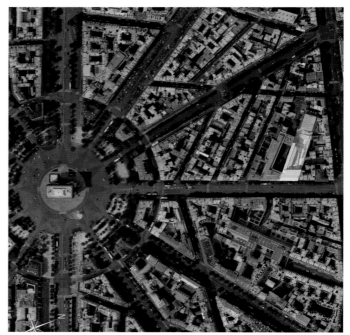

Site plan and aerial view, with building on avenue de Wagram, within 500 meters of the Arc de Triomphe

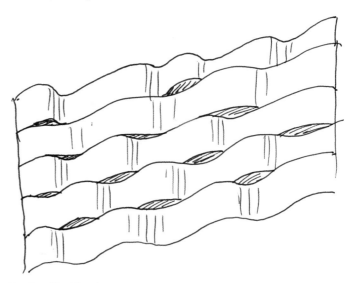

Drawing of front facade

Front façade of the Hotel Renaissance, on avenue de Wagram

top, opposite page: Detail views of the front façade

Second Floor Plan of the Hotel Renaissance

Galeo, Headquarters of Bouygues Immobilier, Issy-les-Moulineaux, France, 2004–2009

This project involved transformation of a large block of garages and stone grit workers' houses located on the outskirts of Issy-les-Moulineaux, opposite the ring road around the center of Paris. Bouygues Immobilier, the French property developer, asked us to built here, at the entry point into Issy-les-Moulineaux from Paris, their Headquarter and offices on the rest of the plot.

I designed three buildings along the street, and opened a public pathway crossing the block to link the existing stone grit houses to the main road. The headquarters is at the entrance position.

Its particular volume respects the urban building code, which requires the upper floors to be stepped back in order to fit in the height limit of 25 meters. Rather than producing a staircase effect, I designed a curved volume, similar to a pebble, with an exterior shell composed of a "double skin" of serigraphed glass scales. This airy, accessible glass mantle reduces heat gain on the office floors, allowing for the addition of wide windows to the rear façade in order to produce a soft and light-filled interior atmosphere. At night, this crystal becomes a "lamp" visible from the highway.

In contrast to the Galeo white glass building, the other office buildings are in red fiber concrete using a mold that we designed and produced in conjunction with Martin Wallace. The result is two architectural "expressions." The entire project is HEQ® accredited for its high standard of environmental performance.

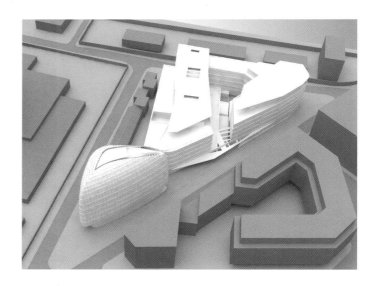

Galeo, Bouygues Immobilier Headquarters, 3, boulevard Gallieni, Issy-les-Moulineaux, France. Program: Multi-program of offices, consisting of three buildings, a business restaurant, retail, multi-function commercial spaces, and a 5-level place car park with 492 parking spots; surface area: 24,000 square meters (Galeo, 5,840 square meters; Dueo, 10,567 square meters; Trieo, 7,275 square meters). Interior Architect: Elizabeth de Portzamparc (Business restaurant, cafeteria). Client: Bouygues Immobilier. Date: Commission, 2004; completion, 2009

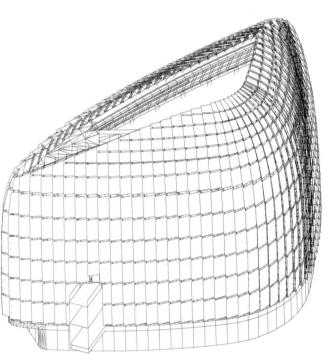

Château Cheval Blanc Winery, Saint-Émilion, France, 2006–2011

This construction rises from the ground to become a hill, promontory or belvedere looking out the long curves of the millennia-old landscape shaped by vines planted by the Romans in Saint-Émilion vineyard.

In 2011, owners Bernard Arnault and Baron Albert Frère asked me to design a new winery for Château Cheval Blanc. The classical nineteenth-century mansion, the "château" of the property, was flanked by a blockhouse which was the unpractical winery where one of the world's finest wines was produced. The new building would be at the other side of the mansion. Pierre Lurton, manager of the property, envisioned it as a new and ideal workshop.

I designed walls as four long concrete sails forming a structure of arches, serving both as columns and girders, accommodating the vat house. A large passage runs across the building into which the grape harvest is brought.

This structure that lifts and drops, houses 6,500 square meters of workshops. It creates an incline leading to the garden and terrace fringed with grass and trees. As you climb the slope, you discover the beauty of the geometric lines planted by human hand.

For the vat house, Pierre Lurton passed over wood and steel and wanted to retain concrete for the vinification process because of its thermal stability and the reaction between the surface and tartaric acid. I produced jar-shaped vats that billow in their center to optimize oxygenation.

Like large sculpture, these vats are central to the architectural design and echo the concrete sails. Lines of overhead openings bathe the interior in a gentle natural light that falls from the ceiling and sculpts the rounded surfaces and vats.

The fifty-two curved vats in nine sizes allow for the precise vinification of grapes according to the size of each vineyard plot and the quantity of the harvest. Shape, types, numbers, material, every element here helps perfect the wine-making process and old expertise practices to enhance the production of an exceptional wine.

The crypt-like barrel cellar with brick moucharaby walls is bathed in a much softer light. It is lined with dozens of barrels.

Indoors and outdoors, the winery is a place of interaction with nature, the air, the climate and the seasons.

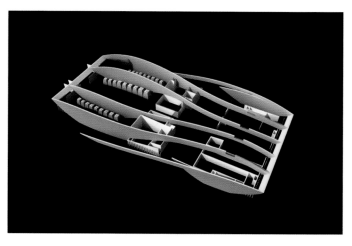

Château Cheval Blanc Winery, Saint-Émilion, France. Program: Cuvier with 52 vats, wine cellars, tasting room, workshops, packaging room, offices; surface area: 5,250 square meters. Client: Château Cheval Blanc. Landscaper designer: Méristème, Régis Guignard. Architect of record: Olivier Chadebost, architect. Acoustic: Point d'Orgue. Light: Captain Spot-Jean-Bernard Favero-Longo; Aartill. Date: Commission, 2006; completion, 2011. Award : Best New Global Design, 2013 International Architecture Awards, awarded by the Chicago Athenaeum, Museum of Architecture and Design

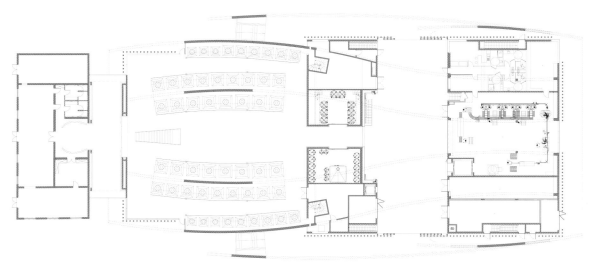

Ground Floor Plan, including vat room

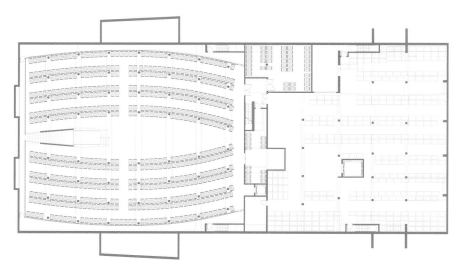

Basement Plan, with barrel cellar and storage area

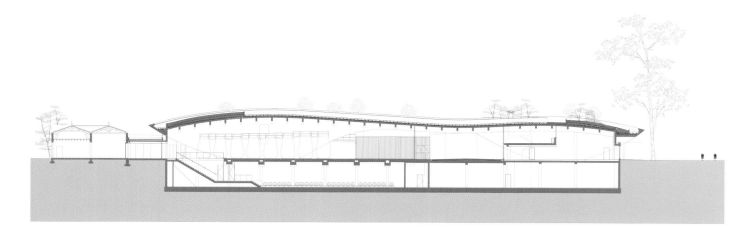

Section

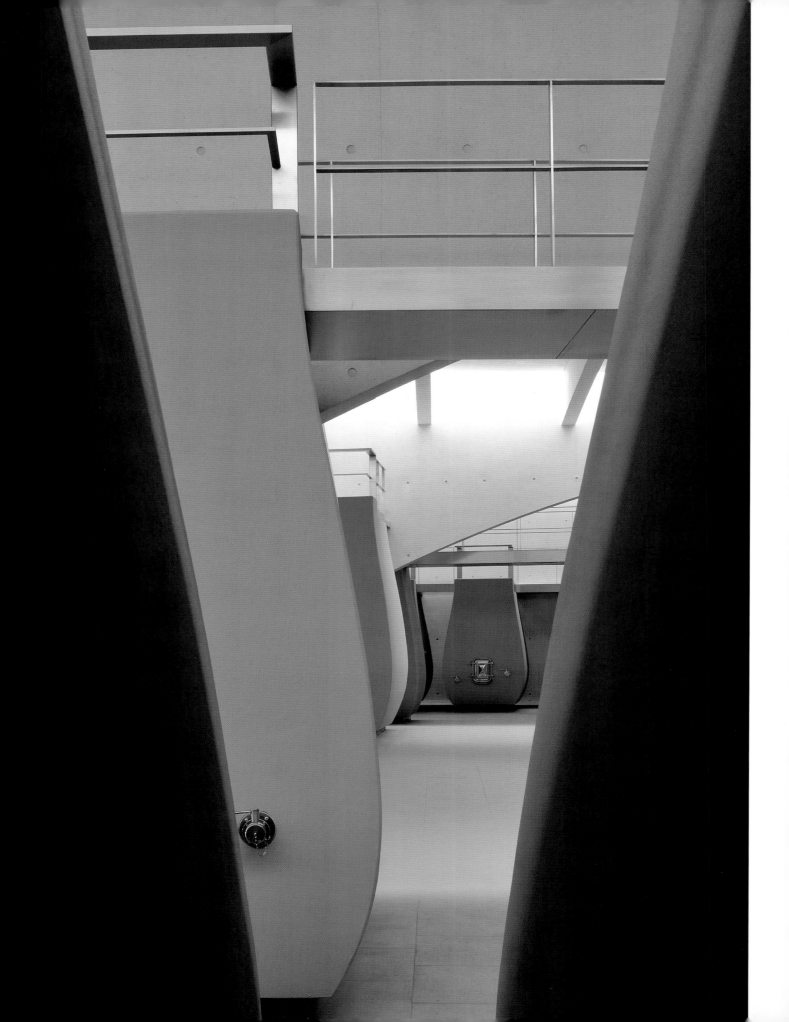

top: View of vat room. For 47 plots, 52 concrete molded vats of 9 different sizes. bottom: Barrel cellar

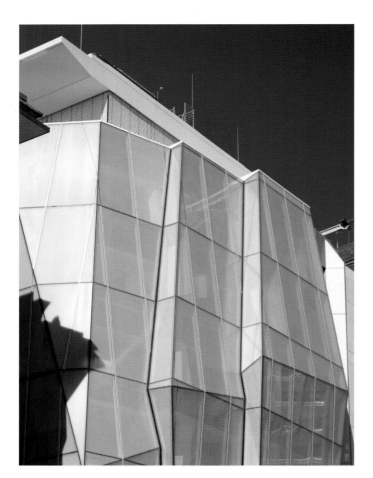

Royal20, Luxembourg, Grand Duchy of Luxembourg, 2012–2016

Leasinvest commissioned us to design a white office building on a deep-set plot on the Boulevard Royal.

We produced two sections: one with a sculptural presence on the boulevard and the other one at the rear of the plot, linked by an inhabited walkway.

This composition takes advantage of the depth by opening up direct views for the offices at the rear of the plot, and creates a small but interesting architectural feature on the alignment with the boulevard, which plays on movement in an environment of straight lines.

For the building's geometry, I shaped the vertical planes in serigraphed white diaphanous glass that drape the façade in an enveloping movement. This reflects local urban planning regulations through an interaction of protruding and set-back sections, in which each plane and ridge scrupulously complies with the rules in force.

This building complies with BREEAM environmental standards, ranking "very good."

Royal20, Boulevard Royal, Luxembourg, Grand-Duchy of Luxembourg. Program: Office building with 8 levels and basement, located on a main axis of the city of Luxembourg; surface area: 7,200 square meters. Client: Leasinvest. Architect of record: Ballini Pitt Architectes. Structure: Schroeder et Associés. Date: Commission, 2012; completion, 2016

House of Dior, Seoul, South Korea, 2011–2015

Apegujeong-ro Avenue in Seoul is an alignment of quadrangular, austere buildings and stores all occupied by global fashion labels housed in enormous box-like buildings, parallelepipeds each with their own façade's graphics and colors. To design the Dior building, I found it possible to break with the parallelepiped at the junction of this avenue and conceived a building as a soft white draping. The building stands out like a large sculptural tribute to Christian Dior. This sculpture is nevertheless a building that invites you to imagine the interior, beckoning visitors inside.

It is made of two complementary parts: the draping on the avenue seems to come from a large metallic quadrangular box situated to the rear, its opposite: a building whose façade walls are decorated with Dior canework.

On the boulevard, at the street corner, the surfaces flow freely skywards, as if brought to life by a movement, crossed by a handful of lines. They are made from long molded fiberglass shells, fitted together with aeronautical precision. They are eleven undulating sections over more than 20 meters high and 7 meters wide, manufactured from a single piece, textured to look like weaving.

They were produced in a plant like boat hulls, strengthened with a steel frame to make it easier to transport and to fix them to the building's basic structure.

The entrance to the store, where two shells come together, is a lancet arch in which two metal mesh surfaces cross in line with the clothing metaphor. It makes us want to go inside and discover the interior design by Peter Marino. The restaurant sky floor and its terrace are characterized by the top lines of the sculptural façade, which here happen to design and frame the vision on the city and the sky.

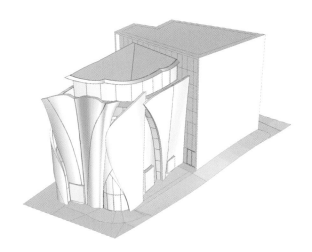

House of Dior, 464 Apgujeong-ro, Gangnam-gu, Seoul, South Korea. Program: Design for Dior fashion house, a flagship on 4 levels, plus living usable space on roof, including retail spaces, private rooms, a gallery and a café on the roof terrace. Client: Dior Couture. Architect of record: DPJ & Partners, David-Pierre Jalican. Interior Design: Peter Marino, Architect. Light: L'Observatoire International. Date: Commission, 2011; completion, 2015. Award: Best New Global Design, 2016 International Architecture Awards, awarded by the Chicago Athenaeum, Museum of Architecture and Design

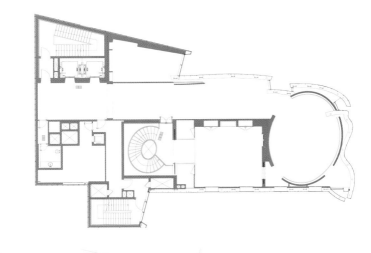

Fourth Floor Plan

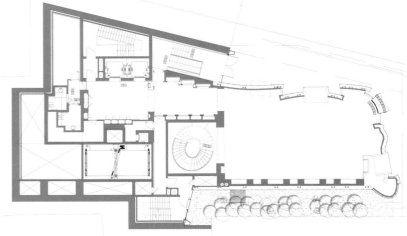

First Floor Plan

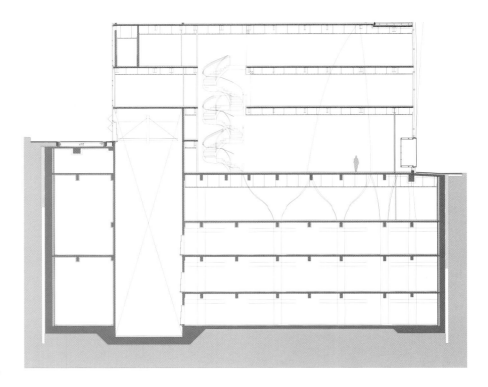

Section

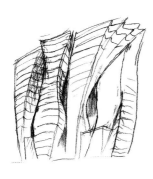 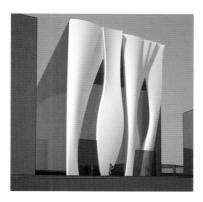  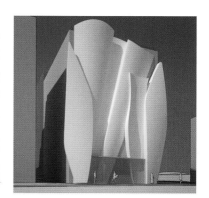

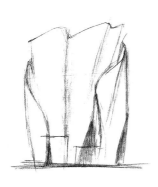 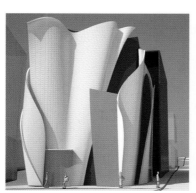  

Evolution of the project durning 2011: Various working sketches and computer renderings of the House of Dior building façade

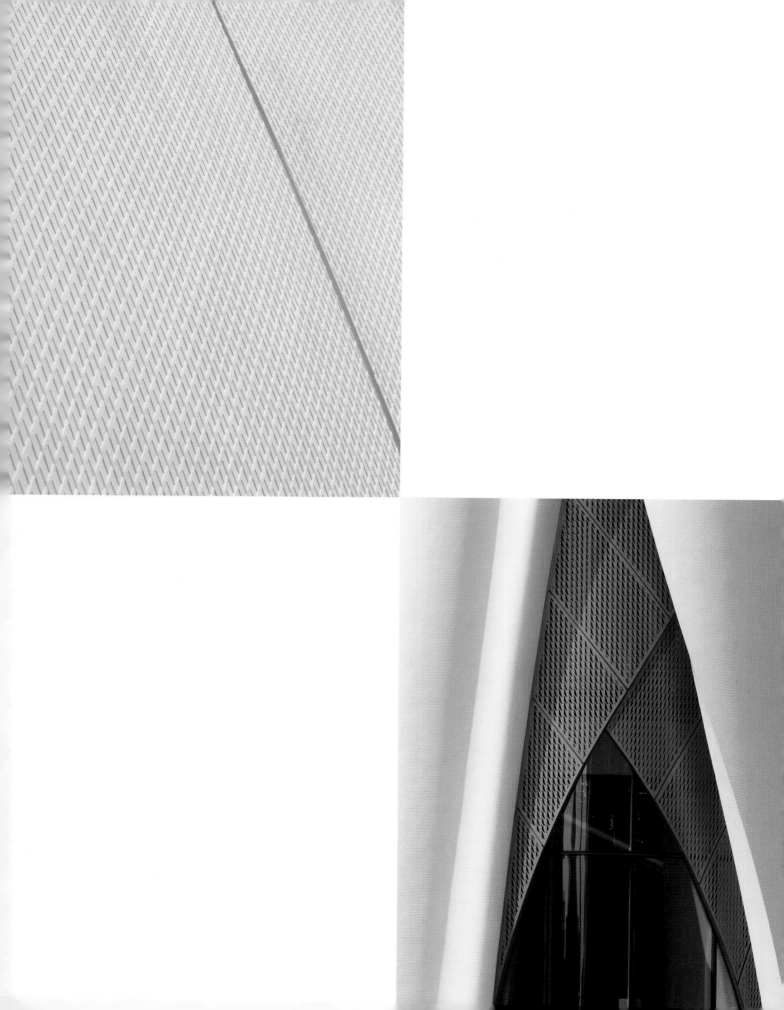

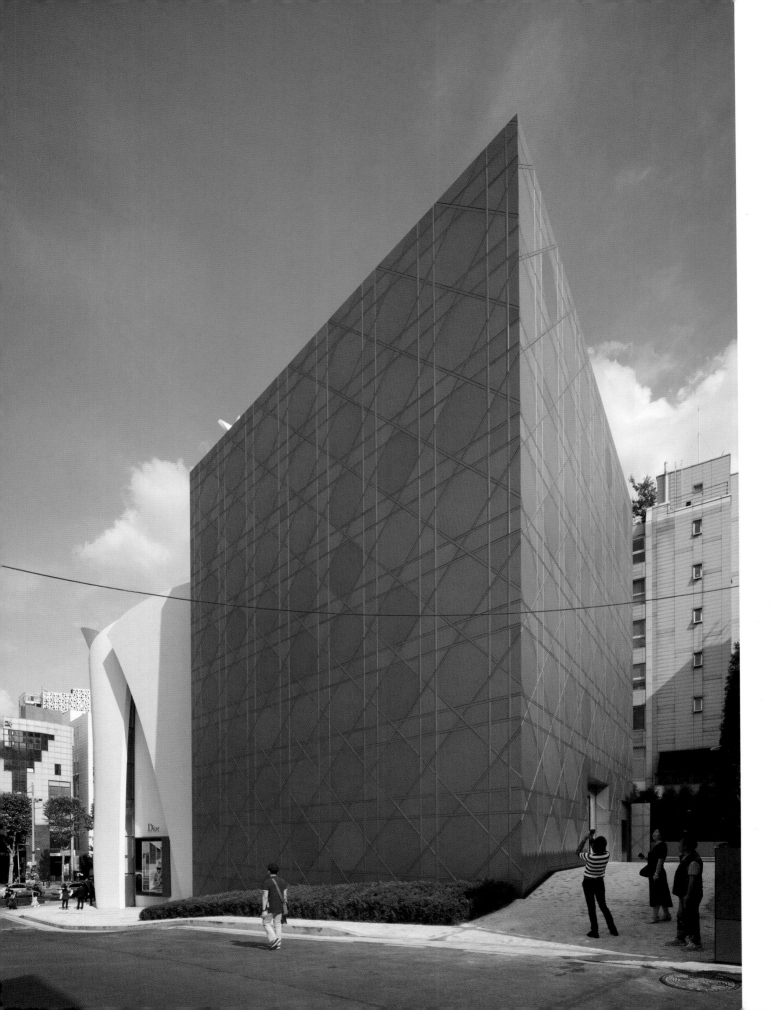

The restaurant sky floor and roof terrace at the House of Dior building

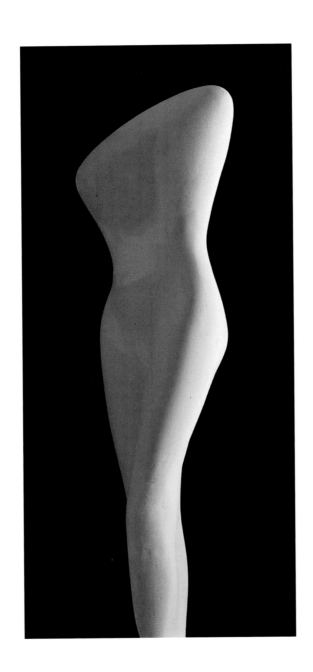

Chapter 6
Verticality

A "vertical dead-end" for some, is the tower compatible with the idea of the street, this fluid, horizontal line, open to all, without obstacle or dead-end? Is the tower a way to prevent energy-hungry, polluting, transport-heavy urban sprawl that destroys our soon-to-be essential local farmland? Urban planning, economics, the environment: the tower touches on all of these issues.

Towers have a basic economic logic. They are distant killers. They are only workable in places where there is a local rationale or need and where the cost per cubic meter of air rights outweighs the construction and maintenance costs. From this economic "window" vertical neighborhoods can emerge. The process is described by Rem Koolhaas as "congestion," an observation people understand as shedding light either on a modern efficiency and fascinating beauty or on an urbanistic pathology that, in some neighborhoods, enhances capacity for action. And there are exceptions to archaic arrogance, I was told by one of the Ben Laden brothers, whose company built the 829-meter Burj Kalifa tower in Dubai: above 200 meters, towers are simply an expression of human pride.

Towers are not viable in forests, on the outskirts of cities, and require carefully adapted urban planning on the ground.

It's in New York that I first fell in love with towers, strolling along Manhattan's grid with its unwavering straight rhythm—a sort of musical bass that allows room for whim and variety. That was a decisive lesson without which I would not have been able to design Les Hautes Formes, many years later.

The straight streets of the Manhattan grid frame the sky from the blue directly above to the light-brimming horizon of the Hudson and East rivers, and in its long corridors of light, the horizontal lines of this network welcome the vertical towers that soar into the sky without eclipsing the light or creating a sensation of claustrophobia. In the south of the island, where the streets are not aligned on a grid, the public space between the towers is claustrophobic.

In different contexts, I think we don't take enough in consideration the value of small towers in a modest vertical cityscape for housing neighborhoods. Towers with ten to fifteen floors combined with buildings with four to six floors allow the sun to shine through. In open blocks, the surface built-in height permits large courtyards or gardens, without sacrificing economically necessary density.

But my introduction to the architecture of vertical signs, starting with the water tower in 1971, came from another idea. Vertical signs have been essential ever since towns began to grow; towers, raised buildings and bell towers all allow you to see into the distance. The sensorial appropriation of the far-away, the landmarks in the city's massive scale, are necessary in the sprawl of large metropolitan areas; seeing the immense panorama, gazing into the distance, is an essential but often overlooked point in these neighborhoods. From Montmartre, Beaubourg, Mont-Valérien and the terrace of Saint-Germain-en-Laye, in Paris you can "embrace" the living landscape.

You can get a feel for the scale of what lies before you, the millions of people who live there, the horizontal

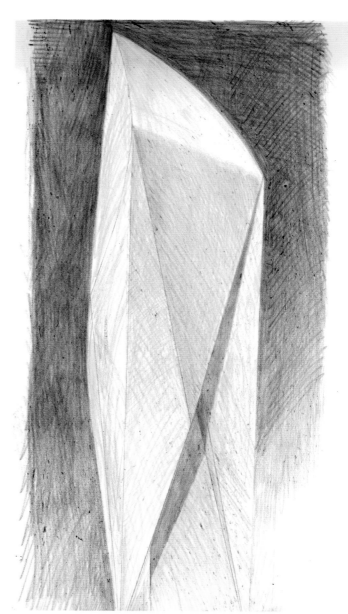

Drawing of T1 Tower competition entry, La Défense, Paris, France, 2001

community of people together. The physical space reconnects us to the world and is no longer the alienating obstacle it too often is in our immense labyrinthine suburbs, where we cannot appreciate distances. That's why we need landmark buildings, hills, viewpoints, towers and extraordinary wind farms.

Riverbanks and cliffs have this quality of making an impression on our senses. They are symbolic forms because they effect a break and because of their spatial location. They have a marked impact on an entire section of the city. When you approach the city as a large form, you intend to reconquer it: the site, the large-scale landmark, is a significant factor in any urban location.

When I was designing on the green tower in Marne-la-Vallée, in the Paris region, I had this in mind. My intention was to resist indiscriminate sprawl of construction in this new city, which was going to happen and eventually did. From a single point, how do you give meaning and shape to a scattered, labyrinthine, urban expanse, sliced up by motorways?

The water tower is a modest thirty-meter tower covered in vegetation but placed it in the middle of a traffic circle. Its location makes it a landmark, a symbolic figure at the junction between two roads. The water tower is not a monument; it does not mean something specific; its shape, the dimensional relationship it forms with the landscape, is what counts. Monumentality, not the monument.

I was interested with the capacity of large-scale, physical landmarks to permit people to feel and understand the space.

This notion had not been adopted by twentieth century modernism, it was never championed as part of a broader conceptual approach, because before the war it belonged to neoclassicism, to a vision of the urban space where the res publica had been affirmed with authoritarianism by totalitarian regimes.

The Pyramide du Louvre and the Arche de La Défense reflect this concept, because they fit into the large-scale perceptive axis. Few were surprised, however, that the discarded idea of monumentality resurfaced silently in the Grands Projets of President François Mitterrand. There are physical realities that go beyond words, and the real history of architecture is not written in books but in silent spaces, in actual constructions.

Bandai Tower competition model, 1994

Lille Tower, Lille, France, 1991–1995

It was twenty years after the water tower when Rem Koolhaas asked me to produce a design for one of the towers he had decided to install on the high-speed train line in his masterplan for Euralille. The tower I had to build was one which had to serve as both tower and as a bridge, straddling the high-speed train station for over 100 meters, without a load-bearing point. The promoter, Michel Lefebvre, immediately explained to me that this bold plan made the tower far too expansive, and that my task was to search for a way to bring down the cost of the bridge loads.

Imagining a lighter weight, I proposed we forget the parallelepiped volume of 100-by-100 meters of the urban plan, and Rem accepted that. That led me to design an L-shaped volume, an angle for a tower that was also a bridge. This permitted us to keep a vertical load under half of the building. But this vertical foundation was tight, in an area reduced by underground train and subway lines, and the bridge itself, the horizontal part, serves as the necessary stabilizer.

Neither tower nor block, the angle was to me more beautiful than a tower, it seemed to float and rise back up to the sky. And it provided the starting point for my continuous work on towers: a large-scale building as a sculpture in space. It introduced the series of prismatic towers that continues even today.

Lille Tower, Cité des Affaires, ZAC des Deux Gares, Lille, France. Program: An office tower for the Crédit Lyonnais bank headquarters, in the Euralille zone within a site plan designed by Rem Koolhaas (OMA); surface area: 18,135 square meters. Client: Nexity-Sari. Developer: Euralille. Owner: Ferinel Industries, Groupe George V. Architect and town planner: Rem Koolhaas–OMA. Height: 116 meters (380 feet). Date: Competition 1991; completion, 1995

Aerial view of site

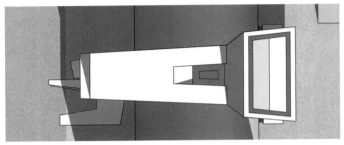
Drawing, view from above

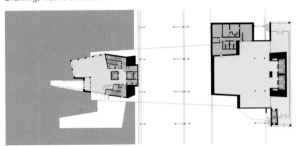
Plan of Lower Floor

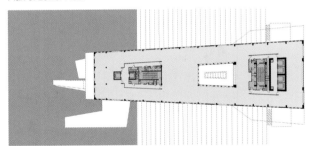
Plan of the Bridge

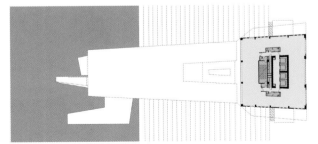
Plan of Tower Floor

opposite page: View of the tower from the street

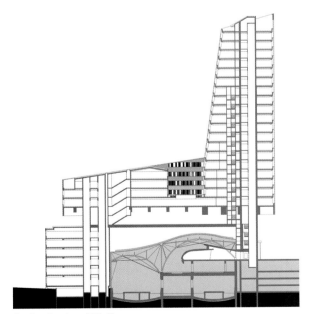
Section drawing of Lille Tower

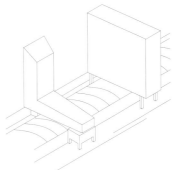

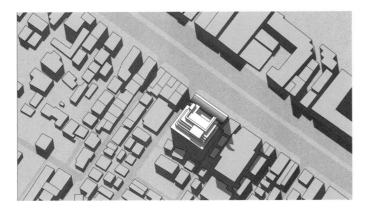

Bandai Tower, Tokyo, Japan, 1994

For the Bandai tower competition, we were asked to create a headquarter on the famous Anoyame Dori street in Tokyo. It was good to give the project a particular visibility. I decided to adopt a theme: the one of the acoustic window in the concert hall of the Cité de la musique, that disseminates passages of colored light, provided me a starting point. It seemed like a good idea to start with even if I felt it naïve and even if it turned out to be ugly at this size.

But the idea of an envelope of petals that intersect with light remained, completely transformed by losing its symmetry on the avenue side with large shells. Behind, this face is the opposite: a series of stepped terraces of housing units facing the interior of the block.

Bandaï Tower, Anoyama-Dori, Tokyo, Japan. Program: Mixed use tower: offices, restaurant, housing, and theater (300 seats); surface area: 7,000 square meters GFA. Height: 80 meters (262.5 feet). Date: Competition prizewinning entry, 1994; abandoned project

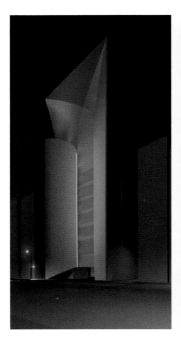

Site Plan, model, and computer generated drawings showing lighting changing slowly, mixing colors

LVMH Tower, New York, USA, 1995–1999

With the LVMH tower in New York, I had the demand from Bernard Arnault to construct a "flagship building"—the head office of the LVMH Group in the US. The first plot of land was a very narrow one. I did a first project, which was a piling of boxes. Then Bernard Arnault could expand the plot, buying the six-meter gallery adjoining the site. Given its width, I sought to create a vertical unity rather than enlarging the superposed boxes. I imagined a building with a real presence, but also well included in the block and "belonging" to the city, and this raised a first challenge: I wanted to avoid the staircase effect on the volume that Manhattan's building regulations led to have at fixed heights. This would have made our building a twin of the adjacent Chanel building of the same width. The second challenge was the light: the plot was located just opposite the absolute black façade of the IBM Tower which would reflect onto any sort of glass building built opposite.

For the setbacks, architect and zoning consultant Michael Parley permitted me to understand that this rule could be interpreted, in order to avoid a staircase effect: in fact, it needed to be designed in such a way that the façade would only touch on a point on the street wall. I tried to find an autonomous, vertical line distinct from the Chanel building. This is why I used a prismatic geometry breaking with the street wall and its horizontal setback line. It permitted to play down the repetitive effect of the setbacks. And it permitted at the same time to break up this reflected image of the black façade, which I soften also when deciding to work with sanded white glass for some of the volumes.

The prismatic form creates a rift in the façade that starts at the base and becomes a ridge at the top. This line hollows out a relief that magnifies the tower from top to bottom and gives a sense of interiority. There was no height or area limit. The tower is topped by a belvedere opening onto Manhattan, a large triple-height space called the "Magic Room."

LVMH Tower, 19 East 57th Street, New York, U.S.A. Program: American headquarters of the LVMH Group, this office tower also accommodates two boutiques on the ground floor and a function room on the top floor; surface area: 8,683 square meters. Height: 100 meters (328 feet), 23 floors. Client: LVMH (Louis Vuitton Moët Hennessy Group). Architect of record: Hillier Eggers Group. Date: Commission, 1995; completion, 1999. Award: Business Week Architectural Record Award, 2001

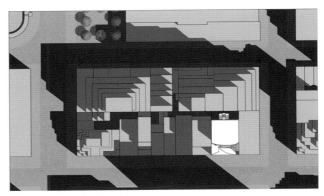

Rendering of the site from above

Aerial view of tower

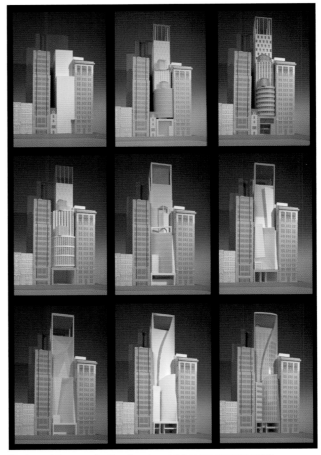

Study models. opposite: Pencil and pastel drawing of tower, 1996

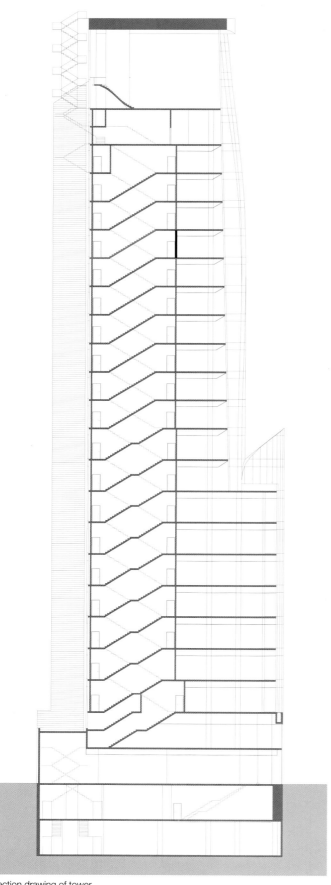

Section drawing of tower

23rd Floor Plan

11th Floor Plan

3rd Floor Plan

1st Floor Plan

opposit page: Streetscape view of tower

Detail views of the façade of the LVMH Tower

The "Magic Room"

Sandblasted glass façade

Septentrion Tower, Paris—La Défense, France, 1997

To renovate the Septentrion Tower in La Défense, I added a large prismatic shell that let visible the original building designed by Pierre Dufau in the 1960s. We transform the thermal isolation efficiency of the façades and also add floors and an atrium at the top.

Program: Office tower extension; surface area: existing surfaces: 32,000 square meters; with extension: 55,262 square meters. Height: 150 meters (492 feet). Client: Unibail. Date: Commission, 1997; unbuilt

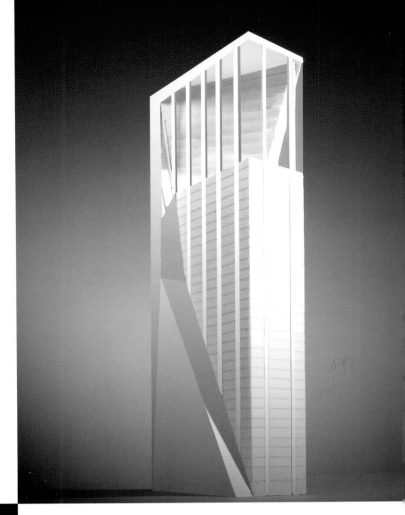

Hearst Tower, New York, USA, 2000

The Hearst Corporation had outgrown its original six-story building in the heart of New York. To extend its premises, an office block was built above the existing historical building, which had to be preserved. Without giving the impression of resting on a base, the project presents a tower rising toward the sky like a flame, a statement on the New York skyline, a landmark for the city, and a strong symbol for the Hearst Corporation. The building was finally built by Norman Foster.

Program: Office tower designed to accommodate the headquarters of the Hearst Corporation. The program planned for the preservation of the existing building façade; 80,000 square meters. Height: 180 meters (591 feet). Client: Hearst Corporation. Date: Consultation, 2000; unbuilt

Zeil Tower, Frankfurt, Germany, 2002

Situated in the dense city center of Frankfurt, the project creates a wide breach across a vast block, opening it up and creating a light-filled street. The tower continues with the prismatic shaping, providing here a dynamic motion growing from ground to sky.

Program: Shops, offices, hotel, cinema, cultural spaces, car parks ; surface area: 210,000 square meters. Height: 148 meters (486 feet). Client: MAB. Date: Competition, 2002; unbuilt

T1 Tower, Paris—La Défense, France, 2001

A cheerful struggle for visibility in La Défense's forest of towers. The T1 project is composed of two vertical wings of varying heights. The shorter one accommodates large open spaces (1,000 square meters) dedicated to front offices. The location of the site beyond the beltway calls for a novel design, and thus for a new landmark in this large business district.

Program: Office tower; surface area: 70,000 square meters. Height: 165 meters (541 feet). Client: SARI. Date: Competition, 2001; unbuilt

Granite Tower, Paris—La Défense, France, 2001–2008

Nexity organized, over the summer months of year 2001, two competitions for towers in La Défense, with separate architects to be selected for each tower. I designed the T1 tower as a monumental sculpture adapted to the plot, integrating large trading rooms as requested. I also entered the other competition for the headquarters of French bank Société Générale at the extremity of La Défense, like a bow marking the start of the "Valmy" sector. Squeezed into a narrow triangular site, the design needed to preserve views of the two existing semi-circular buildings designed by architects Andrault and Parat. I streamlined the main body to safeguard the views from the existing buildings.

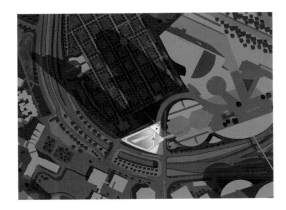

For the last thirty years, towers have been based on slabs supported by a central core and columns around the edges, which are fairly light and spaced to open up the view as far as possible. The core provides the main structure for the bracing.

The static bracing for the Granite tower is supplied by a dihedral structure of "pierced shear walls" (with openings for windows) enveloping the interiors, protecting them from exterior temperatures and ultra violet rays to optimize thermal inertia.

The jury selected my project in October 2001. But at the end of April 2002, the President was unable to convince the board of directors. After September 11, 2001, was it a good idea to build a 50,000 square-meter tower for 17,000 people?

The project was cancelled. A few months later, the bank called me: "We own this land. If we sell it, another tower would block our view and the light, whereas your project resolved these issues." The board gave its backing on condition that it will be constructed at market price. It would no longer be the bank's head office, but a property investment that would be rented or sold off at a profit.

The building needed to be constructed with a 20 percent smaller budget. Engineers came to the studio every day to adapt the design to this new economic reality. I kept my distance. They increased the surface area of the floors to make them more profitable, reduced the height, and the tower shrank until it looked like a sort of potato. On the other hand, we started to have core studies, which were intelligent.

In early August, while I was working on the site of the French embassy in Berlin, the president of Nexity called me: "I've got some good news. The plans have been accepted by Société Générale! We're going to do it!" I told him that this was good news but I couldn't continue with the project as it was, because the shape of the tower and the principle of the façades had lost all logic by artificially retaining the original lines without retaining the mode of construction.

At that time, I was focused on a competition for a huge block in the center of Frankfurt, with a shopping mall, offices, a hotel and a tower. With its simple oblique planes enlarging from ground to sky, the slenderness of the tower I was designing for Frankfurt had struck some of the judges and I thought about moving the Granite project in this direction.

I told Nexity in October that we weren't putting their money in the right place. They quickly came to see a small model of a new design. The dihedral structure was restored to its static role and the rear folds preserve light and views from the existing towers. The project regained its logic and it was less expensive. Oblique lines and slanted prisms were back as features of towers I designed since Lille, LVMH, and Zeil in Frankfurt and later for Prism. It turns this tower into a prow that completes the "Valmy" sector and the ensemble of the Société Générale's head office. The triangular tower conveys a dual image: an independent construction on the Paris—La Défense skyline and a construction attached to two existing towers while unifying the bank's block.

Granite Tower, La Défense, Paris, France. Program: An office tower designed for the French bank Société Générale, located in front of the Alicante and Chassagne towers (built in 1995); surface area: 69,000 square meters. Height: 184 meters (603 feet), 45 floors. Client: Galybet (Sub-company of the group Société Générale). Client Representative: Orcadim (Sub-company of the group Société Générale). Property Developer: Nexity-Sari, Vinci. Bright sculpture within the reception hall: Martin Wallace. Date: Commission, 2001; completion, 2008. Award: First Certified High-Rise Building High Environmental Quality (HEQ®) in France (2010)

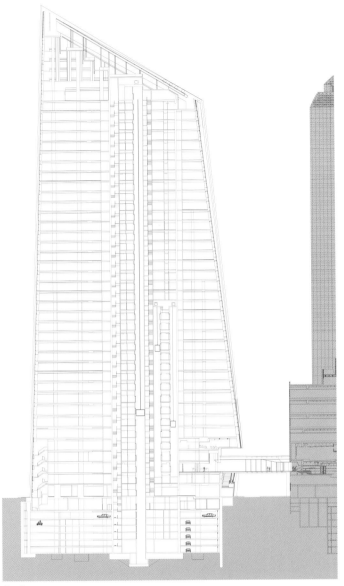

Section

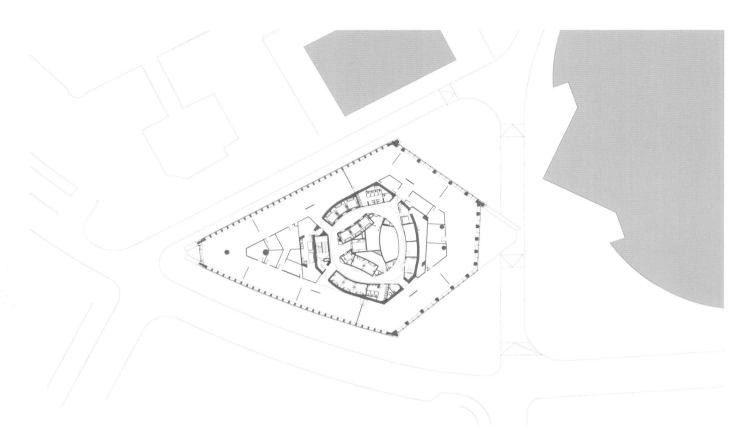

20th Floor Plan of Granite Tower

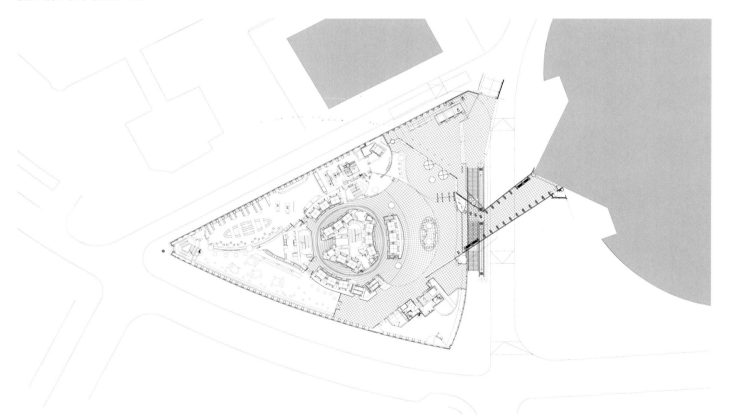

Ground Floor Plan

Prism Tower, New York, USA, 2002–2016

The two-in-one tower, Prism, is an apartment and condominium skyscraper, with part of its space dedicated to affordable housing in Midtown, Manhattan. This interaction of prisms at the corner of Park Avenue and 28th Street in Manhattan is designed to provide many of the housing units with long distance views. None of the angles is "purposeless."

After the opening of the LVMH tower on 57th Street, I received several requests from property developers who wanted me to design buildings for New York. They told me that Amanda Burden, chair of the New York City Department of City Planning, aimed to foster architectural creation and enhance social quality and street life by providing an incentive. The developers would be free to negotiate air rights with the local authorities at the district level, this allowing them to build beyond city regulations at the condition that they would propose a creative project. This procedure was called the Uniform Land Use Review Procedure (ULURP). Developers saw me as someone who could design a building in line with this new approach, since my work for LVMH.

Albert Kalimian wanted to built according to the affordable housing rules that framed his family activity and to share the project with another promoter. As he expressed to the chair of City Planning, his parents were "brick builders" of social housing, and following this tradition, his ambition was "to be a hero" by bringing a landmark in Manhattan. I produced a study including advices from Michael Parley for the zoning code.

The building consists of two main intricated pieces, and two additional vertical pavilions on either side as a connection with the adjacent buildings but without touching them. The building is a "viewing machine" from its interior spaces. The prismatic design of the volumes optimizes views to the far distance and takes into account the necessary recess from the avenue. Each corner or oblique line creates perspectives that optimize the light. On Park Avenue, the continuity of the façades with the one of the historic 1930s buildings is maintained, including with its large neighbors the Metropolitan Life Insurance Building and the New York Life Insurance Co, with which it establishes a dialogue on the New York skyline. At the ground floor are restaurants, and I integrated the subway entrance at the corner into the building, thus enlarging the passageway.

After some presentation of the studies a final design was approved by Amanda Burden and I was given authorization to enter into negotiations for an additional 17,000 square meters in 2003. Gary Handel was the architect of record.

As a European, I didn't anticipate neighbors would accept more height in front of their home. But surprisingly, the community board blessed the project, considering it would bring new value to the neighborhood! Great positive example of the urban democracy in NYC. The project was

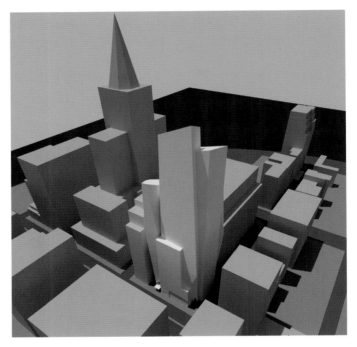

delayed when Albert Kalimian requested us to study a big project on Amsterdam Avenue mixing housing and the New York City Opera.

Suspended in 2008 as a result of the economic crisis, it was only taken up again in 2011 by Equity Residential and Toll Brothers, who retained the initial project unchanged, asking us to only modify some interiors.

The bottom 22 floors, with 269 rental apartments developed by Equity Residential have an access on 28th Street and the top 18 floors with 81 condominium apartments developed by Toll Brothers have an access on Park Avenue. The rental tenants and condo residents share the lower level amenities, which include a pool, fitness center with a sauna, and a lounge.

Prism Tower, 400 Park Avenue South, New York, U.S.A. Program: Tower accommodating apartments, shops on the ground floor, and access to the subway. Surface area: 40,000 square meters. Height: 144 meters (472 feet). Client: Equity Residential and Toll Brothers. Architect of record: Gary Edward Handel & Associates. Zoning consulting development: Michael Parley, Development Consulting Services, Inc. Environmental and planning: Allee King Rosen & Fleming, Inc. (AKRF). Date: Commission, 2002; completion, 2016

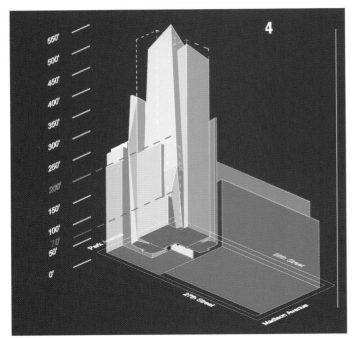

Schema showing Prism Tower footprint and various hight levels in feet

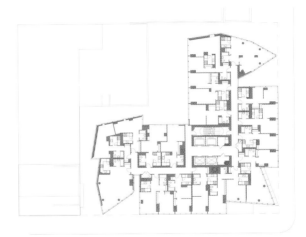

19th Floor Plan

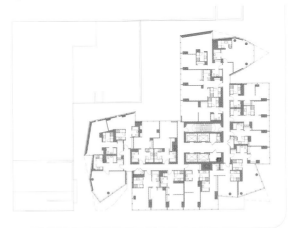

7th Floor Plan

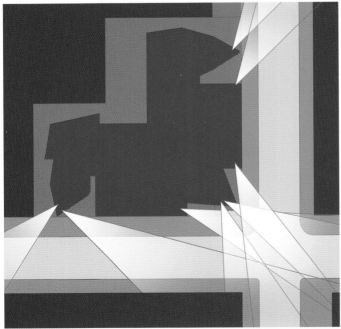

Schema showing sightlines from the tower

1st Floor Plan

Interior views

opposit page: Subway station entrance at base of Prism Tower. top, bottom: Condominium lobby and tower entrance with drawing by Christian de Portzamparc

One57 Tower, New York, USA, 2005–2014

When the Prism project was suspended, in 2005, Gary Barnett, the president of Extell Development, commissioned me to design two towers on 57th Street. The towers' characteristic soaring movement, like arrows in the city, their summits turned toward the immense open sky of Central Park, emerged from the initial study. It was a tribute facing the great void and symbol of the city.

Extell was soon presented with a series of different plot acquisition options, and after four years of testing design schemes and model studies, the tower finally entered into construction in 2009 (after the 2008 crisis, Gary Barnet had courageously rapidly re-launched his plans for the site rather than abandon).

The highest residential tower in New York at that time, it followed the line of 57th Street and looked out onto Central Park, facing it like a simple sign perceived differently from each point of the compass. In fact, the plot forms an angle, and I drew on the complexity of this L-shape to provide the main thrust of the design. The result reflects the structural requirements of a markedly elongated tower, the city's alignment regulations and the air rights specific to this site.

The southern façade is structured into vertical bands of glass in two contrasting colors that express the energy of a waterfall in New York's vertical landscape, linking each unit of volume allowed by the code via curved transitional surfaces containing occupied terraces.

The east and west façades use the random aesthetic of glass and aluminum marquetry and we called this weft of color a "Gustave Klimt" façade in reference to the famous Austrian painter. It fluctuates with the changing light exposure.

The program comprises a Park Hyatt Hotel, for the section without views over the park and, on the upper floors, stunning apartments with views over Central Park. Between the two is a large swimming pool and spa. We drew up core plans and made structural studies and façade studies. SLCE did the execution drawings. The interior design was entrusted by Extell to Thomas Juul-Hansen, thereby covering every aspect of the project.

One57 Tower, 157W 57th Street, New York, U.S.A. Program: Hotel and residential; Surface areas: 79,299 square meters. Height: 306 meters (1004 feet), 75 floors. Client: Extell Development Company. Architect of record: SLCE Architect LLP. Residential interior design: Thomas Juul-Hansen, LLC. Hotel interior Design: Yabu Pushelberg. Zoning consultant: Michael Parley, Development consulting services Inc. Structural engineer: WSP Cantor Seinuk. Fluid engineer: AKF. Exterior performance consultant: IBA Israël Berger & Associates, NY. Landscape architecture: Terrain-NYC. Date: Commission, 2005; completion, 2014

Areal view of tower and site

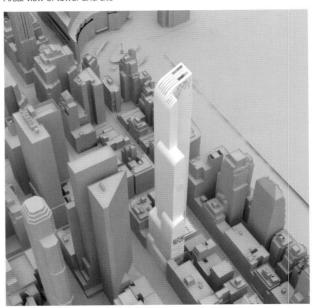
Model showing One57 Tower in context of street

View of Central Park as seen from the tower

opposit page: View of One57 Tower and environs from Central Park

318

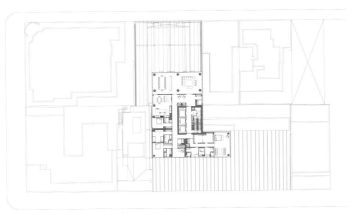

Floor Plan for floors 60 through 70

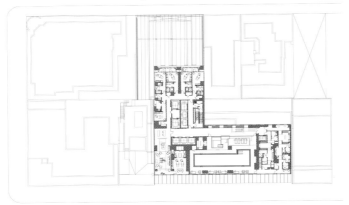

20th Floor Plan

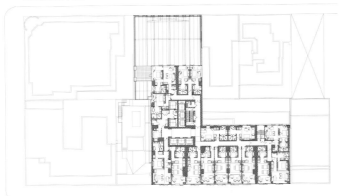

6th Floor Plan

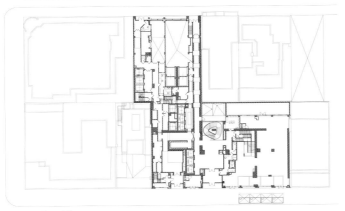

1st Floor Plan

Preliminary sketch of tower

View from Columbus Circle. opposite: View from the Hudson River

Detail views of entrance of One57 Tower

3

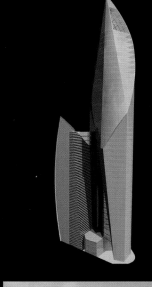

4

5

7

8

9

11

12

Tower

1. Manara Tower, La Défense, Paris, France, 2011
2. Signal Tower, La Défense, Paris, France, 2007
3. Imefa52 Tower, Issy-les-Moulineaux, France, 201
4. T1 Tower, La Défense, Paris, France, 2001
5. CMA-CGM Tower Marseille, France, 2004
6. M-Generali Tower, La Défense, Paris, France, 200
7. Law Court, Paris, France, 2010
8. New Trigone, Issy-les-Moulineaux, France, 2011
9. B3A Massena Tower, Paris, France, 2011
10. Rose Tower, La Défense, Paris, France, 2013
11. Sisters Towers, La Défense, Paris, France, 2013
12. Hafencity, Hambourg, Germany, 2014

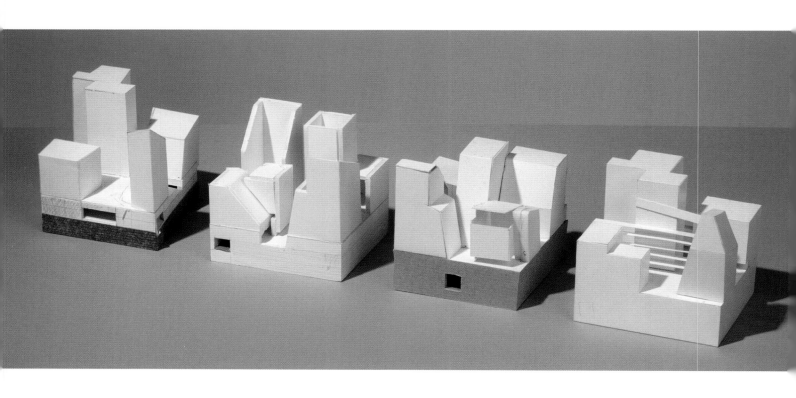

Chapter 7
Blocks and Neighborhoods

At the junction between two disciplines, I work on each of my projects both as architect and as urban planner. Every building contains a vision about the city.

Whether I'm designing individual open blocks in Montreal or Boulogne, or setting the rules for opening up blocks in Paris-Masséna, or working on the interior of a closed block like the French embassy in Berlin; I always work beyond the building, at the dimension of the neighborhood—what is woven between the highways, streets, roads, groups of buildings and public spaces. Furthermore and even though it is a recent trend, we must be aware that the planet's need for protection has a knock-on effect on every aspect of architecture: forms, materials, techniques, distances and urbanistic concepts.

For the last 50 years successful urban planning for a section of any given city turned out to be the hardest to master and the most difficult ambition to put into practice, and yet the most essential. It counts to a far greater extent than designing a successful building.

This thought came to me when I saw the first man walking on the moon. This extraordinary feat of spatial exploration and technological mastery occurred just as we were witnessing our own loss of control over our ability to live in large numbers on Earth.

When you construct a building and create architecture to breathe new life into the way we live, architecture is adapted to how we live today and maybe tomorrow, you can control 90 to 95 percent of what you want to do. Within the mission of urban planning, since working with a large number of actors and not going to build all the neighborhood in question myself, I don't control everything, but I have a decisive influence on what counts most. It requires to share an intended purpose, organizational and esthetic, to tame the "builder ego" of architects, set the rules of the game, and supply the creative energy and ideas. Ordinary buildings have to suite to their place. But more than that, we need to ensure that an esthetic we don't particularly like forms part of a musical ensemble when mixed with a dose of architectural brilliance. Our rules need to accommodate the unpredictable. Randomness is part of my vision of what a current urban esthetic can be; random enters a game with rational and sometimes opens onto a surrealistic reality! This "unintended" side of beauty, when it appears, is the source of a city's grandeur.

Architecture of Blocks

Many of my projects developed the open block idea, either as architect or urban project manager.

Included here are several block exemples such as "L'Atria" in Bordeaux, "Prairie au Duc" in Nantes, and "Pont de Lumière" in Metz. And the "Tripode" mixed block in the Ile de Nantes. Each case is different, following the context. Sometimes the block has a base like in Nantes, sometimes it is partially three-dimensional like in Boulogne.

Architecture alone is not a guarantee of quality, but rather the inhabitable spaces they produce. Beyond this idea to open the blocks is the will to link places, to find one's ways in the city, to reconnect the separated Hestia and Hermes at the scale of the immense wild territories of the metropolis.

Santo André, São Paulo, Brazil, 1988

Santo André is a municipality located in the south of São Paulo. In 1998, advised by Jordi Borga, the mayor organized a consultation to come up with ideas for this huge site composed of industrial wasteland, disused factories and flour-mills that formed a four-kilometer corridor of activity that was running right in the middle of the city. This was organized as a workshop shared with younger architects of São Paulo.

The mayor wanted to avoid this lands from being bought and regrouped by operators who would create closed office, leisure facilities and businesses areas concealed from the public land and which would cut the city in two.

To ensure the continuity of the urban territory and to avoid creating large enclaves, I proposed to define a basic and infallible layout of public thoroughfares that crossed the site and extended, continued and linked the existing street network. From this starting point, and even though the timeframe was unknown, it would be possible to divide the land into plots along the streets, allowing people the freedom to use the blocks as they wished; they could be big or small depending on demand, but would allow the public space to pass through them.

I was careful to take a realistic approach to the project and I did not produce a plan that would immediately require the city to spend money it did not have. The layout defined the roads, which were earth-surfaced to start with. Then I wanted to show that architecture could be simple and that we could create a lively neighborhood out of something people were used to: types of buildings and low or high constructions that were regularly built in the region. This sacrosanct principle of public space would protect the territory. Dividing street sides into plots would open them to life. Quality of life would come from the streets themselves and from the ease with which they encouraged mixed use and construction of varied programs with the open blocks.

The problem with private functional zones, more perhaps than closing and guarding them, arises from their frozen block plan, their absence of road systems, and their tree-structured "clumped" urban planning. Even if their gates would have been left open, these spaces would not have been able to be transformed, whereas in cities, all blocks are indefinitely transformed, divided and unified, and sold in parts, because they have public accessways on each side. We talk a lot about sustainable planning. For me sustainability is about transformability and reversibility.

Logistic Port, Beijing, China, 2003

In 2003 in Beijing urban space was growing at a pace and on a scale no city had ever known before, and urban planning had to reflect that. We were asked to design the plan for a housing district covering one million square meters and to design several building prototypes.

There were hundreds of new closed residential camps under construction in Beijing then, all designed according to the same process: each operation had a type of building— a housing block or tower—extremely well designed on the inside, developed and repeated in parallel series over the plot, and complying with the constant daylight rule that governed the space between buildings. A loop roadway distributed every-thing from a single access point to the site.

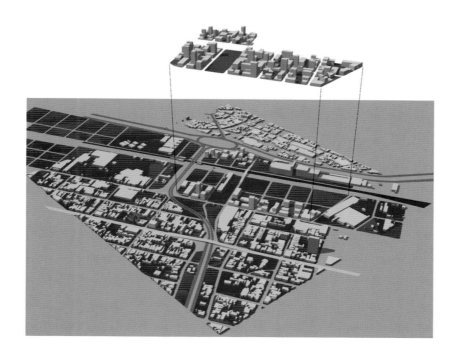

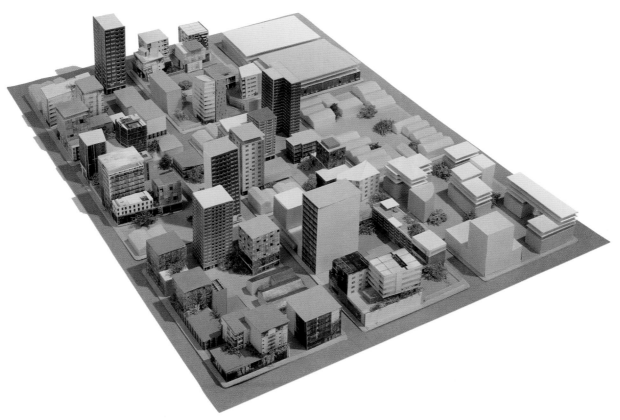

Santo André/Sector Avenida dos Estados, Santo André, São Paulo, Brazil; drawings and model from a workshop devoted to exploring a way to avoid large privatization of the city, 1998

The scale of this phenomenon was impressive. When I proposed a neighborhood with streets, multiple entry points, mixed uses and businesses, the developers said: "This is not our model." I set about imagining the possible future of the condominiums in this model with them. Considering how fast Chinese society was changing, were these egalitarian and serial alignments for Beijing's new middle classes going to be a model for the future? The neighborhood spanned one million square meters. What would happen to these plots once aspirations, tastes or the economic means of their inhabitants will rise or drop? Massified neighborhoods with a single-entry point for ten thousand inhabitants could not be resold as a unit and could not flexibly evolve in the future. It had all the rigidity of zoning.

The developers accepted the idea of a series of entry points and streets for a neighborhood open to modification and capable of accommodating an unknown future. A city that would be able to change one day. The developers asked for time to think it over and when they came back to us they said: "Your idea of the future is interesting. Let's study it!"

So we prepared the "building permits" for the first two blocks and the rules for other architects to apply in the future.

The challenge was firstly to successfully create streets, blocks and a partition of private spaces in a public road network, while taking into account the drastic daylight law implemented across China that prevents the use of streets and causes tall buildings to be spaced far apart. For this purpose, we produced digital models of open blocks with the authorized heights and the Institute of architecture checked if we had two hours of regulatory sunshine a day in the ground floor living rooms. It was a work of volumetric cunning that centered on the daylight rule and it was rather amusing because it led us to open streets, to create open blocks to successfully create north-south streets lined with buildings. From that point onwards, we were able to imagine a variety of architectural designs, a randomness.

The neighborhood is therefore made up of a network of public streets, of which some were adopted by the city's urban planning services. It is a street layout that introduces a rule for the long-term future. I also proposed to add a long central park, a green river that would irrigate the site and become the symbol of the neighborhood. We increased the number of park-side possibilities and the qualities of housing in the city.

In the same block, we can construct buildings that are very different from each other, mainly residential, but we try to ensure they are used for different functions, such as offices, businesses, and sometimes public services. We avoid the obsessive repetition that often characterizes

outlying areas where residential accommodation is built in large numbers. And the idea of making these streets commercial as soon as possible was kept and led developers to halve the large shopping mall planned next to it.

In 2006, the government banned all this housing projects around Beijing to prevent an over production of housing that would have triggered a serious economic crisis.

Public or Private Management?

One wonderful aspect of cities is the fact that they bring together everyone in their incredible diversity within a single form, in a shared atmosphere, in which everything is combined.

I have always thought of urban planning as the result of a struggle between two energies or two currents: on the one side, the disordered, anarchic, living expression of needs and desires and individual pressures, and on the other, a need for the rules of coexistence, for public actions that coordinate us and champion the collective interest while guaranteeing and limiting individual rights. A way of organizing natural disorder without killing it. This is a political action. It also requires us to rely on a lot of shared intelligence. It's the peak of civilization when it works. And this has become quite rare.

At a time when public authorities no longer have the capacity to invest or to control the ground to transform cities, urban development processes are changing and, with them, urban planning practices. Private operators are more in control than before and sometimes interests of cities and communities are ignored: it is an unbalanced expression of interests, where individual pressures can be disastrous.

But cities invent urban planning processes based on project contracts or partnerships to implement a triad of investor, designer and public authority representing the general interest. Private actors fulfill their role differently, as part of a shared and controlled approach.

Cities can therefore initiate, incite and control good projects, and sometimes even control urban planning issues.

This reflects our experience of urban planning projects in the 2000s, such as the Rue de la Loi in Brussels, for the Brussels region, in the European quarter, and for the 60th Street in New York in the Riverside district for Extell Development and with City Planning.

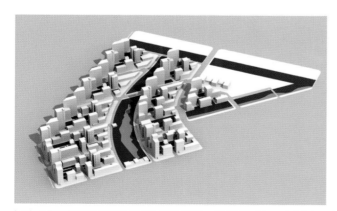

Logistic Port District, Beijing, China. Commission, 2003. Models and digital renderings. A neighborhood of diversity: one million square meters, ten streets; to avoid one single huge private houseing camp to connect the city

Rue de la Loi, Brussels, Belgium, 2008

In the center of Brussels, Rue de la Loi forms along some of its length the city's historic axis, which runs from the Parc Royal and through the Arcades du Cinquantenaire and home to several Belgian public institutions as well as European one's. It is becoming the heart of the European institutions quarter and the site of the future Commission's buildings is waiting there, by this street, its building.

In 2008, a joint international competition was organized by the Brussels Region and the European Commission to transform the street in order to accommodate the Commission's buildings, new office buildings and housing units.

The site of Rue de la Loi was an opportunity for the European Commission because it was going to be at the center of a lively neighborhood, not tucked away on an outlying protected estate that would underline the separation between Europe's executives, representatives and civil servants and the Brussels urban community. It was also an opportunity for Brussels, because it would affirm at its core its city's status as a capital and global metropolis.

However, in the middle of its "course," the Rue de la Loi is a sad gloomy and closed corridor blocked by cars. The perpendicular streets are not crossing it. It is lifeless and I understood the aim of the project as to bring life to this street while providing Europe with the new image of a visible headquarter integrated into the Belgian capital. I believed this was possible through an open-street approach. The idea was to create a new volumetric envelope with a functional and social mix, by adding housing, businesses and public spaces.

My entry for the 2008 competition aimed at steadily creating a new neighborhood based on the spatial concept of opening the street.

We set the "rules of the game" of urban planning that would steadily enable the city to open itself to the sky, to integrate new functions in a vertical local grow, while respecting the height limit of 110 meters. We set rules for street-side squares in order to open the street horizontally and to accommodate higher buildings next to them. Keeping useful or classified buildings, the project opened up free spaces on some plots, created throughways north and south, and pocket parks in plots where buildings are not efficient and without interest.

Rue de la Loi, Brussels, Belgium. Program: The definition of an urban program to restructure and density the Rue de la Loi, and its environs; surface area, 880,000 square meters (former surface: 490,000 square meters of offices)—increase in surfaces: 390,000 square meters (offices: 240,000 square meters; residential: 110,000 square meters; retail: 40,000 square meters). Client: Brussels Region, and the European Commission. Date: International competition's winning project, 2008; work in progress

Bird's-eye view of Rue de la Loi and surrounding areas

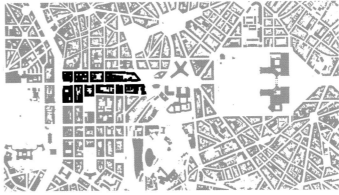

Rue de la Loi before transmofrmation; blocks are enclosed

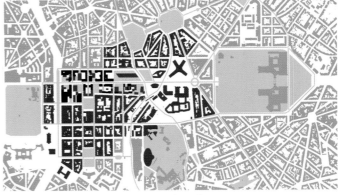

Rue de la Loi after transformation, with parks and greenways

This allows beside them to build vertical buildings and relieve the claustrophobia of the street. This plan set up a dialogue with what already existed, an openness to random elements and to a coexistence of periods and dimensions.

Thus a new built envelope is proposed, including the existing and set back from the street. It allows us to build up to the 100 meter Brussel ceiling in some locations. It transforms Rue de la Loi, with its light, side views, the spectacle of the sky, and verticals mixing with the existing heights without the sensation of being crushed under their weight.

But what means will be efficient for such a transformation? Means were not specified, public money is was limited, we needed a new approach to urban planning since the Region and city were unable to buy all the land and built.

Then, imagining a method with the authority to encourage private investment was is crucial. The project is specifically based on the principle of urban planning negotiated by contract with the actors of real estate and the owners of the various plots, mutualizing the profit block by blocks. It requires the pooling of space rights as part of the planning operation. Whether their lot is freed for trees or built on, interests of the owners need to be preserved and fairly distributed in accordance with the percentage of property. Some buildings were preserved or listed in the current marketplace. They were not affected by the plans. Other buildings were superannuated and they were going to be demolished and rebuilt.

On larger plots were some building could be fruitfully replaced or suppressed we had opportunities according to our plan: either liberating "pockets park" along the street, or building high towers set back from the street alignment.

The new European Commission building, in the "vernacular" concert, plays the role of soloist, located on a plot of land set aside for it. Purer, higher, the symbol of the institution, it stands out and speaks to Europe and the world, while towers of the neighborhood "belong" to Brussels. Street life would be created through a mix of businesses, pavements, trees, pedestrians, terraces, gardens, a tramway and car access ways, and so on, according to a traffic plan to be implemented.

Presqu'Île New District, Grenoble, France. Program: Urban development area on 250 hectares; housing, offices, laboratories, public facilities, public spaces, transport, sport and cultural facilities, learning spaces. Client: SEM Innovia. Conception: Project initiated by Claude Vasconi, taken over by Christian de Portzamparc in 2011. Landscaping: Péna & Peña. Date: Commission, 2010; in progress, anticipated delivery in 2025

Place Nelson-Mandela; an ellipse plaza with ponds

Integration of street, buildings, and park

A lively streetscape

An apartment terrace

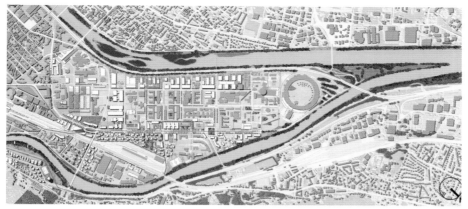

Master Plan

Bird's-eye view of proposed district

De Citadel, Almere, Netherlands, 2000–2006

For this project, I played the role of architect while the urban planning, the rules of the game, had been set by Rem Koolhaas, who had invited me to interpret.

Built forty years ago, Almere is a new town in the Dutch polders. Setting it apart from other new towns of that period, it is laid out on a grid of streets without adopting modern patterns and with a specific characteristic that distinguishes it from other examples like new towns in the suburbs of Paris. Instead of basing it around the "center," it contains the brilliant idea of leaving an enormous empty space in its center to be built on at a later date, when the town had matured. The center is located at the crossroads of two lively main streets. It is impossible to dig down in the polders. Rem Koolhaas won the competition to urbanize this center by proposing to gently raise the ground using a curved slab rising from the natural ground to create a place for pedestrians, leaving the cars to pass underneath. He organized several types of blocks and building in the area.

The natural ground to create a place for pedestrians, leaving the cars to pass underneath, he organized several types of blocks and building in the area.

In the very central block that he asked me to build, later called De Citadel, he had superposed three programmatic layers: automobiles at the ground, pedestrians and stores on the "street" going on the slab level, and housing above the public level. Here, I brought this partition into play by approaching the housing plate like a flying carpet. At one level, I organized a strip of housing units covering the slab around a prairie. A multi-level store crosses it vertically to form a hill in the prairie. I cut the block apart with two perpendicular streets to encourage passers-by to penetrate inside it. By offsetting the alignments at the central crossing point, I gave visibility to the angles of the store windows from outside the block. I also placed a small tower of student apartments at the high point of this "hill."

Forty years after the city was founded, this new center conceived by Rem Koolhaas, is a unique example of mixed uses in this urban "heart."

De Citadel, above the Hospitaalweg, Almere Stad, Netherlands. Program: Commercial and housing, central urban block ; surface area: 45,000 square meters (shops: 35,000 square meters; apartment buildings: 10,000 square meters). From an OMA mass plan based on slab layering and respecting the Dutch city scale. Master Planner: OMA Rem Koolhaas. Client: Ontwikkelings Combinate Chappij, Almere Hart CV. Client Representatives: Shops: MAB; Apartment Buildings: Eurowoningen BV. Architects of record: Beekin + Molenaar. Facade Design: Christian de Portzamparc and Martin Wallace. Date: Commission, 2000; completion, 2006. Award: 30 Years Of Architecture In Almere, 2006

The central block, De Citadel, and environs

An overview of De Citadel

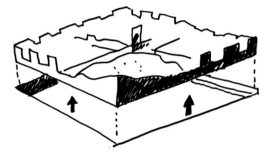

Slab architecture on a Dutch scale

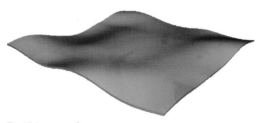

The "flying carpet"

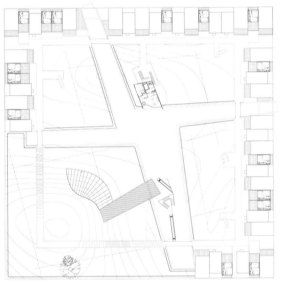

Top Garden Plan

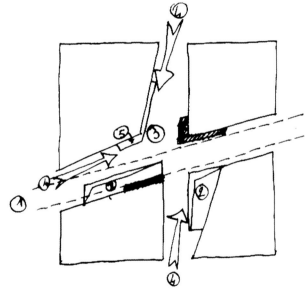

1. Offsetting of streets
2. Opening to the ground floor
3. Triangular square
4. Visual appeal
5. Ramp

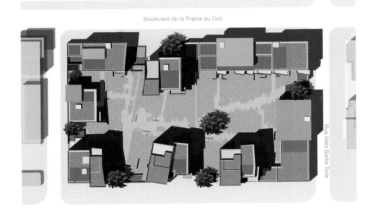

Prairie au Duc Residence, Nantes, France, 2004–2008
An Open Block

Situated in the center of the Nantes conurbation, the Ile de Nantes is a former industrial wasteland covering a surface area of 350 hectares. Following the implementation of the urban area development plan by Alexandre Chemetoff, it is now an extensive new neighborhood. I was invited by Daniel Chabod to build a program of 154 residential units on the site and 500 square meters of businesses. The urban area development allowed us to reinterpret the open block.

A linear texture embraces the block interposed with vertical and horizontal volumes Ground-floor businesses bring façades to life on the boulevard de la Prairie au Duc, which are capped with a private garden at the center of the block.

Each building has two access points: one to the street and another to the garden.

Prairie au Duc Residence, Boulevard de la Prairie-au-Duc, rue Alain Barbe Torte, rue Nouvelle, France. Program: Urban project, 154 residential units (14,500 square maters net floor area) and businesses (500 square meters net floor area). Client: Groupe Gambetta; Société CIPL. Developer: SAMOA with the Atelier de Nantes. Landscape design: Méristème, Régis Guignard. Date: Commision, 2004; delivered, 2008

L'Atria—Bastide Blanche, Bordeaux, France, 2004–2009

In Bordeaux, it was on the "other" bank, in the Bastide neighborhood, an industrial inner suburb which emerged in the nineteenth century after the construction of the stone bridge and the Gare d'Orléans, that Bouygues Immobilier submitted a request to build a housing block within an existing renovation scheme. The project was initiated by the City of Bordeaux and the CUB (Urban District of Bordeaux) in the early 2000s.

The block is situated along an avenue and two streets. The housing units with south-facing terraces are built in four strips and surround a garden. The new construction on the rue Jardel ensures the continuity of the typical Bordeaux street with its light hues and horizontal design, while the new buildings on allée de Serr have a more forceful, vertical presence. It helps form one of the neighborhood's major thoroughfares. Three long built strips stand out, their stepped terraces turned toward the Garonne.

The overall organization of the project hinges on three goals: one, provide two new throughways inside the project for pedestrian through-traffic and punctually for vehicle; two, create a series of three five-story high buildings along the allée de Serr that underscore the avenue; and three, allow for the formation of a large central garden in the ground open to the city, thanks to new throughways. In this way, the block is not closed: it provides passers-by with a view of the central garden and allows for new passageways, it is open to the city.

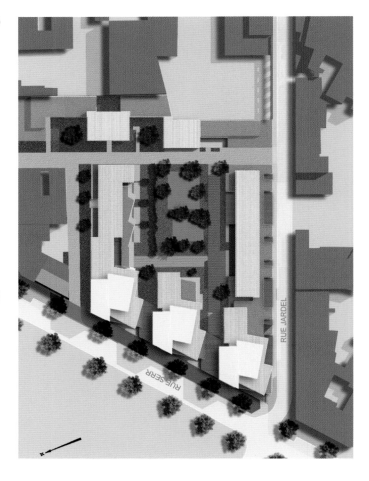

"L'Atria," Bastide Blanche, 11 allée de Serr, Bordeaux, France. Program: Construction of a property development with 108 housing units and commercial units; 11,130 square meters net floor area. Creation of a garden at the center of the blocks. Client: Bouygues Immobilier. Landscaper: Méristème, Régis Guignard. Date: Commision, 2004; completion, 2009

Tripode, Nantes, France, 2006–2013

In this Ile de Nantes, this site formerly occupied by a big building "Le Tripode," is part of the urban area development plan carefully drawn up by Alexandre Chemetoff. It had been programmed there a very large block with the proposal that one builder alone would realize it totally. This type of lot was called a macro-lot. The Nexity group won the commission and asked me to design the whole and realize it. The program combines housing, offices and businesses.

The large dimension of this block led me to make it cross with two transverse throughways. The commercial program allowed only one of them.

The "open block" layout is composed of twelve distinct and detached buildings and a large raised garden over the ground-floor businesses, each with a flat façade strictly aligned with the street and with openings for views and light between them.

The "volume" of the block and its limit on the avenue and canal are clearly legible. It provides alternating near and far views from the buildings. It also allows for light, sunny block interiors, autonomy of the volumes of building, a character and an address for each program: a hotel, a two-star vacation residence, a four-star vacation residence, three office buildings, convenience stores, medium-sized stores, social housing, and home ownership accommodation, along the canal and open to views of the Loire river.

Tripode Residence, Boulevard du Général-de-Gaulle, Nantes, France. Program: Within an urban plan by Alexandre Chemetoff is to be the realisation of a mixed block (12 buildings) of housing, retail, offices, hotel, services, parking. Surface area: 45,850 square meters GFA (housing: 12,200 square meters; offices: 20,900 square meters; hotel: 8,900 square meters; retail: 2,550 square meters. Client: SNC Nantes Tripode; Neximmo 41, represented by Nexity Entreprises and Nexity George V. Landscape design: Méristème, Régis Guignard. Date: Commission, 2006; completion, 2013

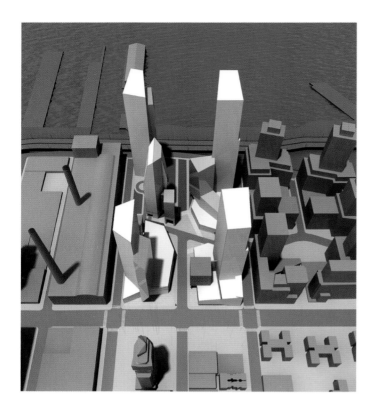

LOW MED HIGH

The Riverside Project, New York, USA, 2005

We studied for Extell Development a project on a huge site formed of four blocks available on the Upper West Side (on the tracks of the former Penn Station).

We have worked several years with Extell Development through regular presentation to the City Planning to guarantee the pedestrian comfort of a nice urban life and a good skylight within a high density of buildings.

Extending the 60th Street, the project is integrated into the Manhattan grid. It is composed of five tower blocks around a square, the heart of this new neighborhood, and a public garden that extends onto Riverside Park, which runs along the Hudson River.

I combined entities of variable heights forming "vertical blocks" or composite towers, gathering low, middle and high level of buildings which of installs something of a human dimension in the middle of this grandeur, on the square and the garden. The tower blocks are vertical residential buildings around which, on the lower floors, are incorporated businesses, schools, a movie theater, restaurants, a hotel lobby, and so on.

Riverside City Center / Between West End Avenue and Riverside Boulevard, between West 59th Street and West 61st Street, along the Hudson River, New York, U.S.A. Program: Urban project; residential and retail: apartment buildings, shops and offices; surface area: 297,289 square meters GFA. Client: Extell Development Company. Architect of record: Costas Kondylis and Partners LLP. Landscape design: MN Landscaping. Date: Commission, 2005

University Campus Sorbonne Nouvelle, Paris, France, 2014-2018

This is a block project for a university that is currently under construction.

This innovative and environmentally friendly, 35,000-squre-meter block of new buildings will be built at the heart of Paris to meet the needs of expansion of the Université de Paris 3, devoted to art, literature and languages, and to human and social sciences. The Université Sorbonne Nouvelle will be rehoused on a site alongside existing buildings with a strong presence. A teaching center, it needs to combine spaces for individual study and group activities and cater for large numbers of students.

I created several units of buildings between which flows a courtyard area, garden and cloister where students and teachers meet, according classical tradition.

The library acts as the unifying element and its triangular form, along with the other buildings, creates a central common space where university activities will take place.

The project underlines the university's presence in the city, its openness to society, and its vocation to promote knowledge. To this end, the library building, which is open to the public and researchers, will play an emblematic role.

Sorbonne Nouvelle University, 10 avenue de Saint-Mandé / 33 rue de Picpus, Paris, 12th District, France. Program: University Campus, "Nation" center of the University of Paris 3; a campus in eastern Paris for an open and innovative university, a place of life and exchange, research and training areas, a library for the new humanities (teaching rooms, amphitheaters, auditoriums, screening rooms, exhibition rooms, cafeteria, university library, staff accommodation, etc.); surface area: 25,000 square meters usable surface; 35,000 square meters gross external area. Client: Ministry of Higher Education and Research, University of Sorbonne Nouvelle, Paris 3. Project owner: EPAURIF, Public Establishment for University Development in the Île-de-France (Paris) region. Landscape design: Régis Guignard, Méristème. Acoustic: A&A, Acoustique et Architecture. Date: Competition winning project, 2014; under construction, anticipated completion in 2018

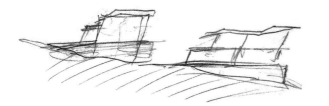

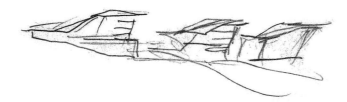

L'Avant-Scène Trésums, Annecy, France, 2008–2018

A neighborhood and a park project is also under construction, on the slopes of Semnoz, in front of the Lac d'Annecy and its stunning mountain panorama. There is was a hard high "block" of building housing an hospital and the mayor has decided to replace it by housing. Then we created L'Avant-Scène Trésums, a series of buildings and terraces stepped around a two-hectares public park that we studied with Régis Guignard, landscape architect. The park crosses the sloping estate, stepping through four wide flat lawns fringed with planted banks. Housing units are grouped into enclosed terraces where shared private garden are surrounded by two or three buildings. "Flowing" over the slopes, buildings are composed of two superposed parts: an elongated base of stone and concrete and an occupied "roof" area in zinc. Each apartment is open to the sun, the park, the lake and mountains.

L'Avant-Scène Trésums, 1, avenue du Trésum, Annecy, France. Program: housing, hotel, retirement home with healthcare facilities (54,398 square meters, GFA total net floor area); 152 social housing units and 480 private accommodations (44,373 square meters), hotel: 110 rooms (4,372 square meters), retirement home: 109 rooms (5,653 square meters), public garden (2 hectacres). Client: Crédit Agricole Immobilier. Social housing: HALPADES. Landscape design: Méristème, Régis Guignard. Date: Commission, 2008; work in progress, anticipated delivery in 2018

Watercolor, 2004

Acknowledgments

I would like to thank those who worked on these projects, engineers, architects, contractors, various managers.

My gratitude to the main collaborators of the Atelier who have worked with me for years to develop and build:

Since the eighties some are still with us Céline Barda, Bertrand Beau, Pascal Boutet, Isabelle Bürck, Marie-Elisabeth Nicoleau, Etienne Pierrès, Odile Pornin.

Some with us since the eighties having been on their own like François Barberot, Frédéric Borel, François Chochon, Paul Guilleminot, Benoit Juret.

Since the nineties and still in the team: Frank Anderle, Frédéric Binet, Barbara Bottet, Jean-Charles Chaulet, Thierry Damez-Fontaine, Hyun-Jung Song; and having gone: Jean-Daniel Boyer, Bruno Durbecq, Julie Howard.

Since the 2000s in the team: Marion Barray, Rex Bombardelli, Morgane Cauchy, Thibaut Clarens, Charlotte Crosnier, Tania Da Rocha Pitta, Olivier Desz, Pierre-Emmanuel Escoffier, Héloïse Ficat, Margarita Frezza, Mohammed Henni, Léa Héraud, Li Jiang, Pierre Lemaire, Guillaume Letschter, Julien Lissarague, Guillermo Lumbreras, Khatir Madjidi, Sébastien Menu, Nikolina Pavlova, Liza Pizzini, Lei Qiao, Jorge Queiros, Bettina Réali, Erwan Saliva-Campion, Delphine Vidon, Ning Wang; and now in the world: Chantal Aïra-Crouan, Duccio Cardelli, Magali Chetail-Baillon, Karol Claverie, Clovis Cunha, Nanda Eskes, Anna Paula Pontes, Burkhardt Schiller, Léa Xu.

Thanks to the architects of record: Pierre Accarain and Thierno Dumbuya (Hergé Museum), Rachid Andaloussi (Casarts), Christian Bauer (Philharmonie de Luxembourg), Beekin + Molenaar (De Citadel), Olivier Chadebost (Château Cheval Blanc winery), Guy Geier and John Mulliken from Hillier Eggers Group (LVMH Tower), Gary Handel (Prism Tower), David-Pierre Jalicon (House of Dior), LDI Institute (Suzhou Cultural Center), Philippe Macary, Ballini Pitt Architectes (Royal20), Luis Antonio Rangel (Cidade das Artes), Tom Sheehan and Salah-Eddine Saidoune (Seat of the Algerian Parliament), Tongji Institute (Music Conservatory of Shanghai).

Thanks to friends: acousticians, Jean Paul Lamoureux, Xu Ya Ying; landscapers, Fernando Chancel, Régis Guignard, Florence Mercier, Daniel Péna; scenographers, Jacques Dubreuil, Findlay Ross and Mark Stroomer from Theatre Projects.

Thanks to Michael Parley.

Thanks to Jean-Marc Verne, Serge Santelli, Octavio Leonido, Nikola Petrovic-Njegoš.

Thanks to Tataaki Matsumoto, Amy Wilkins.

Iconographic choices: Christian de Portzamparc and Étienne Pierrès.

They contributed to the realization of this book: Étienne Pierrès with Alexandra Baron, Camille Henry, Anne Herjean, Thierry Damez-Fontaine, Catherine Rochant.

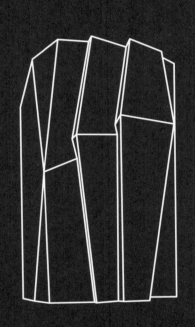